The Beyond Experience

Consciousness in Bhagavad Gita

The Beyond Experience

Consciousness in Bhagavad Gita

Sangeetha Menon

BLUEJAY BOOKS

An imprint of Srishti Publishers & Distributors
New Delhi

BLUEJAY BOOKS
An imprint of Srishti Publishers & Distributors
N-16, C. R. Park
New Delhi 110 019

First published in paper back by *BLUEJAY BOOKS* 2007

ISBN 81-88575-96-8

Typeset in AGaramond 11pt. by Suresh Kumar Sharma at Srishti

Cover design: Suresh Sharma

Printed and bound in India

Unto my Guru

CONTENTS

Foreword

I come from a tradition where 'consciousness' is considered central to any form of study. The heart of that worldview is the subject-object dynamics. The objective world depends on subjective experiences of the self-conscious individual. According to this worldview no study can be considered complete without factoring the subject in the study.

The binary thinking inaugurated by Rene Descartes and the subsequent surge in the field of objective studies at the cost of the subjective has created lopsidedness, in spite of the phenomenal progress in the objective fields, leading to the loss of human soul. The human soul is the window to consciousness. Modern science has succeeded in reducing almost all observable phenomena to measurable units. But the phenomenon of consciousness seems to defy the methodologies developed by science. Scientific inquiry in its relentless march to absolute knowledge seems to be stuck at the ramparts of consciousness. Higher physics has become a set of mathematical assumptions beyond the discipline of experimentation. The looming horizon of consciousness and the increasing role of mind-play in advanced research have made science look like a poor cousin of metaphysics and mysticism. Physicists like Einstein and Schrodinger in their sublime moods talked like mystics to express their profound thoughts about the physical world and laws governing it. Linear thinking has discovered a soul mate in holistic thinking. Science, rational traditions, and knowledge gained from experimental research no more shy away from standing along with other modes of knowing and being in the world. Science has become humble and inclusive.

Today consciousness is one of the greatest puzzles that both science and other disciplines face. Consciousness is so close to human experience, but so far away from human understanding. A part of the puzzle is the insistence that all knowledge should empower the possessor with tools of manipulation in her ego-centered demands of the world. A knowledge that subsumes the knower in a higher experience of ecstasy is dismissed as subjective and therefore irrelevant. The ontological status and universality of the subject remains a distant dream for the objective scientist.

The Vedantic tradition in India explains the problematic as the spiritual indiscipline and ignorance of the enquirer. In a very telling verse the Kathopanishad describes the sad predicament of the objectivist thus: "Not being reflective, and extroverted he is conditioned to see only the outer world and is condemned to think that the outer sensations are the only basis of reality. It is the rare few that come to realize the subjective Self by desiring the Beyond and disciplining the mind". Besides disciplining the mental processes for better methods and hypotheses, the idea of disciplining the whole person is not an agenda of the objectivist.

Brain studies and third person approaches to consciousness have made great strides in understanding consciousness and human behavior. But those studies seldom cover the phenomena of subjective experiences, as pointed out by the Rishis of India and very powerfully expressed as the 'hard problem' by the Australian mathematician and consciousness researcher David Chalmers. The central point in consciousness studies is the nature, role and origin of subjective experience. Though Francis Crick, Richard Dawkins, Daniel Dennett and others try to explain consciousness in terms of the biology of the brain, genetic information, evolutionary biology and neural processes, there appears to be a large community of researchers who tend to think that consciousness studies require a new paradigm approach.

Dr. Sangeetha Menon belongs to this category of thinkers. She brings a variety of knowledge systems to throw light on the puzzle of consciousness. Besides her critical appraisal of the third person scientific methods, Dr. Sangeetha also takes the routes of art and spirituality in her quest for consciousness. *Natya*, dramaturgy, a detached simulation of mental processes; *Bhakti*, self giving love of the world, and; *Jnana*, happily abiding in the Self by the self, are some of the subjective disciplines that she recommends for understanding consciousness in the first person mode and as a healing experience.

Dr.Sangeetha Menon develops her thesis based on the philosophy and psychology of the Bhagavad Gita. The Gita is an exhaustive phenomenological study of consciousness leading to consummate understanding of the experiencing subject, experienced world and the ontological basis of both. The Gita presents many opposing and complementary views and offers an unified integral theory of consciousness. To the readers of Gita, understanding of consciousness should lead to happiness, freedom and spontaneous action. The Gita's position is that consciousness is fundamental, and the ground and being of the material universe. Human consciousness is one form of its myriad expressions. A life integrated in reflection, love and action leading to the experience of expanded consciousness is the vision that the Gita expounds.

In Dr. Sangeetha Menon I find a perfect blend of scholarly rigor, humanly love and spiritual depth. Her words carry profound conviction and convey the puzzle of consciousness in its complexity. What is soothing is that she does not take side in the divided debate; rather she tries to see a valid point in ail views and makes heroic efforts to synthesize a unified theory of consciousness.

This book is a valid study of consciousness from the Indian wisdom standpoint integrating many issues and questions that are raised by both first and third person approaches. I strongly recommend this book for both the researcher and the lay reader.

Swami Bodhananda
Chairman & Spiritual Director, Sambodh Foundation, India
and The Sambodh Society Inc. USA

1

Introduction

prajahati yada kaman sarvan partha manogatan
atmanyevatamana tustah sthitaprajnastadocyate

O Partha, Sthitaprajna is one who has given up desire for happiness and has come to abide happily in the Self by the self.
Bhagavad Gita 2:55

The concept of consciousness is central to the study of human existence. The wide-ranging meanings given to the concept of consciousness have been of interest to traditional as well as modern thinkers. Though consciousness is a theme that demands multidisciplinary intervention, in no field of study it can be alienated from its reference to subjective existence. It is undeniable, philosophically and neurobiologically, that consciousness is the crux of any subjective analysis. Consciousness has logical priority since it is the awareness superintending the subject-object dichotomy. All cognitions are made possible by the cogniser. Consciousness has epistemic priority being the cogniser's self or subject. When the existence of anything and everything can be brought under scepticism consciousness stays an apodictic fact. Hence consciousness has ontological priority too.

The concept of consciousness harbours various interpretations and definitions. Etymologically, the word consciousness has Latin roots. The word consciousness is derived from the Latin 'con' (with) and 'scire' (to know)'.[1] The Oxford English Dictionary finds the first literal use of consciousness to mean "person's thoughts and feelings as a whole."[2] As a foundational characteristic of intelligence and survival consciousness can be defined and described variously according to different perspectives in understanding, awareness, thinking, insight and creativity. The concept of consciousness is vested with diverse meanings and functions from religious, ethical and historical realms apart from philosophical, psychological and scientific standpoints. Religion considers consciousness from a teleological point of view. A religious consciousness implies the faith in a supreme power, to bring about an universal consciousness enveloping all particular existent beings. Ethically, consciousness is interpreted as conscience. "At one time identical with the term 'consciousness', the English term 'conscience' has gained the restriction of standing for consciousness of right and wrong as known inwardly."[3] Consciousness has historical significance too. From an historical and evolutionary perspective, Thomas N. Munson says: "Consciousness is a living reality that we have to think as a movement in which a past is constantly recreated in terms of

[1] W.L. Reese, Dictionary of Philosophy and Religion: Eastern and Western Thought, (New Jersey: Humanities Press, 1980), p.104.

[2] F.G. Fowler and H.W. Fowler, Pocket Oxford Dictionary, 4th ed., (Oxford: Clarendon Press, 1965), p.165.

[3] W.L. Reese, Dictionary of Philosophy and Religion Eastern and Western Thought, (New Jersey: Humanities Press, 1980), p.105.

a projected future. Therefore as a movement, it can be neither securely grounded in something else nor itself absolutized."[4] At the same time, consciousness integrates past experiences of the human self and advances into the future without being relegated into historicity.

The word consciousness is included in the technical terminology of a number of philosophical systems, brain studies, psychology and cognitive sciences. In psychology, consciousness is often presented as a process prescribing different mental acts primarily in the conscious, unconscious and subconscious states of the mind. In the words of Katheleen Wilkes: "Consciousness is a term that groups a thoroughly heterogeneous bunch of psychological phenomena."[5] Cognitive sciences identify consciousness as a knowing function. Consciousness is an embarrassment to functionalistic and computational theories of mind. These theories suggest a causal determinism between human thought and action, which unsatisfactorily explains the freedom of will and spontaneity of consciousness. Reductionists and Structuralists define consciousness as a neurological stimuli or behaviourist response. The materialistic theory of consciousness with which behaviourist theories are associated hold that the functioning of consciousness is intimately associated with the nervous system and functioning of the brain. D.M. Armstrong equates consciousness with a mental state such as that involved in the ability to perceive. He says: "In perception the brain scans the environment. In awareness of perception

[4]Thomas N. Munson, Religious Consciousness and Experience,(Hague: Martinus Nijhoff, 1975), p.100.

[5] Kathleen V. Wilkes, Real People, (Oxford: Cllarendon Press, 1988), p.196.

another process in the brain scans the scanning."[6] According to the automation theory of T.H. Huxley: "Consciousness in man depends upon the integrity of the anterior division of the brain. ... All states of consciousness are immediately caused by molecular changes of the brain substance."[7] Structuralism, which is relatively, a recent advancement of behaviorism holds that "... consciousness ... occurs as a consequence of self-monitoring activity in individual nuclear groups throughout the neuraxis. ... The verbalization of awareness of this process may be related to language centres in the human cerebral cortex...."[8] Functionalistic theories are seriously criticized, as they reduce consciousness into a mere physical function, thereby questioning the very existence of consciousness. David Smith says, "When philosophers question the existence of consciousness, they are out of touch with human experience. Theorizing has cut them off from a basic feature of even their own experience - viz. - consciousness. Their position is intellectually schizoid."[9]

In the history of Western thought, four principal concepts of consciousness have been elaborated. The first is that of empiricism, the classical British school commenced by Locke and brought

---

[6] D.M. Armstrong, A Materialist Theory of the Mind, (London: Routledge and Kegan Paul, 1968), p.94.

[7] T.H. Huxley, The Automation Theory, Eds. Paul Edwards and Arthur Pap, A Modern Introduction to Philosophy, (London: George Allen and Unwin Ltd., 1957), pp.245-256.

[8] Aryeh Routtenberg. Redundancy in the Nervous System as a Substrate for Consciousness, Eds. Julian M. Davidson and Richard J. Davidson, The Psychobiology of Consciousness, (New York: Plenum Press, 1980), p.123.

[9] David Woodruff Smith, Res Cogitans: The Unquestionability of Consciousness, Eds. H.R. Otto and J.A. Tuedio, Perspectives on Mind, (Boston: D. Reidel Publishing Co., 1988), p.25.

to its completion by Hume. Empiricists conceive consciousness as a mosaic of sensory data and images derived from the data. Descartes, Leibnitz and Kant insisted on the activity and spontaneity of mind in terms of perception and apperception and thus established the second principal (rationalistic) concept of consciousness. The two other concept, of consciousness are in the context of phenomenological and existential approaches. Akin to the psychological methodology, phenomenology is also concerned with consciousness in general, as well as with specific conscious acts such as perception, memory, reason etc. Phenomenologists, starting from Husserl, view consciousness as constituting the essence of a being. Henry Ey defines consciousness: "the intermingling of objects, data, lived experiences and the meaning of each constituted reality."[10] Sartre inaugurated the existentialist approach to consciousness. For Sartre: "Consciousness is a plenum of existence.... The existence of consciousness comes from consciousness itself."[11]

Linking phenomenological, existential and behaviourist approaches to consciousness, in more recent trends, there are those approaches grouped under 'identity theory'. Of the identity theories C.O. Evans is the proponent of self-identity theory. Evans holds: "The concept has application for the reader because it applies in his own case. In this sense we can affirm 'There is consciousness' without prejudging the question whether there is

---

[10] Henry Ey, Consciousness – A Phenomenological Study of Being Conscious and Becoming Conscious, Tr. John F. Flodstrom, (Bloomington: Indiana University Press, 1978), p.43.

[11] Jean Paul Sartre, Being and Nothingness, (New Jersey: Citadel Press, 1956), p.XVI.

any subject of consciousness to be revealed through its analysis."[12] The Self or Person is considered as the underlying entity possessing both mental and physical attributes. The Person-identity concepts of consciousness can be traced in the works of C.R. Bukala, Pratima Bowes et.al. In an article Bukala writes: "Consciousness, in our understanding, is one of the aspects of a dynamic subject, in fact, the aspect which is the focal point of a person's identity and experience as a human person."[13] Though Bowes interprets consciousness as pre-personal, it is a modified oı varied version of the personal aspect, and can be accommodated in person-identity theories. According to Bowes, "Consciousness as a primary datum is pre-personal and not personal in the sense that its occurrence is attended by a feeling that it belongs to so and so. Of course it is not impersonal in the sense that it happens as something detached from all moorings. The very intentional nature of consciousness provides it with an individual character and the presence to itself of consciousness gives it identity."[14] In spite of the differences in the wide array of theories conceptualising consciousness, the epistemological and the ontological status of consciousness is agreed to in different theories. Asserting the self-evident nature of consciousness as the subject, Fritjof Capra remarks: "... consciousness is not that can be derived from or explained in terms of something else. It is a primal fact of existence out of which everything else arises."[15]

[12] C.O. Evans, The Subject of Consciousness, (London: George Allen and Unwin Ltd., 1970), p.66.

[13] C.R. Bukala, Consciousness: Creative and Self-Creating, Ed. David Pellauer, Philosophy Today, vol.35:1(Illinois: De Paul University, 1991), p.15.

[14] Pratima Bowes, Consciousness and Freedom, (London: Methuen and Co. Ltd., 1971), p.145.

[15] Fritjof Capra, Uncommon Wisdom, (London: Century Hutchinsons Ltd., 1988), p.150.

The focus of the classical systems of Indian thought when addressing consciousness, is epistemological, ontological or both. Heterodox systems introduce consciousness to account mind-body relationship. Amongst Orthodox systems, Nyaya-Vaisesika interprets consciousness epistemologically in atomistic terms. Samkhya Yoga brings consciousness to a realm of passive reciprocity. Though Advaita Vedanta analyses consciousness from an epistemological perspective, gives it more ontological significance by defining it as the nature of the cogniser's or experiencer's Self.

The Bhagavad Gita, included in the Prasthanatreya, the three foundational pillars of classical Indian thought, presents a distinct theory of consciousness. The Gita presents an elaborate analysis of the psychology of consciousness based on the bedrock of a deep experiential philosophy. The Gita concept of consciousness cannot be categorized solely as psychological, existential, epistemological or pragmatic. Through its teaching, the Gita gives a wholesome definition for consciousness. In Sri Aurobindo's words: "The language of the Gita, the structure of thought, the combination and balancing of ideas belong neither to the temper of a sectarian teacher nor to the spirit of a rigorous analytical dialectics cutting off one angle of the truth to exclude all the others; but rather there is a wide, undulating, encircling movement of ideas which is the manifestation of a vast synthetic mind and a rich synthetic experience."[16] The Gita encompasses wide-ranging experiential meanings of consciousness from an ontological standpoint. By consciousness the Gita means not

[16] Sri Aurobindo, Essays on the Gita, 8th ed., (Pondicherry: Sri Aurobindo Ashram, 1970), p.6.

the ego, non-ego or psychic function but the Self. The very teaching of the Gita is set in the background of an existential situation in the war-front, and the methodology adopted is of a transpersonal dialogue form. It is notable that the existential situation of the individual and the dialogue form of communication are considered essential positive factors in modern methods of psychotherapy.

This book makes an effort to analyse thoroughly the psychological, epistemological, ontological, existential and pragmatic implications of consciousness in the Gita. As far as Indian philosophy is concerned, conceptual studies of consciousness have been made mostly in the field of Buddhism. The study of consciousness in the Bhagavad Gita is a maiden attempt. A comparative study of 'consciousness' with 'action' and 'thought integration' is also a new attempt by which the philosophy and psychology of concepts like action, inaction, non-action, freedom and happiness will be discussed.

The primary aim of this book is to synthesise and coherently present the experiential philosophy of the Gita concept of consciousness. As a supplement to this venture, this study will briefly discuss consciousness as dealt with in classical Indian philosophy. This book does not trace the historical evolution of the concept of consciousness, but enables an experiential and spiritual understanding in the context of human action and predicaments. The first four chapters present an introduction, the concept of consciousness in the Upanishads, the Heterodox and the Orthodox systems of Indian philosophy. The later chapters make an attempt to comprehensively present and synthesize the concept of consciousness in the Bhagavad Gita.

An effort to trace the concept of consciousness in the Vedic and the Upanishadic philosophy is made in the second chapter. This chapter pays special attention to the Upanishadic eschatology, epistemology, creation theories, and the ontologised epistemology of *mahavakyas*.

Heterodox systems of Indian thought do make references to understanding different planes of consciousness and their relation with *karma*. In the third chapter an effort is made to give an exposition of consciousness as presented in the schools of Carvaka, Buddhism and Jainism.

The analysis of the nature of consciousness according to the Orthodox systems such as Nyaya-Vaisesika, Samkhya-Yoga, Purva-Mimamsa and Advaita Vedanta is attempted in the fourth chapter. In this chapter, the concept of consciousness in Advaita is studied with special reference to Samkaracarya's theory of superimposition (*adhyasa*) in his commentary on the Brahmasutra. This chapter also presents the Samkhyan concept of *purusa* and *prakrti* in contrast with the same concepts in the Bhagavad Gita.

The proceeding chapters focus on the concept of consciousness in the Bhagavad Gita. The original verses of the Gita and the ideas are presented in the backdrop of Samkaracarya's commentary to the Gita. In chapter five, the concept of consciousness in the Gita is presented to trace its epistemological, ontological and hermeneutical imports.

The relation between consciousness and materiality is a subject of keen interest to scientists, philosophers and psychologists. The sixth chapter makes an effort to present the Gita view of the relation between consciousness and matter.

The ontological pragmatism of the Gita brings forth a theory of action that is grounded in freedom through its technique of *karmani-akarma darsanam* (freedom in action). The pragmatics of *karma* given in the Gita is to be understood in the light of its ontology of the identity of the Self and consciousness. The seventh chapter is devoted to the examination of the Gita theory of action, and its reference to mental purity, renunciation and meditation.

The eighth chapter examines the Gita concept of freedom. The Gita allocates freedom to the ontological realm than to the existential situation of the individual. This chapter tries to present the Gita theory of identity between freedom and happiness, and the integral experience of consciousness.

The ninth chapter makes an appraisal of consciousness. It enumerates, substantiates and reiterates the prominent features of the Gita concept of consciousness comparing with Upanishads, Darsanas, and recent discussions. This chapter brings to attention the distinct and novel characteristics, definition and scope of consciousness as developed in the Bhagavad Gita.

The final chapter, Epilogue, gives a brief account of the current discussions in consciousness studies in a multidisciplinary context, and its impact on larger questions asked and challenges faced in neuropsychiatry, philosophy, psychology and cognitive sciences.

The primary work for this book started during the days of my doctoral research. Over a period of 10 years I have modified it many times without losing the focus, which is a discussion on the concept of consciousness in the Gita from an experiential point of view. Though the Epilogue briefs the current discussions on consciousness, I have not gone into the details of the challenges and puzzles that these discussions present in their entirety.

To enable an easy reading for scholars as well as general readers I have not included diacritical marks for Sanskrit words. At the same time, I have avoided popular spellings. Extensive references from the original and secondary sources are expected to help the reader for further reading.

From the start to the finish of this book I was blessed to have many dialogues with my Spiritual Guru Swami Bodhananda. Without the many discussions with him and his guidance and insightful thoughts this book would not have been possible. Beyond the help to complete this book he taught me to live the epitome values in the Bhagavad Gita. And that is the greatest gift this study has given me. My pranams to him. I dedicate this book unto his holy feet. I also thank Gurudev for agreeing to write the foreword for this book in spite of his busy schedule.

The calm and serene air of National Institute of Advanced Studies helped me bring the book to this final shape. I fondly acknowledge the inspiration and encouragement I received from the late Dr Raja Ramanna, the then Director when I joined the Institute. Many thanks to my senior colleague and friend-philosopher-guide Prof BV Sreekantan for scholarly exchanges on Bhagavad Gita. I am fortunate to see a person whose life reflects many practical teachings of the Gita. In the last 10 years few days have gone, in our discussions, without some reference to the profundity of the Bhagavad Gita.

I thank Dr K Kasturirangan, Director of National Institute of Advanced Studies, and Member of Parliament, Upper House, for his continuous motivation and support.

Thanks also to all colleagues at the Institute and my friends.

Without the support and understanding of my family I would not have completed this book.

The support of the *Global Perspectives on Science and Spirituality Award* programme (GPSS) managed by Interdisciplinaire Universite de Paris, Elon University North Carolina, and supported by Templeton Foundation, helped me to finalise this book and also to extend this study for the forthcoming book which will focus on current discussions on consciousness studies in the context of agency and spiritual experience.

Writing this book was a great experience to me, not just from an academic perspective, but from a spiritual perspective too. I present this book to you to explore the meaning of the Gita ideal of 'freedom in action', and its basis that our true nature is pure consciousness.

Sangeetha Menon
27 March, 2007

2

Consciousness in the Upanishads

tan me manah siva sankalpamastu

On that – the auspicious will of the divine – may my mind dwell
Shukla Yajurveda, Vajasaneya Samhita 34-1

Beyond the ephemeral experiences but revealing through each and every cognitive act is the one unifying principle of consciousness – the cogniser's Self. This is the epitome of the teaching conveyed by the Vedic sages and the Upanishadic seers through a vast corpus of sacred literature. A continuing identity in all experiences, holding different experiences and states together, the mind-body relationship, the nature of the individual, her relationship with the world etc. have always been subjects demanding an intensive inquiry. In this context the Upanishadic Rishi puts forth the theory of encompassing consciousness and the identity of consciousness with the Self. The Rishi presents a new discipline of psycho-ontology. He presents a psychology that explains and forms the basis of ontology and axiology. Thus we have profound Upanishadic statements like *aham brahmasmi* and *anandam brahma*. This chapter attempts to trace the concept of consciousness in the pre-Upanishadic period by an analysis of the Samhitas, Brahmanas and Aranyakas, followed by an account of the concept of consciousness in the Upanishads.

Consciousness in the Pre-Upanishadic Literature

Vedas constitute one of the earliest documents of the Indian mind. The Rig Veda deities represent the possibilities of infinite human relationships with the fundamental truth of existence namely consciousness. The Vedic people were able to reflect its cosmic dimensions in their daily life. They lived a comprehensive life full of feelings, urges, passions and joys. To them the external nature was not a rival to their inner aspirations, but a medium for free expression.

Earliest Signs

The earliest signs of a psychological inquiry into the first principle, can be noted in expressions like: "Who has seen that the boneless bears the bony when being born first? Where may be the breath, the blood, the soul of the earth? Who would approach the wise to make this enquiry?" (Rig Veda: I.164.4)[1] "In the beginning there arose the Golden Child (*Hiranya-garbha);* as soon as born, he alone was the Lord of all that is. He established the earth and this heaven: Who is the God to who, we shall offer sacrifice?"(Rig Veda: X.121.I) "Unsupported, unattached spread out downwards – turned – how is that he does not fall down? By what power of his does he move? Who has seen (that)? Erected as the pillar of

[1]Rig Veda: I.164.4. Quotations form the Vedas are taken from F. Max Muller, Ed. Sacred Books of the East, (Delhi: Motilal Banarsidass Publishers, 1978).

Heaven he protects the firmament" (Rig Veda: IV.3.5). In these verses a metaphysical and epistemological distinction in inquiry is made. The metaphysical distinction made is between the manifest and the unmanifest nature of reality. The epistemological distinction made is between direct and indirect knowledge. These verses initiate a psychological inquiry too into the nature of reality.

Speech and Mind

An attempt to explain the relation between the material world and the psychosomatic person is made by identifying physical powers and psychic faculties with the portfolio of various deities.

Among the deities goddess Vac is of psychological import. Vac is the Vedic term referring to both speech and speech-consciousness. The hymn to Vac says that all actions and powers are grounded in speech. It is the primordial energy-stuff out of which all existence originates and subsists. At the same time it goes beyond the heavens and the earth. Speech is also recognised as the first expression of truth when the hymn says: "When I partake a portion of this speech, the first products of truth come to me" (Rig Veda: I.164.37). Dirghatamas proceeds: "From her (Vac) flows the oceans; through her exist the four regions; from her flows the ground (*aksara*) of the Veda; on her the entire universe stands"(Rig Veda: I.164.32). But three verses later, he reminds us that only the manifested forms of speech can be known and the deepest levels remain hidden. He further adds that prayer is the highest heaven in which speech dwells. Thus we find innumerable Vedic hymns in the form of prayers. Through prayer – the fundamental mode of speech consciousness – the individual mind tries to resonate with the cosmic mind.

The *yajna* performances are based on the psychology of speech-consciousness. Through the liturgical knowing-acting of sacrificial celebration, the limitations of ordinary existence and the grounding of human existence in the more fundamental levels of consciousness are recognised and experienced. The Vedic sage offers his oblations unto: "He who gives breath, he who gives strength, whose command all the bright gods revere, whose shadow is immortality, whose shadow is death…"(Rig Veda: X.121.2). The Vedic concept of *rta* comes as a result of this recognition of a comprehensive and unifying principle. Vedic sages recognise *rta* as the rhythm behind the structuring of the dynamic aspects of the universe.

A more comprehensive nature of reality is admitted when in later Samhitas and Brahmanas, the superior nature of mind to speech is recognised. In a dialogue between the Speech and the Mind, Prajapati is made to describe speech as "Thou art the messenger of mind, for what one thinks of in the mind, one utters in speech" (Taittiriya Samhita: II.5.11).[2] In a later version Taittiriya Samhita recognises the limitations of both speech and mind to define the first comprehensive principle. It says: "Finite are the hymns, finite the chants, finite the ritual formulae, to what constitute Brahman however there is no end" (Taittiriya Samhita: VII.3.1.4).

In Satapatha Brahmana, we find an analysis of sleep

[2] Taittiriya Samhita: II.5.11. Quotations from the Taittiriya Samhita are taken from F. Max Muller, Ed. Sacred Books of the East, (Delhi: Motilal Banarsidass Publishers, 1978).

consciousness where the superiority of *prana* is recognised. The verse says: "And when he is asleep he does not, by means of them, know of anything whatever, nor does he form any resolution with his mind, or distinguish the taste of food with (the channel of) his speech, or distinguish any smell with (the channel of) his breath, neither does he with his eye, nor with his ear, for those (vital airs) have taken possession of him"(Sathapatha Brahmana: X.5.2.15)[3].

Satapatha Brahmana thereafter gives a negative description of the First principle as *apurvam* and *aparavat* as to which there is noting earlier and after. "This Brahman has nothing before it and after it" (Sathapatha Brahmana: X.3.5.11). In a later verse it adds: "It is this that the Rishi saw when he said, I praise what hath been and what will be, the Great Brahman, the one *Aksara*; for indeed, all the gods, all kings pass into that *Aksara*..."(Sathapatha Brahmana: X.4.1.9). It is *ekam* and *purnam*. It is the One principle which is given various names by the poets. Here we find a hint to the fundamental thought of the Upanishads.

Principles of Knowledge

An analysis of cognition is found in the Satapatha Brahmana. The whole universe is depicted as coextensive with the universal principles of name and form. "These, indeed, are the two great manifestations of the Brahman; and verily, he who knows these two great manifestations of Brahman becomes himself a great

[3] Satapatha Brahmana: X.5.2.15. Quotations from the Satapatha Brahmana are taken from F. Max Muller, Ed. Sacred Books of the East, (Delhi: Motilal Banarsidass Publishers, 1978).

manifestation. One of these two is the greater namely Form; for whatever is Name is indeed form; and verily, he who knows the greater of these two, becomes greater than he who wishes to surpass in greatness" (Satapatha Brahmana: XI.2.3.5). Cognition of objects is made by name and form. Name comes from speech and form from mind. It is by mind that one knows form. The Brahmana also says that he who understands this, understands the universe comprehensively. In a similar context Atharva Veda says that the indescribable is the ground of all names and forms, the support of the whole creation. The same text in another verse describes the indescribable as "Desireless, self-possessed, immortal, self-proved, ever full of Bliss, inferior to none, ever young and everlasting is he, the soul of this universe, through his knowledge alone can one spurn death" (Atharva Veda: X.8.44).

The nature of the personal identity is a subject dealt in detail in the Upanishads. The earlier Brahmanas and Samhitas give a prologue to the Upanishadic psychology of the individual. Satapatha Brahmana notes: "Let him meditate upon the 'true Brahman'. Now, man here, indeed, is possessed of understanding, and according to how great his understanding is when he departs this world, so does he, on passing away, enter yonder world. Let him meditate on the Self, which is made up of intelligence, and endowed with a body of spirit...that Self of the spirit (breath) is my self..." (Satapatha Brahmana: X.6.3.1-2). Apart from the words *kratu*, *manas* and *samkalpah* used in this verse, denoting psychical faculties, *manas* appear in the verse: "Let us know each other's mind" and "Let our minds be the same"(Satapatha Brahmana: X.191.2). This verse also imply that the sages did conceive of a relation between the individual mind and the cosmic mind. Satapatha Brahmana further says: "One becomes, what one meditates on" (Satapatha Brahmana: X.5.2.20). Here we find the Vedic insight into the subject of Knowing and Being that is later discussed in the Upanishads in a pivotal manner.

The First Principle

The first principle that belongs to the last phase of Vedic cosmogony is considered less in personalistic terms and more as a psychic principle. The whole world is a sacrifice and the Gods perform their function through sacrifice. The concept of sacrifice leads to the analysis of the relation between the creator and the created. This analysis is elaborately done in the Purusasukta and the Nasadiyasukta. As far as the inquiry into the nature of consciousness is considered, these hymns demand a study.

In the first verse of Purusasukta reality is depicted as the *Virat Purusa* or Cosmic Person, pervading the whole universe but still beyond it. "*Purusa* is all this world, what has been and what shall be" (Purusasukta: X.90.2). The Vedic poet conjures a vast picture to present the nature of Purusa. The Purusasukta speaks of an eternal sacrifice that sustains the whole world. World is one single being of incomparable vastness and immensity enlivened by the Purusa.

Vedas interpret creation as the manifestation of the First principle. It is not the becoming of something not hither to existent. "Verily, in the beginning this (universe) was, as it were. Neither non-existent nor existent, in the beginning this (universe), indeed, as it were, existed and did not exist: there was then only that Mind" (Satapatha Brahmana: X.5.3.1). The

Nasadiyasukta explains the universe as evolving out of the primary principle. In the first verse *kama* or desire is identified as the creative energy. But the last two verses, with an agnostic touch exclaim: "*ko vedah*" (Nasadiyasukta: X.129.6-7) – who knows? – from where the creation came, for only one who was before creation can really know that. The hymn marks the boundaries of a conceptual categorisation in terms of cause and effect. It simply says that wholeness which can only be pointed as 'That one' is the ground of all existence – *sat* – and non-existence – *asat*. The mystery of creation can never be discovered conceptually. The only solution as given by the Upanishads is to know the nature of the Self as the basis of reality.

Mind in Vajasaneya Samhita and Aitareya Aranyaka

When in the Purusasukta and Nasadiyasukta, reality is indicated by the expressions '*purusa*' and '*tad ekam*', the Vajasaneya Samhita uses another description to distinguish between the knowing and willing functions of *manas*. The Samhita uses the word '*manah*' not in the sense of mental faculty, but as pure awareness. (Sukla Yajurveda, Vajasaneya Samhita: 34-1).

Consciousness illumines both the waker and sleeper (waking and sleep states), but is also beyond it. "May that mind of mine be of auspicious resolve, which is divine; which goes out afar when I am awake, and which similarly comes back when I am asleep; that which goes far and wide, and is the light of lights."[4] The introductory verse also gives a theory of perception when it says that in the waking state, consciousness goes out far – *duram*

[4] Jwala Prasad, History of Indian Epistemology, 3rd ed., (New Delhi: Munshiram Manoharlal Publishers Pvt. Ltd., 1987), p.16.

udaiti – to the world of objects and remains in ourselves during sleep. *Manas* is described as the power that helps in performing sacrifices and other duties. It is the unique – *apurvam* – and sacred entity in the heart – *antah*. It is the inner core of all beings.

Consciousness is also expressed as the tripartite mental faculty like intelligence (*prajnanam*), feeling (*cetas*) and resolution (*dhrtih*). It is experienced as cognition, affection and conation. Consciousness is the eternal – *amrtam*, light and life breath in all beings, without which nothing is accomplished. The fourth verse describes consciousness as the eternal principle and hence holding in it together the past, present and future. Here the transcendent and the immanent nature of consciousness are recognized. Consciousness is conceived as the unifying principle of knowledge, which brings about the continuity of experiences. It is the basis – *otam* – of all thoughts – *cittam sarvam*.

The sixth verse gives an analogy of the charioteer. "May that mind of mine be of auspicious resolve, which leads and controls men; just as a good charioteer does the horses with his reins; that which residing in the heart of men is the swiftest and free from decay."[5] Consciousness controls men, like a charioteer who leads and controls his horses. Consciousness not only resides in the heart – *hrdipratistam* – but also ramifies by going out swiftly – *javistam* – and it never decays – *ajiram*. By referring to the heart as the seat of consciousness, the intimacy of consciousness to the Self is underlined. The primacy of consciousness is specified when it says that it alone goes out swiftly. All the six verses of the Samhita end with the refrain 'May my mind be of auspicious

---

[5] Jwala Prasad, History of Indian Epistemology, 3rd ed., (New Delhi: Munshiram Manoharlal Publishers Pvt. Ltd., 1987), p.18.

resolve, which is of the nature of this consciousness'. Prayer is made for the abidance of the mind in its real nature. It is clear that the Upanishadic Rishi was encouraged to see the (functions of) mind not as cognitively isolated but as experientially capable of revealing something that is higher.

Aitareya Aranyaka in the initial chapters brings the concept of *ukta* as the essence and the symbol of the universe. *Ukta* etymologically signifies that from which things arise, and therefore where things do depart. Later in the Aranyaka, *ukta* is replaced by *Atman*. *Atman* is that from which the five-fold *ukta* (the five elements) arise and resolve. The second Aranyaka emphasises consciousness and intelligence. From the fourth chapter of the second Aranyaka begins the Aitareya Upanishad that gives a remarkable analysis of the mental faculties and consciousness.

The Brahmanas and Aranyakas bring the concept of a fundamental and inclusive principle, which is named variously. In these descriptions we find an approach to understand the absolute as that which includes and transcends divisions.

A significant concept in the Vedic hymns is that which describes reality as 'one' – *ekam sat* – that which includes variety of existences. It is the idea of 'oneness' that is metaphysically described as Pure Consciousness and ontologically presented as Self in the Upanishads. In contrast to a discrete and object-centred empirical approach that prevails to a large extent in contemporary analytical philosophy and cognitive psychology, Upanishadic psychology insists upon an orientation towards subjectivity. With the emphasis on consciousness as the foundation of thoughts, the Upanishadic philosophy forms the basis for the psychological principles developed in later systems of Indian philosophy.

Consciousness as the Ultimate Reality

The word used in the Upanishads to indicate the Supreme Reality, that is uncl angeable and eternal, is Brahman. The word Brahman is derived form the root *brh – atisayana* – to exceed. Brahman is that which 'grows' and hence includes more. The same definition can be related to consciousness too. From the form in which it is presented, Mandukya Upanishad is one of the latest among the Upanishads that describes Pure Consciousness in its immaculate notion, unmixed with sectarian views. The descriptions indicate the absence of any uncertainty. Consciousness is "not that which cognises the internal (objects), not that which cognises the external (objects), not that which cognises both of them, not a mass of cognition, not cognitive, not non-cognitive. (It is) unseen, incapable of being spoken of, ungraspable, without any distinct marks, unthinkable, unnameable, the essence of the knowledge of the one Self, that into which the world is resolved, the peaceful, the benign, the non-dual, such, they think, is the fourth quarter. He is the Self; he is to be known" (Mandukya Upanishad:7).[6] Consciousness is not that which knows the external objects during the waking state. It is not that which knows the internal objects during dream

[6] Mandukya Upanishad: 7. Quotations from the Upanishads are taken from S. Radhakrishnan, Ed. and Tr. The Principal Upanishads, (Delhi: Oxford University Press, 1989).

state. A mere function of knowing cannot be attributed to it. At the same time it is not ignorance. Samkaracarya explains *naprajnam* as *acaitanyapratiseta*. Consciousness is that in which the whole world resolves, since it is not qualified by the experiences in the waking, dream and deep sleep states. The Mandukya concept of consciousness is different from the superego, ego and id of Freud, and the conscious, subconscious and collective unconscious concepts of Jungian psychology. Consciousness is *santam* since it is *avikriyam* – without any modifications. The prime nature of consciousness is that it is the invariable factor in all experiences. The Self is to be known as this consciousness.

A significant idea of the Rishis is the inclusion of all experiences in consciousness, and, maintaining it as beyond and untouched by them. In various terms and expressions, we find this nature of consciousness, depicted in the Upanishadic literature. The Peace Invocation for Brhadaranyaka Upanishad describes the unmanifest Brahman (God) and the manifest Brahman (world) as whole. From the unmanifest *Brahman* comes the manifest Brahman. And retaining the wholeness of the world, the whole (Unmanifest *Brahman*) remains ever. Samkaracarya in his *bhasya* to this verse, says, *yat svarupam*, *purnatvam*, *paramatmabhavam*. Neither the immanence of consciousness lowers it nor its transcendence alienates it from the world. Consciousness is *purnam* – mere fullness.

In Candogya Upanishad, Prajapati emphasizes the nature of Self as pure consciousness. It is unaffected by the changes of experience, but runs in and through the differences. The

Self is not an abstract formal principle, but an active universal consciousness. It is the sole reality.

Is this consciousness established on something else? In Candogya Upanishad, Narada asks Sanatkumara: 'On what is *Bhuman* established?' and Sanatkumara answers, 'It can only be established on its own greatness or not even on greatness'. Bharadvaja adds onto this statement in Arseya Upanishad, "That light which shines incessantly suffusing everything ... when near it looks far away, when far away it looks near; None can transcend its greatness."[7] Consciousness is self-sufficient, self-explaining and self-supporting. There is nothing exterior on which it depends. Hence it is "the Real, Knowledge and the Infinite" – *satyam jnanam ananatam* (Taittiriya Upanishad: II.1.1). Therefore if a person knows consciousness as not existing, he becomes as it were, herself non-existing; if a person knows consciousness as existing, then it is known that he exists. It is "by which the unhearable becomes heard, the unperceivable becomes perceived, the unknowable becomes known"(Candogya Upanishad: VI.1.3). Yajnavalkya describes consciousness as a given fact of all experiences and as the innermost Self, which is the imperishable – *aksaram*. Consciousness is the very principle of knowledge, in the light of which everything else is illumined. Yama rhetorically asks in Katha Upanishad, 'what else remains here?' – '*kimatra parisisyate*' – and answers, 'This is verily that'.

Candogya Upanishad and Katha Upanishad further describe consciousness as the one, the infinite (*bhuma*) and the bliss. It is the eternal amidst the transient, one amidst the many and is the

[7] S.K. Belvalkar and R.D. Ranade, History of Indian Philosophy, vol.I, (Poona: Bilvakunja Pulbishing House, 1927), p.298.

principle of Intelligence. It is the Infinite. "Infinite is Bliss" (Candogya Upanishad: VII.23.1). And "to the wise who perceive him as abiding in the soul, to them is eternal Bliss" (Katha Upanishad: II.2.13). On this description of Consciousness as Bliss, Gispert-Sauch makes an interesting remark: "From the highest peak of the integration of being, therefore, when one has achieved the perfect unity in which the totality is possessed, and all pluralism of dispersion is excluded, there flows the experience of the blissful character of existence."[8]

Consciousness and Creation

The mind-body and consciousness-matter relations often witness polemic discussions between the realist and the idealist, and the behaviourist and the centralist. The attempt to develop a theory of everything in terms of ideas has landed the idealist in a state where he is unable to explain the feel of the world in which he lives. The attempt of the behaviourist to reduce everything to neurological stimuli and responses, condemn herself to a situation of retrogressive evolution and self-negation. In the context of questions like 'what is the nature of the world?', 'what is the nature of its basis?', 'what is the relation between the world and the individual?', Upanishads present some interesting theories.

The West so as to maintain a rigid distinction often labels the Upanishadic concept of reality as Pantheism. Such an idea strikes at the root of all distinctions. Such a labelling is not justifiable. The Upanishads do not speak of a unitary principle that is opposed to the multiplicity of creation. The 'transcendence' that

[8] G. Gispert-Sauch S.J., Bliss in the Upanishads, (New Delhi: Orient Publishers and Distributors, 1977), p.202.

the Upanishads highlight does not signify an aloofness or exclusion. The Upanishadic ideas of immanence and transcendence, creation and creator are best understood with the help of the principle of consciousness.

Rishis expound consciousness as the ultimate reality, and identifies it with the Self. At the same time, the Upanishadic seer gives a substantial explanation for the world. In the attempt to explain world as the heartthrob of consciousness, many doctrines on creation are enumerated. But the goal aimed by these doctrines is not the analysis of the world in discrete parts, but the integral realisation of the Self as consciousness, as the warp and woof of the world. A rigid categorisation in terms of cause and effect is cut asunder by the Rishi. The Upanishadic Rishi considers the story of creation or causality as a myth to explain the mystery.

The uncertainty on the origin of the world will stay till the Self is realised as consciousness, as the One behind the many. It is consciousness that which illumines all experiences and cognitions expressed through psychic faculties – *jyotisam jyoti*. The world is meaningful only if it is seen in the light of its underlying substratum. The Brhadaranyaka Upanishad therefore describes consciousness as *satyasya satyam*. Mundaka Upanishad says in personified terms: "He who is all knowing, One, the all-wise whose is this greatness the earth" (Mundaka Upanishad: II.2.7). "Brahman, indeed, is this universe. It is the greatest" (Mundaka Upanishad: II.2.12).

The problem of the co-existence of plurality and unity is explained by Upanishadic psychology from the standpoint of two apparently contradictory angles. Non-existence before creation is maintained, along with the description of the unmanifest and manifest states of reality. The Rishi introduces this apparent contradiction as a psychological puzzle, to quieten the mind and to establish the sole reality of consciousness.[9]

From the first standpoint of explanation, that is the non-existence of anything prior to creation, we can find references like. "There was nothing what so ever here in the beginning" (Brhadaranyaka Upanishad: I.2.1), "Non existence verily was this (world) in the beginning" (Taittiriya Upanishad: II.7.1), "In the beginning this (world) was non-existent" (Candogya Upanishad: II.19.1). These references are made to emphasize the existence of the Self which is of the nature of consciousness. The Upanishads annul the independent existence of duality. It says there is no plurality here – *na iha nanasthi kimcana* (Brhadaranyaka Upanishad: IV.4.19), change is a mere matter of words, a simple name – *vacarambhanam vikaro namadheyam* (Candogya Upanishad: VI.1.4).

From the second standpoint of creation and creator, Aitareya Upanishad speaks of the creator's entrance into the body by the opening in the skull – *vidriti*. Brhadaranyaka Upanishad adds that the creator entered up to the very tip of the nails. This *anupravesa* has for its object, "to become everything that there is" and for "assigning names into the objects and the evolution of their functions" (Candogya Upanishad: VI.2.1). Taittiriya Upanishad says: "Having entered it, He became both the actual (*Sat*) and the beyond (*Tyat*), the defined and the undefined, both the founded and the non-founded, the intelligent and the

[9] Similar puzzling questions and contradictions are termed 'koans' by the Zen Buddhists and are employed as a technique for meditation.

non-intelligent, the real and the un-true. As the real He became whatever there is here" (Taittiriya Upanishad: II.6.1). Mundaka Upanishad also gives a unitary description of reality, as in the Purusasukta, when it says that the fire is his head, wind is his breath, moon and sun his eyes. He is the inner spirit that dwells in things.

The Upanishads give metaphors like spinning of the web by the spider, the production of notes from musical instruments etc. It is the intimate relationship, *tadatmya*, or oneness between consciousness and its creative power that is conveyed, through these similes. Consciousness is not only the operative cause but also the material cause. It is not only the energising power but also the very substance of the universe. The Taittiriya Upanishad describes consciousness: "That, verily from which these beings are born, that, by which, when born they alive, that unto which, when departing they enter" (Taittiriya Upanishad: III.1.1).

Is the glory of consciousness confined to the spatio-temporal world? Mundaka Upanishad answers that its glory is something that not only transcends the world but also is very intimate to one. Consciousness manifests the mind and thoughts. The psychic and vital energy functions in and through it. For a unitary explanation of consciousness and world the Candogya Upanishad introduces the cosmological picture of consciousness as *tajjalan*. Samkaracarya in his commentary to this verse summarises consciousness as that from which matter (world) comes, in which matter dwells and finally that into which it is resolved. From consciousness (*tad*) has the world arisen (*jan*). Therefore it is called *taj-ja*. And also it disappears (*li*) in the very same consciousness. It is absorbed into the essence of consciousness. Therefore consciousness is *tal-*

la. The world at the time of its origin breathes, lives and moves in consciousness. Therefore in the three time scales of past, present and future, matter (world) is not separate from the essential consciousness. There is nothing that is outside and beyond consciousness. The attempt of the Upanishadic Rishi is to show the continuity of human life with that of universe. It is the *sambhuti* or the holistic vision that is spoken about.

Immortality and Upanishads

Rishis define the state of immortality as the realisation of the Self, and mortality as being ignorant of it. The Kena Upanishad says that man attains energy and vigour through consciousness and immortality through the knowledge of the Self as consciousness. The Isa Upanishad adds that Self-knowledge rids one off all sorrow and error. Not to attempt to win it is tantamount to suicide, and a life of blind darkness forever onwards. Verily self-knowledge is immortality.

Is Immortality a post-mortem phenomenon? The Kena Upanishad and the Katha Upanishad answers otherwise. "If here (a person) knows it, then there is truth, and if here he knows it not, there is great loss. Hence, seeing or (seeking) (the Real) in all beings, wise men become immortal on departing from this world" (Kena Upanishad: II.5). The phrase 'departing from this world' in this verse implies not the physical death, but the psychological death. It is the death of the false notion of separateness. If so who suffers form physical death? The Katha Upanishad reminds: "Whoever perceives anything like manyness here goes from death to death" (Katha Upanishad: II.1.10). The same Upanishad says, that by realising the Self as eternal and immutable, one is liberated from death. And this realisation has to occur, in the very present life, while the body lasts. No future life is to be relied upon. According to the Upanishadic eschatology, *jivanmukti* is the real immortality. It seldom speaks of *videhamukti* or liberation after death. Liberation from death is immortality. Liberation is the knowing of the Self as never born.

Again, mortality is conjured by the feeling of the 'other', something separate from consciousness. And immortality is seeing everything as the throb of consciousness. The Candogya Upanishad remarks that, where one does not see the other, does not hear the other, does not understand the other, that is the Infinite. But where one sees the other, hears the other, understands the other, that is small. What is fullness is immortal and what is small is mortal.

The same Upanishad says: "In the beginning ... this was being alone, one only without a second" (Candogya Upanishad: VI.2.1). Any sense of duality creates fear, the extreme of fear being fear of death. The Brhadaranyaka Upanishad says that primeval self feared, as he was alone. But on finding out that since there is nothing other than him whom he should fear, he became fearless. "It is from a second that fear arises" (Brahadaranyaka Upanishad: I.4.2). Hence, according to the Katha Upanishad, the *dhira* – the fearless – looks inwards, desirous of immortality. The nature of this inward vision is the realisation, "the self, indeed is all this" (Candogya Upanishad: VII.25.2). According to the Upanishadic eschatology, liberation is enjoying the continuity of ones existence with the universe, knowing the Self as infinite consciousness.

Epistemology of Consciousness

Self-knowledge is the key concept in the Upanishads. We find a frequently occurring refrain, '*yo evam veda*' – ' he who knows thus'. The remarkable note of Upanishadic psychology is the concept of the Self as the Pure subject, which never becomes an object. It is endowed with all psychical faculties usually attributed to mind in modern psychology. When in the West mind is often considered to be the seat of psychical faculties Upanishadic philosophers present mind itself to be a psychical faculty. Consciousness is that which is beyond mind and its functions. The Upanishads give clear and distinct place for mind and its functions, its relation to the individual and the nature of Self-knowledge.

Mind and its Function

The Upanishads refer to *manas* as the coordinating factor that governs the five organs of perception and five organs of action. It is ascribed of material origin. It also accounts for *buddhi* as the intellect, the organ of discrimination, *ahamkara* as the organ of personal ego and *citta* as the sub-conscious mind.

In the Aitareya Upanishad a distinction is drawn between consciousness as the real knower and mind as a sense organ. Various functions classified under the three categories of cognition, affection and conation are enumerated with much precision. "Perception, discrimination, intelligence, wisdom, insight, steadfastness, thought, thoughtfulness, impulse, memory conception, purpose, life, desire, control" (Aitareya Upanishad: II.1.2) – all these are identified as the operative names of consciousness. A further point of psychological import is the analysis of the cognitive act in the context of the knower (*praajna*), intellect (*prajna*) and cognition (*prajnana*).

Do these psychic functions have any separate existence? The same Upanishad says mental processes are only the many names of consciousness. The Brhadaranyaka Upanishad says: "When breathing he is called the vital force, when speaking voice, then seeing the eye, when hearing the ear, when thinking the mind; These are merely the names of his acts" (Brhadaranyaka Upanishad: II.4.2). Consciousness appears in various forms through which it manifests, but also transcends it.

The Kena Upanishad starts with the psychological enquiry as to what must be regarded as behind all psychical functions, namely thinking, breathing, speech, vision and action. Why is that the mind is able to think? Who regulates the vital breath? How is that the mouth, eye and ear enable to speak, see and hear? Are the sense organs autonomous or is there an entity that lies at the back of these? To these enquiries, the Rishis reply that it is consciousness that is behind all psychic functions. But the sense organs or the mind cannot know it. Consciousness is beyond not merely what is known, but also what is unknown. It is beyond the reach of knowledge as well as ignorance.

Consciousness and Conceptual Reason

Two major reasons can be cited for contending consciousness as beyond conceptual reason:

i. Rigid concepts work only in the context of a spatio-temporal framework of mind.

ii. Consciousness is the innermost subject that illumines

everything and hence cannot be an object.

Substantiating the first reason the Taittiriya Upanishad and the Kena Upanishad say: "Whence words return along with the mind, not attaining it", (Taittiriya Upanishad: II.4.1), "There the eye cannot go, nor can speech reach" (Kena Upanishad: I.3). Consciousness is not an object to be grasped by *tarka*, because it is the subtlest (*anupramanat*). Hence, it is said in the Brhadaranyaka Upanishad, "You cannot see the seer of seeing, you cannot hear the hearer of hearing, you cannot think of the thinker of thinking, you cannot understand one who understands understanding" (Brhadaranyaka Upanishad: II.4.2).

Consciousness is the very principle that imparts meaning to all concepts and statements. Though it is unmoving, it is faster than the mind. Thus moving faster it is beyond the reach of senses. Ever steady it outstrips all that run. Thus it "is the ear of the ear, the mind of the mind, the speech, indeed of the speech, the breath of the breath, the eye of the eye" (Kena Upanishad: I.2).

Consciousness is given the best epistemological definition, at the same time its ontological purity maintained, when it is described as "*pratibodhaviditam*" (Kena Upanishad: II.4), by the Kena Upanishad. Samkaracarya explains this description as *bodham bodham prati viditam* – which is known through every act of cognition. Every mental modification reveals the light of consciousness. Consciousness is co-inherent and co-existent in every piece of cognition. Consciousness is the witness of all states. It is *sarva-pratyaya-darsi-cicchakti-svarupa-matrah*. The Katha Upanishad describes it as the seer (*vipascit*), the Prasna Upanishad as the all-beholder (*paridrastur*) and the Svetasvatara Upanishad as the spectator (*saksi*).

Owing to the self-revealing nature of consciousness, the Upanishads discourage any categorical definition of it. By describing consciousness using paradoxical phrases the Rishi endeavours to show that it is in everything, but also beyond everything. Attributes both in positive and negative terms are attributed to it and finally all negated. It is not a logical acquaintance that is aimed at by the Upanishads but a concrete experience of consciousness.

On this Upanishadic style, Deussen remarks: "The opposite predicates of nearness and distance, of repose and movement are ascribed to Brahman in such a manner that they mutually cancel one another and serve only to illustrate the impossibility of conceiving Brahman by means of empirical definitions."[10] According to Samkaracharya, consciousness is without any empirical attributes – *sarva-samsara-dharmavarjita.*

Consciousness and Pure Reason

According to the Upanishads, if consciousness is misconceived as an object of knowledge then it can never be known. The Upanishad speaks of the self-luminous nature of consciousness. Such a nature of consciousness is revealed not to the logical reason, but to a pure reason – *suksmabuddhi.* It is the reason that does not try to create something, but comprehends that which is already there. The Upanishad prays: "May the Supreme endow us with clear understanding" (Svetasavatara Upanishad: III.4). The Katha Upanishad says that the Self reveals to a quiet and tranquil mind. In the words of the Brhadaranyaka: "Therefore

[10] Paul Deussen, The Philosophy of the Upanishads, Tr. A.S. Geden, (Edinburgh: Morrison and Gibb Ltd;1906), p.149.

... having become calm, self-controlled, withdrawn, patient and collected (one) sees the Self in his own self" (Brhadaranyaka Upanishad: IV.4.23). The word 'self' with which the verse ends denotes the mind.

In this context comes the Upanishadic idea of *tapas*. *Tapas* is not 'self-torture' as translated by Archibald Gough, but is mental discipline. The Rishis do not give a methodology to 'capture' the reality. The greatness of the Upanishadic concept of Self-knowledge is that it is *vastutantrajnana* and not *purusatantrajnana*. It is the knowledge of the reality as it is. The goal of *tapas* is to allow the mental equipment to shine in its real nature. It is the mental-stillness that is meant by *tapas*. Thus, in the Prasna Upanishad, Rishi Pippalada sends away six inquirers for *tapas* before starting any spiritual instruction. In the Candogya Upanishad, Satyakama-Jabala is asked to tend his teacher's cattle, enabling him to withstand the most difficult circumstances. Following the injunction of progressive *tapas*, by Udalaka, we see in the Taittiriya, Brghu finally realizing everything as his Self. In the Katha Upanishad, Yama puts Naciketas to a test of patience for three days. The Maitri Upanishad even says that control of thought is liberation. "By freeing mind from sloth and distraction and making it motionless he become delivered from his mind (reaches mindlessness) then that is the supreme state.... Mind, in truth is the cause of bondage and liberation for mankind" (Maitri Upanishad: VI.34). *Tapas*, thus is not ritualism, but the competency for Self-realisation.

Consciousness and Progressive Inclusion

The Upanishads synthesise the knowledge of the within and the knowledge of the without in a total comprehension of reality. It presents an integral vision by which the discordant notes of experience are held in harmony. And for the same reason it advocates the full and complete expression of personality.

In this regard the Upanishadic psychology gives a clear analysis of the 'person' and his 'persona'. The Upanishadic words *atman* and *purusa* denote the person. Samkaracarya defines these words. Atman is that which pervades all, the subject that knows, and illumines objects and that which remains immortal and always the same. *Purusa* is *sarvapuranat* – that which fills everything. These two definitions imply consciousness. The person is therefore identified with consciousness.

The persona comprises of sense organs, mind and intellect. The Katha Upanishad says that sense objects are higher than the sense organs, the mind is higher than the mind. And the unmanifest (*avyakta*) is higher than the intellect. Above all, *Purusa* is higher than the *avyakta*. There is nothing higher than *Purusa*.

In the Candogya Upanishad, Sanatkumara gives instruction for progressive meditation on Brahman. He gives the inclusive hierarchy of name, speech, mind, will, thought, contemplation and understanding. He who meditates on name (material knowledge) becomes independent so far as it goes. He who meditates on speech as consciousness goes so far as speech goes. Will, thought and contemplation can take one only up to the respective limits.

The Taittiriya Upanishad describes the human being as vested with *kosas* or sheaths. These are the *annamaya* or the physical body, the *pranamaya* or biospherical, *manomaya* or psychical, *vijnanamaya* or noospherical body. The Prasna Upanishad, the Candogya Upanishad and the Maitri Upanishad give systematic explanation for waking, dream and deep sleep states. The waking state relates to the physical body and the gross objects. In the dream state, sense organs rest in the mind and the mind creates its own spatiotemporal world and subtle objects. During deep sleep, mind also reposes and rejoices in the unconscious. Thus we have the conscious, subconscious and unconscious states. Consciousness is not any of these states, but runs in and through it. The Mandukya Upanishad names the self in these states as *Vaisvanara*, *Taijasa* and *Prajna*, and Consciousness as the fourth 'stateless state'. Consciousness is *Turiya*. Ranade describes *Turiya* as the 'fourth dimension of psychology'. None of the states colour consciousness, but they work in the light of consciousness, and hence it is *Turiya*. In the Prasna Upanishad it is said that we are united with consciousness everyday without being aware of it – *ahar ahar brahmagamayati*.

It is in the light of this psychology that the Upanishad speaks of the ontologised epistemology or the continuing and inclusive realisation of consciousness.

Ontologised Epistemology of Mahavakyas

In the West two lines of epistemological discussions are engaged in such as the analysis of the concept of knowledge within the framework of epistemic concepts, and study about the relation between knowledge and existence. In the Upanishads we find a holistic study. There is not much place for the dualistic presentation of epistemology and ontology. The Upanishads, infact, ontologise epistemology.

Thus the student in Taittiriya Upanishad declares, '*aham annam ... aham annadah*'. Matter, breath, mind and intelligence are no more alienated existence for her. She realises herself as everything. She overcomes the false notion of finitude. In her infinitude, she recognises herself as Consciousness-Bliss, from which everything is born, in which everything lives and unto which everything depart.

Exposition of Mahavakyas

The psychological discoveries of the Upanishadic Rishi is epitomised in four mystic statements such as:

prajnanam brahma – Brahman is Consciousness (Aitareya Upanishad: II.1.3)

ayam atma brahma – This Atman is Brahman (Brahadaranyaka Upanishad: II.5.19)

tattvamasi – That Thou Art (Chandogya Upanishad: VI.16.3)

aham brahmasmi – "I am Brahman" (Brahadaranyaka Upanishad: II.5.19).

The Upanishads introduce ideas of immanence and transcendence to establish the sole reality of consciousness. Ontologically it is the whole world. Epistemologically it is intelligence, and axiologically it is Bliss. Such a sole reality cannot be other than the inclusive principle of consciousness. Hence according to the teaching of the Rishi, '*tattvamasi*', the student realises herself as '*aham brahmasmi*', and understands the whole world as *aham eva idam sarvosmi*. In the words of Barnett: "the sum of Upanishadic teaching is that Brahman, the cosmic force manifested as a universe to the thought, is in essence one with that same thought, with the Atman or self."[11] Zaehner regards that "the great achievement of Upanishads is the ... *Brahman Atman* Synthesis, that is the identification of the individual soul with the ground of the universe."[12] Annie Besant summarises: "*Brahma-vidya* ... is the central truth of the Upanishads. It is the identity in nature of the Universal and the Particular Self...such is the final truth, such the goal of all wisdom, of all devotion, of all right activity: That thou Art. Nothing less than that is the Wisdom of the Upanishads; nothing more than that – for more than that there is not. That is the last truth of all truths; that is the final experience of all experinces."[13]

Knowing is Being

The Upanishads give no time lag between Knowing and Being. It considers Self-knowledge as *saksat aparoksa* or immediate. The immediacy of knowledge surpasses all mediateness of senses. *Atmajnana*, knowledge of *atma*, is being *atma*. The knower and known coalesces in Being. Hence the Upanishads make statements such as: "*brahmavid brahmaiva bhavati*" (Mundaka Upanishad: II.2.9) and "*brahmavid apnoti param*" (Taittiriya Upanishad: II.1.1). The act of knowing applies only for the removal of the false notion of separateness. Samkaracharya considers Self-knowledge as eternal, universal and necessary. It cannot be destroyed, though it may be obscured. The knowledge

[11] L.D. Barnett, The Heart of India, 2nd ed., (London: North Book Society, 1913), p.27.

[12] R.C. Zaehner, Hinduism, 2nd ed., (New York, Oxford University Press, 1966), p.18.

[13] Annie Besant, The Wisdom of the Upanishads, 6th ed., (Adyar: The Theosophical Publishing House, 1974), p.2.

of the Self does not create emancipation, but is emancipation. The Upanishadic Moksha hence is not a loss, but recognition of the true nature of the Self. It is not *having* an idea of the Self, but the *experiencing* of it. It is an experience of the present and not a prophecy for the future. The Upanishads describe it as seeing everything in oneself and oneself in everything. This vision is not a distinct knowledge but is spontaneous. It is the revelation of the whole in an instantaneity of moment. Now, is such knowledge indispensable? The Upanishad cautions, that no calamity is greater than the absence of Self-knowledge, for it is the knowledge by which whatever is to be known is known. According to the Upanishads perfection is not an attainment of something alien. It is a state of mind. It is Self-abidance.

From the Brahmanas to the Upanishads we find a cosmology which with more consistent analysis of creation reaches a psychology identifying the First Principle with consciousness, the Self. To criticize this psychology as agnosticism or solipsism as Jhonston and Deussen do is not in place. To describe the fountainhead of knowledge, that is consciousness, as something unknowable can only be a perversion of metaphysical language. Ranade says: "Existence is not existence, if it does not mean self-consciousness. Reality is not reality if it does not express throughout its structure the marks of pure self-consciousness. Self-consciousness thus constitutes the ultimate category of existence to the Upanishadic philosophers."[14] A.L. Basham says in his book *The Wonder that was India*: "The great and saving knowledge by which the Upanishads claim to impart lies not in

[14] R.D. Ranade, A Constructive Survey of Upanishadic Philosophy, (Poona: Bilvakunja Publishing House, 1926), p.270.

the mere recognition of the existence of Brahman, but in continual consciousness of it.... Brahman is the human soul, is Atman, the Self." [15]

[15] A.L. Basham, The Wonder that was India, (Calcutta: Rupa and Co., 1967), p.252.

3

Consciousness in Heterodox Systems

priyam padhyam vacastadhyam sunrtam vrtamucyate
tattadhyamapi no tadhyamapriyam caahitam ca yet

A kind, salutary, and truthful speech is called the 'vow' of *sunrta.* That truthful speech is not truthful, which is unkind to others and prejudicial.

Sarvadarsana Samgraha of Madhavacarya 3:23

This chapter will give a synoptic view of the concept of consciousness in the heterodox systems of Indian philosophy.

Carvaka Materialism

Carvaka is the Indian school of materialism that holds the primacy of matter and denominates consciousness to an emergent product. The Carvaka view of matter and consciousness springs from its epistemological position. For Carvaka, perception is the only means of valid knowledge. Hence what is real is the perceptible. "Whatever is arrived at by means of direct perception, that alone exists. That which is not perceivable is non-existent, for the (very) reason that it is not perceived."[1] For

[1] M. Rangacarya, Trans. The Sarva-siddhanta-samgraha of Samkaracarya, (New Delhi: Ajay Book Service, 1983), Ch.II. Verse 2.

this reason, the earlier school of Carvaka accepted only four of the basic elements such as earth, water, fire and air, and discarded space as an inferred element.

Earth, water, fire and air constitute the ultimate perceptibles. Therefore the material body constituted by these is the ultimate reality. "The atman (or self) is the body itself" (Sarva-siddhanta-samgraha: II.6). The physical body is the Self, the death of which marks the death of the Self. Therefore liberation lies in enjoying all luxuries of the world. Bondage is the experience of suffering inflicted by diseases, enemies and other causes. "The final beatitude of *moksa* is, however, death (itself); and that consists in the cessation of (breath) the principal vital air" (Sarva-siddhanta-samgraha: II.10).

The Susikshit Carvaka or the later school of Carvaka attributes eternal knowledge to the Self that enjoys different experiences. But it also agrees that the Self perishes with the body. All matter as such is inert. But certain compositions of it can generate consciousness. Carvaka considers consciousness to be an epiphenomenon that subsists with the body and disappears when the body disintegrates. "The four elements, earth, water, fire and air are the ground of consciousness."[2] Hence consciousness is produced only when there is a body. When there is no body, consciousness too is absent. Quoting Brhaspatisutra, Samkaracarya elucidates the theory:

"That intelligence, which is found to be embodied in the (various) modified forms consisting of the non-intelligent elements – (that) is produced in the same way in which the red

[2] Haribhadra, Sad-darsana-samuccaya., 2nd rev. ed., Tr.K. Satchidananda Murty, (Delhi: Eastern Book Linkers, 1986), Ch. VII. Verse.82.

colour is produced form the combination of betel, areca-nut and lime" (Sarva-siddhanta-samgraha: II.7). The hedonistic philosophy of Carvaka that reduces consciousness to a mere emergent product of material collocation is vehemently criticized by other Darsanas.

Buddhism and no-self

All schools of Buddhism accept the unreality of the individual self – *pudgala nairatmya.* Later Buddhism extends *nairatmya* to individual objects too – *dharma nairatmya*. "There are four truths in this world: first, all living beings rise form ignorance; second, all objects of desire are impermanent, uncertain and suffering: third, all existing things are also impermanent, uncertain and suffering; fourth, there is nothing that can be called an 'ego', and there is no such thing as 'mine' in all the world."[3] Accordingly, the individual though is dynamic, is essenceless (*an-atta*). Material objects are also devoid of any permanent principle (*anatmattva*). Therefore, "To believe in the existence of an ego is an erroneous belief that supposes the existence of non-existence…."[4] Along with the theory of the non-substantially of the Self, the transient nature of consciousness is also agreed by different schools, as said in the Tripitaka literature.

The Buddha rejected the notion of consciousness as a permanent entity. The Majjhima Nikayasutta points out that: "…consciousness is the product of conditions, in the absence of

---

[3] Bukkyo Dendo Kyokai, The Teaching of Buddha, (Tokyo: Buddhist Promoting Foundation, 1985), p.94.

[4] Bukkyo Dendo Kyokai, The Teaching of Buddha, (Tokyo: Buddhist Promoting Foundation, 1985), p.94.

which there will be no origination of consciousness."[5] The Nikayasuttas identify consciousness as one of the four sustenances, *adhara*, for the maintenance of beings. In the Buddha Carita, Asvaghosa explains consciousness as an influx conditioned by a causal pattern. He says: "consciousness is the causal condition form which name-and–form is produced. Name-and-form again is the support on which consciousness is based.... Consciousness and name-and-form are causes of each other."[6] It must be this mutual relation that influenced the schools of Buddhism in referring to a 'stream of consciousness' (*vinnana sota*) or a 'stream of becoming' (*bhava sota*). At any case, the Buddhist concept of consciousness is undoubtedly based on *nairatmyavada* or the theory of no-self. "Though both body and mind appear because of co-operating causes, it does not follow that there is an ego-personality. As the body of flesh is an aggregate of elements, it is, therefore impermanent. ... Neither is the mind the ego-personality. The human mind is an aggregate of causes and conditions. It is in constant change" (The Teaching of Buddha: p. 90). Asserting this stand, Ananda K. Coomaraswamy holds: "the effect of series is to show that *vinnana*, the consciousness of I, does not reside in an eternal soul, but is a contingent phenomenon arising by way of cause and effect."[7]

---

[5] Padmasiri De Silva, An Introduction to Buddhist Psychology, (London: The Macmillan Press Ltd., 1979), p.76.

[6] Asvaghosa, Buddha Carita, Tr. E.H. Johnston, Acts of the Buddha, 1st ed. rpt., (Delhi: Motilal Banarsidass Pubs., 1972), Ch.XIV.74-75.

[7] Ananda K. Coomaraswamy, Buddha and the Gospel of Buddhism, 2nd Ind. Ed., (New Delhi: Munshiram Manoharlal Pub. Pvt. Ltd., 1985), p.87.

Stream of Consciousness in Theravada and Vaibhasika

The Abhidhammmatha-sangraha of Aniruddha gives a detailed account of consciousness as dealt with by the Theravadins. Abhidhamma includes everything under four categories. "In reality, the categories of the Abhidhamma are four: (i) Consciousness, (ii) Psychic factors, (iii) Matter and (iv) Nibbana. All things are included under these four heads."[8] It also speaks about five *skandhas* such as *rupa* (material aggregates), *vedana* (feeling), *sanna* (perception), *sankhara* (impressions) and *vinnana* (consciousness). World can be reduced to the composition of these *skandhas*.

Analysing the process of cognition, Aniruddha outlines two major courses of cognition such as *panca-dvara-vithi* and *mano-dvara-vithi*. The former includes sensations got through the eye, ear, nose, tongue and skin. It is due to the difference in *vipaka* or the karmic result of pervious life that different people have different sensations. Aniruddha explains also the modes of mind involved in sensations. *Sampathicana* is the recipient consciousness or the mind receiving the stimulus of an independent object. "... the mind reflecting over the object and trying to understand it in the light of its previous experiences...is called *santirana* or 'the investigating conscousenss'" (Abhidhamatthasangaha: p.11). According to Aniruddha, the most lively state of consciousness is that in which, "... the subject is fully conscious of itself and determines its own attitude towards the object. This is called *javana* or 'the active consciousness'" (Abhidhamatthasangaha: p.4). On the explanation of

[8] Aniurddha, Abhidhamatthasangaha, Tr. Bhikkub J. Kashyap, The Abhidhamma Philosophy, (Delhi: Bharatiya Vidya Prakashan, 1982), p.11.

consciousness relating to mental states Lama Anagarika Govinda says: "A state of consciousness is either connected with knowledge (*nan-sampayutta*) concerning the nature of its object and the consequences of its acceptance or its rejection, or consciousness is not connected with knowledge (*nan-vippayutta*), or it is directly bound up with erroneous views (*ditthi*)."[9]

Abhidhamma defines different grades and planes of consciousness on the basis of *nibbana*. *Kamavacaracitta* is consciousness invested with desires. "This is the first plane called *paritta bhumi* or the plane of weak consciousness" (Abhidhamatthasangaha: p.8). *Nibbana* is not possible in this plane. After due yogic practices one is able to concentrate his mind perfectly on the object. This plane of consciousness is called *rupavacaracitta*. *Arupavacaracitta* is the third stage of meditation on the formless. The latter two planes of consciousness constitute the *mahaggata bhumi* or the higher grade of consciousness. The Yogavacara or the practitioner then "... meditates upon the *anicca* (impermanent), *dukkha* (miserable) and *Anatta* (substanceless) nature of all existence; and therby attains *Jnana* upon *nibbana*" (Abhidhamatthasangaha: p.9). *Nibbana* is attained in the highest plane of consciousness called the *lokottara bhumi*. Consciousness at this plane is called *sotapanna*, meaning that which has come in the stream, leading to *nibbana*.

From the analysis of the different planes of consciousness and *nibbana* it can be affirmed that Abhidhamma posits the existence of consciousness as of transient nature. Commenting on this feature Rhys Davids says: "Out of this idea of transience ... grew

[9] Lama Anagarika Govinda, The Psychological Attitude of Early Buddhist Philosophy, (London: Rider and Company, 1969), p.101.

the notion of momentariness, especially in man's inner world of mind."[10] Theravadins in an implicit manner accept consciousness as of the nature of a momentary series. *Nibbana* is considered more as a resultant state of yogic practices.

The psychology of Theravada is taken up by Vaibhasika and is developed into a clear line of thought. Vasubandhu belonging to the Vaibhasika order presents the nature of consciousness and its relation to the cogniser in his Abhidharmakosa. In affinity with the Vaibhasika structuralism, Vasubhandu describes matter as atomic. There are simple atoms (*dravya paramanu*) and combined atoms (*sanghata paramanu*). All categories are classified under two dimensions namely the *samskrtadharmas* or the phenomenal categories and the *asamskrtadharmas* or the eternal categories. Matter or *pudgala* is but the concealed Self. Vasubandhu says that there is no difference between *pudgala* and atman. Of the two categories *nibbana* is covered by *asamskrta dharma*. *Nibbana* is possible by two ways. *Pratisankhya nirodha* is of the nature of *nibbana* by the destruction of worldly sufferings through knowledge. *Apratisankhya nirodha* is liberation by the automatic removal of the cause of suffering (*klesa*).

In his translation of Abhidharmakosa, Stcherbatsky describes: "... consciousness is a conventional name for a chain of conscious moments."[11] Consciousness is a series of successive states. The apparent identity of an individual is an illusion due to the continuity of consciousness (*santana*). "A continuity is a

---

[10] Rhys Davids, A Manual of Buddhism, 1st Ind. Ed., (New Delhi: Oriental Books Rept. Corporation, 1978), p.155.

[11] Vasubandhu, Abhidharmakosa, Tr. Theodore Stcherbatsky, The Soul Theory of the Buddhists, 2nd rev. ed., (Delhi: Bharatiya Vidya Prakashan, 1976), ch.15, p.57.

continually reverting of (new moments of) consciousness which are following on an action" (Abhidharmakosa: 16.72). Consciousness, to the Vaibhasika, constitutes a stream in which the succeeding moment is necessarily different from the preceding moment. Apprehension of an object is consciousness changing its place and appearing in coordination with an objective element. Vasubandhu explains this by the metaphor of the 'uninterrupted production of the series of flames in a lamp'. There is no real apprehension by consciousness, nor there is a cognising agent. "There is nothing that does cognise apart from the evanescent flashing of consciousness itself" (Abhidharmakosa: 14.58). Both Theravada and Vaibhasika cut root at the presence of a subsisting consciousness.

Consciousness as Vinnana and Sunya

The Sautrantika school of Buddhism comes midway between the Hinayana and the Mahayana. Along with the Vaibhasika, Sautrantika also accepts the reality of external objects. Sautrantika differs from Vaibhasika only in minor details as said in Sarva-siddhanta-samgraha. "Vaibhasika declares that external objects are established through direct perception. But the Sautrantika (Buddhists) says that external are (merely such things as are) inferred from forms of consciousness" (Sarva-siddhanta-samgraha). To the Sautrantika, *nibbana* is not a state of the extinction of consciousness, but is only an annihilation of the life process. They admit the presence of a subtle consciousness devoid of any phenomenal consciousness in the state of *nibbana*. This subtle consciousness seems to be similar to the Alayavinnana as expounded by the Yogacaras.

Yogacara and Madhyamika schools express a marked difference from early Buddhism in their treatment of consciousness. Yogacara is idealism in sharp contrast to Theravada Vaibhasika realism. To the Yogacara what exists is only intelligence (*vijnaptimatrata*). External objects are only the forms of intelligence. Thought externalises itself and creates the illusion of objectivity. Objects have no more existence than images seen in a dream. According to Yogacara, *vinnana* is of two kinds such as the *pravarttivinnana* and *alayavinnana*. *Pravarttivinnana* gives the false perception of external objects. Both the external objects and their consciousness are momentary, and hence the moments of *pravarttivinnana* are constantly born and destroyed. "Each moment of consciousness is determined by the past moments, and the series extends to the time of birth or even before."[12]

Yogacara concept of *alayavinnana* is noteworthy in that it brings forth the theory of the unconscious. *Alayavinnana* is the storehouse of all ideations. It alone exists though in its dynamic aspect it reveals itself through individual things and objects. Objects are experienced as externally existing, not because of their real existence. It is the memory in the form of the beginningless subtle impressions that cause their illusory existence. Vinnana therefore "...is the total consciousness, which includes the conscious as well as the residual mental events of the individual."[13]

Though Yogacara considers consciousness as the ultimate, it

---

[12] A.K. Chatterjee, Readings on Yogacara Buddhism, (Varanasi: Centre of Advanced Study in Philosophy, Banaras Hindu University, 1971), p.4.

[13] Padmasiri De silva, An Introduction to Buddhist Psychology, (London: The Macmillan Press Ltd., 1979), p.19.

is not in the sense of an abiding substratum, but as fleeting cognitions. In the Samyutta Nikaya, the Buddha referring to the *parinibbana* of Vakkali Bhikku, says: " the wicked Mara was searching for the *vinnana* (consciousness) of Vakkali, who had been just dead, and adds that, Mara's attempt would not be successful because Vakkali had passed away (*parinibbuto*) with *vinnana*, which cannot be localised (*apatitthita*)."[14] But this transient nature of consciousness does not rule out the possibility of a transmigrating self. Regarding transmigration, A.K. Warder quoting the Samyutta says: "Transient though consciousness is it will continue to serve as a condition for more consciousness as long as there is anything to do, much more so any actual volition. Before it ceases it will have produced a support, a station or resting place, for a further impulse of consciousness."[15]

The Madhyamikas (Sunyavadins) replaced the transient nature of consciousness by voidness or sunyata. Nagarjuna, the founder of this school denies altogether the external and the internal objects. *Sunyata* is extended to *pudgala* as well as *dharma*. There is no such thing as world or consciousness. What exists is only *sunya*. The concept of *sunyata* is brought to bring about a complete cessation of the world. "The realisation of *sunyata* brings about the complete cessation of all *prapancas*, and so it is said that the realisation of *sunyata* is the same as the realisation of *nirvana*."[16] Nagarjuna points out that *sunyata* is not to be

---

[14] Nalinaksha Dutt, Mahayana Buddhism, 1st ed. rpt., (Calcutta: Firma Klm Private Ltd., 1976), p. 199.

[15] A.K. Warder, Indian Buddhism, 2nd rev. ed., (Delhi: Motilal Banarsidass Pubs., 1980), p.128.

[16] Nalinaksha Dutt, Mahayana Buddhism, 1st ed. rpt., (Calcutta: Firma Klm Private Ltd., 1976), p.263.

taken in the sense of *nastitva* or *abhava*, but is to be equated with *pratitya samutpada* and *nibbana*. According to the original teachings of Buddha, "... *Sunyata* means non-substantiality; the un-born, having no form or characteristics that we can speak of them as neither being born or being destroyed. There is nothing about the essential nature of things that can be described in terms of discrimination; that is why things are called non-substantial" (The Teaching of Buddha: p.118).

A really existent entity like *vinnana* must suffer death and decay. Hence, Nagarjuna says that *nibbana* that has no death and decay cannot be identified with consciousness. *Nibbana* is not a *bhava*. Also *Nibbana* cannot be described as *abhava*, since if it is non-existence, then it invites the explanation for an existent substratum. Existence or on-existence cannot be predicated of what is not produced. *Nibbana* is neither existence nor non-existence.

The description of *Nibbana* as voidness can be traced to the *suttas*. In the Maha-parinibbana suttas, references are made to the teachings given to Ananda by the Buddha on the eight steps of liberation. The sixth stage is described: "By passing quiet beyond the mere consciousness of the infinity of reason, he, thinking 'nothing at all exists', reaches (mentally) and retains in the state of mind to which nothing at all is specially present."[17] In the final stage the consciousness of non-existence is also absent. The Sutta proceeds: "By passing quiet beyond the state of 'neither ideas nor the absence of ideas' he reaches (mentally) and remains in the state of mind in which both sensations and ideas have

[17] F. Max Muller, Ed. sacred Books fo the East, vol.XI, rpt. Buddhist-sutras, Tr. T.W. Rhys Davids (Delhi: Motilal Banarsidass Pubs., 1980), Ch.III.39

ceased to be."[18] The identification of liberation with the annihilation of consciousness can also be found as described in the Hridayasutra. The Sutra says: "A man who has approached the *pragnaparamita* of the Boddhissattva dwells enveloped in consciousness. But when the envelopment of consciousness has been annihilated, then he becomes free of all fear, beyond the reach of change, enjoying final *Nirvana*."[19]

The concept of consciousness as momentary flashings could have certain problems. The Yogacaras explain consciousness as momentary cognitions. But they miss the fact that the structure of consciousness is such that it reveals the uniqueness of two momentary cognitions and also the gap in between. Yogacaras fail to fill the gap in between two moments of consciousness. If it is said that the gap in between is void, then Yogacara does not give a theory other than the Sunyavada of Madhyamika. Sunyavadins also suffer inherent discrepancies in their explanation of the ultimate as *sunya*. The final stage of liberation is described ass the state of Boddhisattva, which is a state of utter nothingness. But if nothingness is described as a positive state of liberation that only shows that consciousness is still present as the witness of that state of nothingness.

Consciousness as the Quality of the Self

The Jainas attribute consciousness as the essential quality of the Self. "... in saying that consciousness is the very nature, the

[18] F. Max Muller, Ed. sacred Books fo the East, vol.XI, rpt. Buddhist-sutras, Tr. T.W. Rhys Davids (Delhi: Motilal Banarsidass Pubs., 1980), Ch.III.41.

[19] F.Max Muller, Tr and Ed., Sacred Books of the East, Vol.XLIX, rpt., Buddhist Mahayana Texts, (Delhi: Motilal Banarsidass Pubs., 1965), p.154.

essence, of the soul, Jainism is opposed to the Nyaya theory that atman is neither conscious or unconscious in itself" (Sad-darsana-samuccaya: p.63). Consciousness or *upayoga* is the defining characteristic of the Self. *Upayoga* can be determinate (*sakara*) as well as indeterminate (*anakara*). The former is called *jnana* and the latter *darsana*. It is called *jnana* when it is the knowledge of the outer particulars. It is called *darsana* when it is the intuitive knowledge of the Self. *Jnana* and *darsana* ultimately drop their identity in the Self.

Consciousness is not an adventitious quality of the Self, dependent upon external factors. Consciousness cannot be separated form the Self nor can the Self exist without consciousness. Consciousness is the basis of the functions of the Self. Nemichandra, the author of Dravyasamgraha defines Self as: "*Jiva* is characterised by *upayoga*, is formless and an agent, has the same extent as its own body, is the enjoyer (of the fruits of *karma*), exists in *samsara*, is *siddha* and has a characteristic upward motion."[20] Haribhadra also agrees with this relationship between consciousness and the Self, when he says that "*Jiva* is...the doer of auspicious and inauspicious action, the enjoyer of the fruits of action and is characterised by consciousness" (Sad-darsana-samuccaya: IV.48).

As far as the relation between body and consciousness is concerned Jainism holds an intermediate position. In Bhagavatisutra, Mahavira advises his disciple: "The body, O Gautama, is (identical with) the soul as well as it is different from it."[21] Consciousness is discernible in four different states

[20] Nemichandra Siddhanta-Chakravartti, Dravya-Samgraha, rpt., Tr. And Ed. S.C. Ghoshal, (Delhi: Motilal Banarsidass Pubs., 1989), v.2.

[21] Nathmal Tatia, Studies in Jaina Philosophy, (Varanasi: P.V. Research Institute, Jainashram, Hindu University, 1951), p.23.

of physical existence (*gati*). The different levels of consciousness representing the various states of existence are that of animals, humans, internal beings and celestial. The Self passes through these states of evolution (*paryayas*) before attaining perfection.

Consciousness and Karma Pudgala

In describing the relation that exists between consciousness and liberation Jainism takes a midway position. It endorses neither eternalism nor nihilism. Each and every entity is related to all entities other than itself in the universe in some relation or the other. Hence the complete knowledge of an entity involves the complete knowledge of other entities as well. To overcome the dualism between matter and consciousness Jainism attributes "some psychical functions to the body and some material functions to the spirit."[22]

The Jainas accept six categories constituting the substance. The six *dravyas* such as *jiva* (Self), *pudgala* (matter), *dharma* (principle of motion), *adharma* (principle of rest), *akasa* (space) and *kala* (time) are real and independent. Of these *Jiva* is conscious but has no form. *Pudgala* is unconscious and material, but has form. The other categories are both unconscious and formless. The categories other than *jiva* are classified under the broader category of *ajiva*. In elucidating the distinction between *jiva* and *ajiva* Devendra Muni Shastri says: "... in the lowest possible stage of development [the *jivas*] possess an infinite part of *kevalajnana* (omniscient knowledge). If that part of omniscience is also covered by

[22] Jagat Prakash Atreya, Mind and its Functions in Indian Thought, (New Delhi: Classical Publishing Company, 1985), p.35.

the karmic particles, it would become *ajiva*, but such a contingency never arise."[23]

According to the Jainas consciousness and matter are two distinct principles. But there is a concrete identity between consciousness (Self) and karmic matter in the state of bondage. Haribhadra elucidates: "Bondage is the relationship of both *jiva* and *karma*, which is of the nature of interpenetration of each by the other" (Sad-darsana-samuccaya: IV.51). The *karmapudgala* mixes with the Self just as milk mixes with water. The Jaina takes *karmapudgala* to be the subtle body that mediates between the Self and the matter. It "... correspond[s] to the *sanskaras* and *vasanas* of Vedanta."[24]

The bondage of the Self is caused by the various passions (*kasayas*). The change of material atoms into karmic matter makes up the bondage of matter. The nature of *karmapudgala* is determined by the *kasayas* of the Self and that of karmic matter in turn determines the nature of *kasayas*. In Dravyasamgraha, Nemichandra defines bondage as a conscious state. "That conscious state by which *karma* is bound (with the soul) is called *Bhava-bandha*" (Dravya-Samgraha: 32). Bondage of the Self with the *karma* is made by conscious states of mind. The translator of Dravyasamgraha, S.C. Ghoshal, quotes from Vardhamana-Purana to substantiate this striking description of bondage: "That modification of consciousness consisting of attachment or aversion by which *karma*s are tied (to the soul), is

[23] Devendra Muni Shastri, A Source Book of Jaina Philosophy, Tr. T.G. Kalghatgi, Ed. T.S. Devodoss, (Udaipur: Sri Tarak Guru Jain Granthalaya, 1983), p.105.

[24] Raghunath Safaya, Indian Psychology, (New Delhi: Munshiram Manoharlal Publishers Pvt. Ltd., 1975), p.314.

known as *bhava-bandha*" (Dravya-Samgraha: p.85). Liberation therefore implies that of both matter and Self. Nemichandra says: "That modification of the soul which is the cause of the destruction of all *Karma*s, is surely to be known as *bhava-moksa* and the (actual) separation of the *karma*s [is] *dravya-moksa*" (Dravya-Samgraha: V.37).

Jainism gives a detailed analysis of matter in order to explain the relation between matter and the various planes of consciousness. Matter is ascribed the name *pudgala*. The karmic matter is called *pudgala* because "they fill (*pur*) and dissolve (*gal*)."[25] Haribhadra defines it as that which "can be experienced by the senses" (Sad-darsana-samuccaya: IV.49). The Jainas enlist eight main types of *karma*, that which obscure the purity of consciousness. Those that obscure knowledge and intuition of the Self are called *jnanavarnana* and *darsanavarana*. The karmic matter that which holds up the natural bliss and produces pleasure and suffering is called *vedaniya*. *Mohaniya karma* causes the metaphysical and ethical delusion. *Ayuska karma* breaks up the immortal continuity of existence into various life spans. The embodiment of the bodiless is caused by the *namakarma*. *Gotrakarma* produces various differentiations and gradations. The infinite energy of the Self is obstructed by the *antaraya*. There is a constant influx of *karma* in the Self (*asrava*). This influx of *karma* is stopped by *samvara*. In Dravyasamgraha it is said: "That modification of consciousness which is the cause of checking *Asrava* (influx) of *karma*, is surely *Bhavasamvara*" (Dravya-Samgraha: 34).

---

[25] Madhavacarya, Sarva-darsana-samgraha, new ed., Tr. E.B. Cowell and A.E. Gough, Ed. K.L. Joshi (ahmedabad: Parimal Publications, 1981), p.70.

The *karmapudgala* is attracted and bound to consciousness (self) due to vibrations (*yoga*) and passions (*kasaya*). The space occupied by the Self is densely filled with karmic matter and there is incessant influx of *karma*, which is ever involved in activity (yoga). The influx continues till the soul is completely freed from all activity. Activity functions in two ways n causing bondage. It conditions space bondage (*pradesa bandha*) and also determines the nature of bondage (*prakrti-bandha*). *Pradesa bandha* is bondage with reference to the volume of matter attracted and space occupied by the Self. *Prakrti-bandha* is the bondage with the reference to the obscuration of the respective functions of the Self like *jnana*, *darsana* etc. in the absence of activity no kind of bondage can take place. Emancipation lies in the removal of *karma* by various yogic practices. To quote the Jain scholar Haribhadra: "That which is the destroyal of the *karmas* that bind is considered as *nirjara*; and the absolute separation (of the soul) from body, etc., is called liberation" (Sad-darsana-samuccaya: IV.52).

Planes of Consciousness

The Jaina thinkers discuss fourteen stages of the Self through which the purity of consciousness is experienced. These stages are referred to as *gunasthanas*. In the primary stage of *mithya-drstigunasthana*, the individual thought is devoid of any idea of truth and goodness. The Self in this stage is characterized by blind delusive knowledge due to *darsanavaranakarma*. *Sasadana-samyagdrsti* is the second stage where the individual gets a slight vision of his higher planes. In the third stage of *misragunasthana*, the individual makes conscious efforts to get over the conflicting situations. In the next four stages comprising *avirata samyagdrsti*, *desavirat samyagdrsti*, *pramatta samyata* and *apramatta samyatagunasthanas*, the individual cultivates mental control and approach the complete annihilation of the effects of *karma*. in the eighth stage of *nivrttibadara samparyayagunasthana,* the Self acquires a psychical force for the removal of the binding *karma*. In the *amvrttibadara samparaya*, *suksma samparaya* and *upasantakasaya vitaraga* stages there is the total subjugation of passions. *Ksinakasaya vitaraga* is the stage that represents the end of the journey of the Self. It is the summit of annihilated passions. The thirteenth stage of *sayogikevali* marks the attainment of *kevala-jnana*. *Ayogikevaligunasthana* is the final stage of getting right faith, right knowledge and right conduct.

In this stage, the Self transcends all limitations and enjoys the purity of consciousness. With this stage, the disembodied liberation is gained. The Abaranga sutra says: "(The liberated) is not long nor small… he is without body, without resurrection, without contact (of matter). … he perceives he knows."[26] The Kalpasurta of Bhadrabahu describes the liberation of the Jina called Parsva in a similar note: "… in *Visabha* he obtained the highest knowledge and intuition called *Kevala*, which is infinite, supreme, unobstructed, unimpeded, complete and full; in *Visabha* he obtained final liberation." [27]

---

[26] . F. Max Muller, Ed. Sacred Books of the East, Vol.XXII, rpt., Jaina Sutras, Part I, Tr. Hermann Jacobi, (Delhi: Motilal Banarsidass Pubs., 1980), p.52, sutra 1.5.6

[27] F. Max Muller, Ed. Sacred Books of the East, Vol.XXII, rpt., Jaina Sutras, Part I, Tr. Hermann Jacobi, (Delhi: Motilal Banarsidass Pubs., 1980), p.271. sutra.149.

4

Consciousness in Orthodox Systems

anitya asuci dukha anatmasu nitya suci sukha atmakhyati avidya

To mistake the self which is eternal, pure and pleasant as the not-self which is non-eternal, impure and painful is ignorance.

Patanjali Yogasutra 2:5

This chapter gives a brief presentation of consciousness in Nyaya-Vaisesika, Samkhya-Yoga, Purva Mimasma and Advaita Vedanta.

Nyaya Vaisesika Realism

Nyaya Vaisesika represents an absolute realistic trend in its philosophy. As a development of the Carvaka materialism, it presupposes the real nature of matter. The attempt of this presupposition is to epistemologically and ontologically establish the reality of the world. Gotama gives the detailed work on the sixteen topics of logic (Nyayasutra) and Kanada on the six categories (Vaisesikasutra).

Emergence of Consciousness

With the materialists, Nyaya maintains that plurality is ultimate, but against them, insists on the reality of both material and immaterial substances. To the Nayyayikas consciousness is an adventitious product of an assemblage of events. It has a dependent existence and is evanescent. Consciousness is dependent upon a suitable collocation of circumstances. In Kanada's view: "Consciousness is produced in the same way as the quality of redness is produced in a jar through its connection with fire."[1] It is only an adventitious quality of the Self that makes objects known to it. Kanada holds that consciousness inheres in the Self just as sound inheres in *akasa*. Consciousness is not essential to the Self, just as sound is not essential to ether. Consciousness cannot exist without the Self. But the Self can exist without the manifestation of consciousness, in its atomic form. They are not conjoined accidentally, but one resides in the other.

Consciousness and Self

Both Nyaya and Vaisesika have common views on the atomic theory of the universe and the nature of the Self. Vaisesika psychology has its bearing on atomistic philosophy. The world is produced by the aggregation of the primal cause – the atom. An effect has only a temporary existence. Before its production and after its destruction it is non-existent.

The Self is a unique substance to which all cognitions, feelings and conations belong as its qualities. "Desire (*icca*), aversion

[1] S.K. Seksena, Nature of Consciousness in Hindu Philosophy, 2nd ed., (Delhi: Motilal Banarsidass Publishers, 1971), p.52.

(*dvesa*), volition (*prayatna*), pleasure (*sukha*), pain (*dukha*) and intelligence are the marks of the Soul."[2] Consciousness though is a quality, is not a quality of the body. It is a quality of the Self. All qualities are psychical. Hence they do not belong to the body but to the Self that is eternal (*nitya*) and all-pervading (*vibhu*). The Self knows that it has these qualities only when the mind and sense organs conjuncts with it. This contact or *sannikarsa* is termed *samyukta-samavaya*. The Self is the ground of all thoughts and experiences. It is the knower, the doer and the enjoyer. The Self is the knower – *jnata* – endowed with an instrument of knowledge. It controls the mind, sense organs and synthesises their functions.

It is through the Self's association with the mind and the body that consciousness emerges. A body whether living or dead possesses qualities such as colour. But consciousness is absent in a dead body. It is not because consciousness is the quality of the body that it exists in the body. It exists in the body just as water appears to be warm, not because warmth is its intrinsic quality, but because of fire associated with it. Gotoma says: "If the body were soul there should be release from sins as soon as the body was burnt" (The Nyaya Sutras of Gotama: III.I.202) Consciousness is not the quality of the mind, since mind itself is controlled by the Self. "It does not also belong to the mind the existence of which is inferred from the knowables not being perceived simultaneously" (The Nyaya Sutras of Gotama: II.II.290) It is the Self that cognises and not the mind. Mind is only an instrument of perception, mediating between the Self

[2] M.M. Satish Chandra Vidyabhusana, Tr. The Nyaya Sutras of Gotama, Ed. Nandalal Sinha, (Delhi: Motilal Banarsidass Publishers, 1930), I.I.10.

and sense organs. The Self cognises through the mind. "Cognition cannot properly belong to the non-conscious instrument, *buddhi*, if it did, *buddhi* would become conscious; but here is one conscious entity, different from the aggregate of the body and the organs".[3]

Jayanta in Nyayamanjari says that it can be inferred that consciousness belongs to the Self. He names this kind of inference as *parisesanumana*. Gotoma also recognises this kind of inference. He says "... Knowledge etc. must be admitted to be the qualities of the soul by the principle of exclusion."[4] It consists in asserting anything of something, because it is found not to belong to any other thing. According to this inference, consciousness belongs to the Self, since it cannot belong either individually or collectively to the body, sense organ or mind. Sridhara gives the analogy of cloth to explain this. "... even as a cloth produced by the thread and the shuttle, inheres in the thread and not in the shuttle likewise, the self is not of the nature of consciousness, but still consciousness inhere in it."[5] Though consciousness is produced by the contact of the Self, body and mind, it inheres only in the Self. Vaisesikasutra describes consciousness as a quality of the Self supported by and generated in it by a combination of *manas*, *indriya* and *visesa*. The relation between the Self and consciousness like any other substance and attribute is of *samavaya*. Gotoma contends that consciousness is an activity and is ephemeral. "Knowledge perishes instantly because all

[3] N.S. Junanakar, Gautama, The Nyaya Philosophy, (Delhi: Motiala Banarsidass Publishers, 1978), p.409.

[4] S.K. Seksena, Nature of Consciousness in Hindu Philosophy, 2nd ed., (Delhi: Motilal Banarsidass Publishers, 1971), p.51.

[5] The Nyaya Sutras of Gotama: III.II.313.

actions are found to be transitory" (The Nyaya Sutras of Gotama: III.II.313).

Regarding transmigration Nyaya holds that the Self transmigrates with the aid of *manas* (The Nyaya Sutras of Gotama: III.II.330) which is atomic in nature. *Manas* being atomic is eternal, unproduced, indestructible and without parts. After death the body perishes, but *manas* proceeds to the new abode by the force of *adrsta*. The Self is different in different bodies. But the same Self subsists in the different bodies of a particular individual as a single agent. "On the cessation of the activity of (its) instruments, the soul exists in a condition similar to that of a sotne."[6] The earlier Nyaya is not clear about the distinction of the individual self and the supreme Self. But Annam Bhatta makes this distinction clear in Tarkasamgraha. This distinction is also recorded in Sarva-siddhanta-samgraha (V.31: *atmah dividah, jivatma paramatma ceti*) of Samkaracarya. The supreme Self is devoid of pleasure and pain. It is the individual self that is subject to pleasure and pain.

Consciousness is not self-manifest

Consciousness is not self-manifest. It manifests only other objects. The Self is the subject. But it is not conscious. It has consciousness as the quality to illumine other objects – *praprakasaka* . All sense organs and sense objects are the objects of the Self. The existence of Self is also an object of knowledge. It is the first *prameya*. Haribhadra says: "Soul, body, objects of senses, cognition, senses,

[6] M. Rangacarya, Trans. The Sarva Siddhanta-Sangraha of Samkaracarya, (New Delhi: Ajay Book Service, 1983), verse 36.

pleasure etc., are the objects of right knowledge."[7] Knowledge involves a subject-object relation, but is not the outcome of this relation. According to the Nyaya theory of perception, no cognition can be directly apprehended. They are not self-cognisable. "It is according to circumstances that anything can become an object of perception as well as an instrument of percieption."[8] Therefore under one condition the Self is the cogniser and under another, the cognised. "Knowledge is neither a mode of the permanent intellect nor identical with it" (The Nyaya Sutras of Gotama: III.II.275). Knowledge for the Self is always secondary. Therefore to cognise one cognition another cognition is necessary. It is the *anuvyavasayajnana* that brings about such cognition. To produce the *anuvyavasaya* is the function of the mind.

Pleasure and pain are perceived by the mind as immediate perceptions. But knowledge is always characterised by doubt (*samsaya*) and assurance (*niscaya*). These are absent in the experience of pleasure and pain. They are not causally connected with the antecedents of perceptual and inferential forms of knowledge. But for both cognitive and emotive experience conjunction with the *manas* is the *asadharanakarana*. Still they are heterogeneous activities though arising from the same cause. Knowledge is both cognitive and affective. An object is bound to create the feeling of either pleasure or pain in the knower.

Following the *paraprakasakavada* is the *paratapramanyavada*

---

[7] Haribhadra, Sad-Darsana Samucaya, 2nd ed., Trans. K. Satchidananda Murty, (Delhi: Eastern Book Linkers, 1986) II.24.

[8] S.K. Seksena, Nature of Consciousness in Hindu Philosophy, 2nd ed., (Delhi: Motilal Banarsidass Publishers, 1971), p.78.

of Nyaya Vaisesika. Truth and falsity depends upon extraneous factors. Therefore they are *paratapramanya* or are of extrinsic validity. They are extrinsic to knowledge in respect of genesis (*utpattih*) and ascertainment (*jnaptih*). Truth and falsity are the specific qualities of cognition itself. These specific qualities are the merits (*guna*) and demerits (*dosa*). These are additional properties added to knowledge to make it valid or invalid. Jayanta says that the essential nature of cognition is to manifest its object. Thus for Nyaya the nature of knowledge is presentative.

The Nayyayikas with a pragmatic stance hold that the ascertainment of truth depends on some extraneous factors. At the time of the origination of cognition its validity is not presented. Validity is verified by fruitful activity – *pravrttisamarthya*. However, practical efficiency is only the test of truth and not the nature of truth. It is only the verification and not the definition of truth. Successful activity is the ground of inferring validity, while validity itself consists in cognising a thing as possessing the attributes that it really has. The former relates to the knowing of the validity of cognition – *pramanya* – while the latter shows the mere validity of cognition – *prama*. It is the former that needs a pragmatic test, while the latter needs a mere correspondence.

The epistemology of Nyaya is a result of its belief in the objective order of real objects external to and independent of the knowing subject. Knowledge is a reality corresponding to the objective universe. Therefore all objects have an unerring objective reference. The very possibility of knowledge depends on the existence of the real object prior to itself. Nyaya asserts that knowledge is grounded in the object – *jnanamarthajanyam*.

It is on this ground that Nyaya presents its theory of *anyathakhyati* to explain error. Accordingly an illusion is the manifestation of a real object in the form of a different object. It is the misapprehension of one thing as another.

Nyaya Vaisesika deals with epistemology to understand the ontological truth. This leads it to pluralistic realism – the categorisation of predicables in the universe. In this categorisation, body, mind and consciousness are given a static and specific place. The specificity demands the perception of the real – the world – with accuracy and precision. Vaisesika therefore gives the structural detail and Nyaya the logical detail of the world.

The Vedantin criticizes the possibility of *anuvyavasayajnana*, maintaining that it will lead to infinite regress. Nyaya rejects the self-manifestation of consciousness considering that it has to become an object for self-manifestation. But when Svatahprakasavadins speak of *aparoksatva*, it is not in the sense of the manifestation of consciousness as another object, but its essential nature as the subject. Nyaya accepts knowledge as a property of the Self. But the Self is not regarded as the conscious subject, but only as a category among other categories. Of this concept P.S. Sastri says: "... once we admit knowability to be a property of reality we have also to accept all that which knowability implies. The significant implication is that an entity is not knowable in the absence of a conscious...subject."[9] It can also be objected that if consciousness is not self-luminous, how can it manifest other cognitions. The criticism against Nayyayikas

[9] P.S. Sastri, Indian Idealism, vol.I, (Delhi: Bharatiya Vidya Prakashan, 1975), p.29.

is that they confuse between the subject and the object, the atman and the jiva, pure consciousness and ego consciousness.

Samkhya Dualism

While Nyaya Vaisesika upholds pluralistic realism, Samkhya of Kapila presents reality in dual terms. Consciousness (*Purusa*) and matter (*Prakrti*) are the twin, primal, independent entities that explain the world. Neither is consciousness dependent on matter nor matter on consciousness. Nothing but *Purusa* and *Prakrti* are eternal. They appear as the subject and the object, the knower and the known. Heinrich Zimmer says: "The two principles *Prakrti* (composed of the *gunas*) and *Purusa* (the collectivity of radiant but inactive life-monads) are accepted as eternal and real on the basis of the fact that in all acts and theories of knowledge a distinction exits between subject and object, no explanation of experience being possible without the recognition of a knowing self as well as of an object known."[10]

Purusa – the Static Consciousness

Purusa is pure consciousness. But it is non-active. *Purusa* is distinct form *Prakrti* and is untouched by the *gunas*. It is entirely different from the insentient *Prakrti*. The existence of *Purusa* as consciousness is indubitable. "Spirit exists (as distinct from matter)...since there must be an enjoyer..."[11] , for whom *Prakrti*

[10] Heinrich Zimmer, Philosophies of India, Ed. Joseph Campbell, (London: Routledge and Kegan Paul Ltd., 1951), p.326.

[11] S.S. Suryanarayana Sastri, Ed. and Tr. The Sankhya Karika of Isvara Krsna, 2nd ed. rev. rpt., (Madras: University of Madras, 1973), verse 17.

and its evolvents exist. There must be a conscious *Purusa* besides the composite *Prakrti*.

By itself *Purusa* is inactive. But it is that which excites the activity of *Prakrti*, upsetting the equilibrium of *gunas*. Haribhadra says in "Sad-darsana Samuccaya" that *Purusa* is "...eternal consciousness, who is a non-doer, devoid of *gunas* and enjoyer" (Sad-darsana-samuccaya: III.41). Qualities like knowledge, pleasure, pain, desire etc. that are accepted as qualities of the Self by Nyaya are taken away from the *Purusa* by Samkhya. Nyaya attributes both doership and enjoyership to the Self. Samkhya differs in giving doership to the *Prakrti* and enjoyership to the *Purusa*. *Purusa* is only a perceiver, remaining as a witness – drsta (Samkhya Karika: 19 – *drastrtvam akartrbhavasca*). *Purusa* is not a substance in the form of the substratum of consciousness. *Purusa* itself is of the nature of consciousness. According to Vacaspati Misara, the conscious nature of *Purusa* is natural and not adventitious as regarded by Nyaya. "Consciousness...according to Samkhya refers to an existent that is different from the tripartite process and thus differentiated from all of the transactions of awareness (intellect and so forth), transcending all objectivity whether specific or unspecific, utterly unique or uncharacterisable, sentient or intelligent and incapable of producing anything."[12]

The individual according to Samkhya is a composite of *Purusa* and *Prakrti*. The self-sense of *Purusa* appears due to its association with *Prakrti*. "Hence from their association, the non-intelligent

[12] Karl Potter, Gen. Ed. Encyclopaedia of Indian Philosophies, vol.IV., Samkhya: A Dualist Tradition in Indian philosophy, Ed. Gerald James Larson and Ramshankar Bhattacarya, (Delhi: Motilal Banarsidass Publishers, 1987), p.79.

linga (comprising the intellect, individuation etc.) becomes intelligent as it were;...becomes agent, as it were" (Samkhya Karika: 20). Each jiva possesses a gross material body that suffers dissolution at death, and a subtle body that transmigrates. Due to the multiplicity of jiva there is the multiplicity of *Purusa* as well. "The plurality of spirits certainly follows the distributive (nature) of the incidence of birth and death and of (the endowment of) the instruments (of cognition and action), from (bodies) engaging in action..." (Samkhya Karika: 18).

Prakrti – the Dynamic Matter

Prakrti is the primordial matter. It is the cosmic substance and is the first cause of the universe, which is uncaused. It is the active principle. "The *Prakrti* is eternal, one and non-intelligent" (Samkhya Karika: 11). It consists of three constituents called *gunas*. The complexity of *gunas* explains the diversity of objects. The potential consciousness or "Satva is considered to the buoyant and illuminating, Rajas to be stimulating and mobile; Tamas alone is heavy and enveloping" (Samkhya Karika: 13). *Gunas* support one another, intermingle with one another and are intimately connected. When one *guna* becomes predominant, the others remain latent. Thus whenever there is disturbance of equilibrium of *gunas*, manifestation occurs. The return to the quiescent state of *gunas* is called pralaya of the *Prakrti*. According to Ṣamkhya the material *gunas* are the basis of all emotions and actions. Satva gives rise to pleasure, but by itself cannot produce any impulsion to action without rajas. Tamas functions for inhibiting activity. Activity is a process confined to the realm of *Prakrti*. *Purusa* or consciousness has no role in determining actions, since it is inactive.

Interaction between Matter and Consciousness

For Samkhya, the universe owes its existence to the interaction between *Prakrti* and *Purusa*, the principles of materiality and consciousness. The Samkhya Karika uses the world *samyoga* and Samkhya Pravacanasutra uses sanidhya to indicate the interaction. It is the presence of *Puruṣa* that upsets the equilibrium of the *gunas* and thus passively starts the evolutionary process in *Prakrti*. Samkhya recognizes the mutual association of consciousness and matter as essential for creation. It is said in Sarva-siddhanta Samgraha that: "Through the association (of *Prakrti*) with that (atman) possessed of consciousness there arises creation" (Sarva-siddhanta-samgraha: IX.15-16) Metaphorically illustrated, the 'lame *Purusa* cannot operate without the blind *Prakrti*'. "The association of the two, which is like that of a lame man and a blind one, is for the purpose of Pirmal Nature being contemplated (as such) by the Spirit" (Samkhya Karika: 21).

Creation, for Samkhya, is not a new formation, but a transformation of the already existent. "The effect subsists (even prior to the operation of the cause) since what is non-existent cannot be brought into existence by the operation of a cause" (Samkhya Karika: 9 – *asad akaranad*). Transformation (*parinama*) proceeds form an unmanifest (*avyakta*) cause to a manifest (*vyakta*) effect. World is real and is the actual transformation of the material *Prakrti*. Since the effect is pre-existent in the unmanifest *Prakrti* it can be said that cause and effect are identical. But in the manifest *Prakrti*, there is the difference as the cause and effect. Hence, for Samkhya, the relation between cause and effect is neither of pure identity nor of pure difference. It is identity in difference.

Creation is teleological. Creation is for the experience of *Prakrti* and its evolutes by *Purusa*, and for the final release of *Purusa* from the consequent bondage. "Primordial materiality, therefore provides both ordinary experience and the extraordinary knowledge that consciousness exists."[13] Samkhya Karika makes the purpose singular, when it says that the ultimate aim is the release of each spirit. "The creation from the intellect down to the gross elements is brought about by Primal Nature, to the end of the release of each spirit" (Samkhya Karika: 56). To the question how long is the evolution, Samkhya answers with the help of the famous analogy. When *Purusa* has enjoyed all manifestations of *Prakrti*, *Prakrti* ceases to act. It is like "a dancer [who] desists from dancing, having exhibited herself to the audience" (Samkhya Karika: 59).

Through the cosmological evolution of *Prakrti* Samkhya presents a list of psychic principles. *Mahat* or cosmic intelligence is the first evolute. In the individual it functions as buddhi, for ascertainment and decision – *adhyavasaya* (Samkhya Karika: 23). Ahamkara is the individuating principle, and *manas* the principle of cognition. Samkhya, in total, enumerates twentyfour principles. *Purusa* is the twenty-fifth principle that is "neither the evolvent nor the evolute" (Samkhya Karika: 3).

Samkhya accepts buddhi as the first evolute, that mediates

[13] Karl Potter, Gen. Ed. Encyclopaedia of Indian Philosophies vol.IV., Samkhya: A Dualist Tradition in Indian Philosophy, Ed. Gerald James Larson and Ramshankar Bhattacarya, (Delhi: Motilal Banarsidass Publishers, 1987), p.83.

between *Purusa* and *Prakrti*. Knowledge is the cognitive modification of *buddhi*. Samkhya views that knowledge is characterized by both truth and error. Nothing new is produced at any time. Hence error consists not in misapprehension but in non-apprehension (*akhyati*). If both validity and invalidity belong to knowledge, them no knowing is possible as a valid cognition or invalid cognition. If it is said that circumstances reveal the nature of knowledge, is again depending on something else to prove its validity.

Knowledge and Release

For Samkhya, bondage is due to the ignorance of consciousness and matter as dual realities. The inactive *Purusa* can have no real bondage. *Purusa* is neither bound nor liberated. It is *Prakrti* itself attached to different *Purusa*s that migrates. "... it is Prmal Nature, abiding in manifold forms that is bound, is liberated and migrates" (Samkhya Karika: 62). Bondage and release are superimposed on consciousness, since it is not discriminated form matter. Hence bondage ends by the proper discrimination of *Purusa* and *Prakrti*. Due to the proximity of *Purusa* and *Prakrti*, *Prakrti* which is insentient appears as if sentient and *Purusa* which is inactive appears as if active. This contact of the discrete principles and the enjoyed-enjoyer relation is due to beginningless ignorance. Therefore release consists in the discriminative knowledge of *Prakrti* as inert and *Purusa* as conscious. Liberation is "the separation of *Prakrti* by *Purusa*'s discriminative knowledge" (Sad-darsana-samuccaya: III.43). On this theory of Samkhya, A.B. Keith remarks: "The spirit not being really connected with the nature there is no ground on which there can be produced the lack of discrimination of spirit form nature which causes bondage ... a non-existing connection cannot create a lack of distinction which produces a connection."[14]

The realistic schism between *Purusa* and *Prakrti* confronts many objections. A.B. Keith and Karl Potter make similar observances on the dualistic psychology of Samkhya. "Samkhya designates ... a dualism between a closed, causal system of reductive materialism ... and a non-intentional and contentless consciousness."[15] "Starting from the fact of normal consciousness the whole content of consciousness is attributed to nature."[16]

By emphasizing the mutual dependence of *Purusa* and *Prakrti*. Samkhya presents a position, that in order to understand one the other is necessary. Either *Purusa* and *Prakrti* come to contact or they do not. If they come to contact then that is mediated by buddhi. But it could be asked how buddhi that is a material evolute can mediate the relation. "If the second alternative that *Purusa* and *Prakrti* do not come into contact, is taken then consciousness will be reduced to mere epiphenomenona."[17] Max Muller says: "The reality of matter reduces the purity of consciousness.... Once this relational nexus is achieved the *Purusa*

---

[14] A. Berriedale Keith, A History of the Samkhya Philosophy, 1st Indian rpt., (Delhi: Nag Publishers, 1975), p.99.

[15] Karl Potter, Gen. Ed. Encyclopaedia of Indian Philosophies, vol.IV., Samkhya: A Dualist Tradition in Indian Philosophy, Ed. Gerald James Larson and Ramshankar Bhattacarya (Delhi: Motilal Banarsidass Publishers, 1987), p.77

[16] A. Berriedale Keith, A History of the Samkhya Philosophy, 1st Ind.rpt., (Delhi: Nag Publishers, 1975),p.87.

[17] R.D. Ranade, Vedanta The Culmination of Indian Thought, (Bombay: Bharatiya Vidya Bhavan, 1970), pp.50-51.

looses its pristine purity ... its non-relational, structureless character."[18]

Yoga and mind

The concept of consciousness as dealt with by the Yoga of Patanjali is similar to the major tenets expounded by Samkhya. But unlike Kapila, the founder of Samkhya, Patanjali believes in the existence of God. He brings forth the concept of God to explain the initiation of contact between *Purusa* and *Prakrti*. *Purusa* is consciousness attributed of enjoyership and *Prakrti* is matter, which is the active principle. "The states of the mind are always known, because the Lord of the mind, the *Purusa* is unchangeable."[19]

Patanjali describes consciousness as the witness of all mental modifications. Commenting on the Yoga-sutras Archie J. Bahm notes: "Whereas a thing may be either known or unknown, the functions of the mind which knows consist in its conscious activities which are wholly apparent to the soul, since the awareness constituting consciousness is supplied by the soul. Without the presence of the soul's awareness, the mind not only would neither know itself nor objects but would not even exist as an evolute of *Prakrti*."[20]

Similar to the term *mahat* as referred to by Samkhya, Pantanjali Yoga introduces the term *citta*. According to Patanjali,

[18] Friedrich Max Muller, The Six Systems of Indian Philosophy, 1st Ind.ed., (New Delhi: Associated Publishing House, 1973), p.XXIII.

[19] Swami Vivekananda, RajaYoga, 19th imp., (Mayavati: Advaita Ashrama, 1990), p.259, Yogasutra:IV.17.

[20] Archie J. Bahm, Yoga Union with the Ultimate, 1st Ind. Ed., (New Delhi: Arnold Heinemann Publishers, 1978), p.153.

Yoga is the control of thoughts – *cittavrtti*. "Yoga is restraining the mind-stuff (*citta*) from taking various forms (*vrttis*)."[21] "The object of Yoga is to divest mind of all its impurities, so that the stream of consciousness is clear as crystal capable of reflecting whole reality."[22] As the preliminary step to Yoga, Patanjali gives the Astanga Yoga or the eight-fold path that includes *yama*, *niyama*, *asana*, *pranayama*, *pratyahara*, *dharana*, *dhyana* and *samadhi*.

Purvamimamsa and Self

The metaphysics and epistemology of Puruvamimamsa follows that of Nyaya with slight modifications. In agreement with Nyaya, Prabhakara Mimamsaka holds that consciousness is an attribute of the Self and is not its essential nature. But Kumarila Mimamsaka accepts consciousness as the nature of the Self. "Kumarila…regards the soul to be of the nature of pure consciousness … while according to Prabhakara, consciousness is only a quality of the soul."[23] Kumarila explains the Self as the knower, doer and enjoyer. It is not cognized by any other thing but by itself. Prabhakara disagrees with this view. He holds that the Self cannot be both the knower and the known. Cognitions reveal only objects. In the process Self is revealed as the knower. It is cognized "… not as object of cognition but as cognition."[24]

---

[21] Swami Vivekananda, RajaYoga, 19th imp., (Mayavati: Advaita Ashrama, 1990), p.115, Yogasutra: I.2.

[22] Raghunath Safaya, Indian Psychology, (New Delhi: Munshiram Manoharlal Publishers Pvt.Ltd., 1976), p.270.

[23] Ganganath Mahamahopaddhyaya Jha, The Prabhakara School of PurvaMimamsa, (Delhi: Motilal Banarsidass Pubs., 1978), p.80.

[24] A. Berriedale Keith, Trans. The Karma Mimamsa, 2nd ed., (New Delhi: Oriental Books Reprint Corporation, 1978), Mimamsasutra: I.16.

All cognitions as such are valid. Invalidity rests on the circumstance in which an object is perceived. According to Prahhakara, error is the non-apprehension of distinction (*bhedagraha*) between what is in contact with the sense organ and what is remembered. For Kumarila error is a case of false perception of identity (*abhedagraha*) of the remembered element with the perceived element. The falsity of cognition is discovered when it leads to unsuccessful action. With Nyaya, Mimamsakas also accept action as a test for finalising truth.

For the Purvamimamsakas, Self is the doer and enjoyer of action. They uphold *jnanakarma samuccaya* as the means to liberation of the Self. By performing actions instructed by the Vedas the Self accumulates dharma, the fruits of which may bring prosperity either in this world or in the heaven. Quoting Slokavarttika, Raghunath Safaya remarks: "Consciousness cannot reside in the body or in the senses, as even at the death of the body and cessation of senses, the permanent entity persists and takes another birth. This permanent entity is the soul, bearing the potentialities of Ideas, capable of migrating to another body."[25]

Advaita Vedanta and Non-duality

Advaita Vedanta resolves the dichotomy of matter and consciousness, variously approached by other systems, through the concept of non-dualism. Samkaracarya establishes the theory of Advaita or the non-separateness of the supreme Self and the individual self by critically examining other theories, primarily

[25] Raghunath Safaya, Indian Psychology, (New Delhi: Munshiram Manoharlal Publishers Pvt. Ltd., 1976), p.183.

in his commentary to the Brahmasutra. Samkaracarya regards consciousness as the Supreme Self. In Brahmasutra Adhyasa Bhasya, he establishes that the concept of the Self as physiological (Carvaka), psychological (Vijnanavadin), psychophysical (Nyaya Vaisesika and Samkhya Yoga) deal with the empirical self and not the real Self. For Samkara, the Self is the ultimate basis of all existence and is of the nature of foundational consciousness.

The Self is different from the body and it does not depend upon body for its existence. Consciousness is the essential nature of the Self. Carvaka is wrong when it says that consciousness is a quality and is dependent upon matter. Consciousness cannot be identified with that which it illumines. It cannot be treated as an object among other objects. Nyaya by reducing consciousness to a category eliminates the very possibility of knowledge. In his commentary to Brahmasutra, criticizing the Sankhyan theory, Acarya establishes that the existence of consciousness as the Self "...distinct from the body is beyond criticism."[26]

Samkaracarya prefaces his bhasya to Brahmasutra with a discourse on adhyasa or superimposition. Adhyasa Bhasya outlines the central teachings of Advaita. It epistemologically and logically analyses the criterion for truth, falsity, the relation between subject and object, and the primacy of consciousness as the Self. Samkaracarya's theory of superimpostion explains the problem of appearance and reality from a different perspective.

---

[26] Brahmasutra Samkara Bhasya: 3.3.54. V.H. Date, Vedanta Explained Samkara's Commentary on the Brahma-sutras, vols. 1 and 2, (Bombay: Book seller's Publishing Com., 1954).

Paradigms of Thought

As a prelude to the psychology of illusion, Samkaracarya posits the fundamental principles of subject and object. All cognitions are made possible by these two principles. But the relation between the two cannot be possible at all. "The subject or *asmad pratyaya* and the object or *yusmad pratyaya* are by nature contradictory as light and darkness" (Brahmasutra-adhyasa-bhasya: *asmad yusmad pratyaya gocarayoh visaya visayinoh tamaprakasavat viruddha svabhavayoh*). These two paradigms, "are not only different form each other but diametrically opposed and mutually exclusive, so that what is conceived as the object can never be conceived as the subject...and vice versa."[27] There is a fundamental incompatibility between what is subjective and what is objective.

Samkaracarya uses the words *asmad* and *yusmad* not in their mere logical sense, but in their psychological import too. The word *yusmad* comprises all that can be objectified. *Asmad* denotes the subject which objectifies everything, but which can never be objectified. *Yusmad* includes not only the objects outside, but also the qualities objectified in the act of introspection. Thus ones sense organs, mind and intellect can be addressed by the epithet *yusmad.* But *asmad* as the Pure Subject can never be brought in the field of the object. It is the Self and is of the nature of consciousness – *visayini cidatmake*. James Ward makes a parallel remark when he says that "to identify these two is impossible, but the 'me' cannot be there without the 'I'".[28]

---

[27] F. Max Muller, Three Lectures in Vedanta Philosophy, (London: Longmans Green and Co., 1894), p.63

[28] James Ward, The Psychological Principles, (Cambridge: Cambridge University, 1918), p.379.

With this terminology, Samkaracarya makes a clear definition of the subject and the object. In Existential philosophy the subject is considered as the 'ego' and the object as the 'non-ego'. Samkaracarya brings the 'ego' along with the 'non-ego', to the objective field. To the Advaitin the self is the ego. Max Muller makes an appropriate remark on this foundational difference. "Psychologists may imagine that they can treat the soul as an object of knowledge, dissect and describe it. The Vedantist would say, that what they dissect and weigh and analyse and describe is not the soul, . . . is not the subject, it is not the self in the highest sense of the world. What they call perception, memory, conception ... will and effort, all this ... is outside the self."[29]

There is absolute contradiction between *asmad* which is the *visayi* and *yusmad* which is the *visaya*, since they are opposites by very nature. The subject can never become the object. And the object can never be thought of as the subject. One being, associating or becoming the other – *idaredarabhava* – is absolutely impossible. Also the qualities of one can never become the qualities – *dharma* – of the other. In the field of objects, one can have mistakes. But one can never mistake oneself as the other nor can one mistake the other as oneself. Having classified the subject and its qualities, and the object and its qualities under two classes, Samkaracarya introduces the term *adhyasa* to explain falsity. Since the intermingling of the subject and the object nor their qualities is impossible, "... it will be wrong ... to superimpose the objects and their attributes on the self-illuminating subject ... equally wrong will be the

[29] F. Max Muller, Three Lectures in Vedanta Philosophy, (London: Longmans Green and Co., 1894), p.63.

superimposition of the subject and its attributes on the object."[30]

Now though it is not logically possible to mix up or mistake the object and its properties, for the subject and its properties or vice versa, it has experientially become possible. Samkaracarya says: "superimposition is to be understood as false" (Brahmasutra-adhyasa-bhasya: *adhyasa mithya iti*). It is due to the lack of discrimination between "...the absolutely different subject, object and their qualities" (*itara itara avivekena viviktayoh dharmadharminoh*) that superimposition has become experientially possible. Due to false knowledge – *mithyajnana* (Brahmasutra-adhyasa-bhasya: *mithya jnana nimittah*) – the mixing up is made between the true and the false, resulting n mutual superimposition. Thus we contend, "I am this, and this is mine" (Brahmasutra-adhyasa-bhasya: *ahamidam mamidam*). Two kinds of superimposition have become possible, *dharmi adhyasa* in the realm of the subject and dharma *adhyasa* in the realm of qualities. "We are prone to superimpose', Paul Edwards elucidates, 'the properties of the object of awareness on its subject and vice versa."[31] Samkaracarya qualifies this error as the habitual error – *naisargika* (Brahmasutra-adhyasa-bhasya: *naisargikoyam lokavyavaharah*) – that has no beginning.

Having said that superimposition is false and is due to false knowledge, Acarya examines the definitions given by various Darsanas for superimposition. All the system builders however agree in apprehending adhyasa as the appearance of one of having

---

[30] V.H. Date, Vedanta Explained: Samkara's commentary on the Brahmasutras, vol.I, (Bombay: Book Seller's Publishing Company, 1954), p.1.

[31] Paul Edwards, Ed. The Encyclopaedia of Philosophy, vol.17, rpt.ed., (New York: Macmillan Publishing Co., Inc. and The Free Press, 1972), p.69.

the attributes of another. T.M.P. Mahadevan explains: "It is the cognition of 'that' in what is 'not that'."[32] The system builders differ with regard to the nature and the cause of adhyasa. *Anyathakhyati*, *akhyati* and *viparitakhyati* explain error as an existent real. Samkaracarya rejects this explanation, for it denies the very possibility of error. He criticizes Vijnanadin's intense solipsism, for, "... the non-existence of external things cannot be maintained, on account of our consciousness of them" (Brahmasutra-adhyasa-bhasya: 2.5.28).

Samkaracarya defines superimposition as *mithya*, the "cognition of something as some other thing" (Brahmasutra-adhyasa-bhasya: *atasmin tatbuddhih*). *Mithyajnana* or false cognition is due to the ignorance of the substratum, *atma ajnana*. Knowledge or *vidya* consists in the "... ascertainment of the real nature of the substratum" (Brahmasutra-adhyasa-bhasya: *vastusvarupavadharanam*) concerning the nature of superimposition, it is described as neither real nor unreal – *sadasad vilaksana*. Anything that which is experienced is real in some sense. But the absolutely real is that which that which cannot be contradicted at all times – *abadhita* – and is the locus on which the unreal is sublated. The object of superimposition is not real, since it is sublated on the knowledge of the substratum. It is not unreal, since it appears in experience. It cannot be both real and unreal, since that will be a contradiction. It cannot be first unreal and then real since that will violate the definition of the real and the unreal. It cannot be first real and then unreal since real cannot become unreal, and unreal cannot become real.

---

[32] T.M.P. Mahadevan, Superimposition in Advaita Vedanta, (New Delhi: Sterling Publishers Pvt. Ltd., 1985), p.1 — *anyasya anyadharmavabhasah.*

The object of superimposition and the real cannot be sequentially real and unreal or unreal and real. Therefore it can only be described as *anirvacaniya*. In Vivekacudamani Samkaracarya says: "It is not sat (real), not asat (unreal), not both. It is not bhinna (different), not *abinna* (not-non different), not both. It is not *sanga* (with parts), not *ananga* (without parts), not both. It is very wonderful and of a form which is inexpressible."[33]

The empirical existence of the world can be described neither as wholly existent nor as wholly non-existent. It is not absolutely unreal like 'the son of a barren woman', since it is experienced. The totally unreal cannot appear. The world is not absolutely real since it is sublated by the knowledge of its non-separateness from consciousness, which is the experiencer's self. Against the gross realist Acarya says that the world is not absolutely real and against the nihilist, he maintains the reality of the world. Reconciling realism and idealism he ascribes the world to the category of *anirvacaniya*.

By an analysis of superimposition, Samkaracarya establishes the sole reality of consciousness. It is consciousness that which agrees with the definition of the absolutely real. Consciousness is not sublated at any time. It is the locus of that which is sublated. Consciousness is absolute – *paramarthika* – and all other experiences are relative, since they are substrated and sublated on consciousness. Consciousness is the Self which is self-evident – *aparoksa* (Brahmasutra-adhyasa-bhasya: *aparoksatvat svadasiddhatvat*) – and is present in the three periods of time – *sarvadavartamana* (Brahmasutra-Samkara-bhasya: 3.1.7). In his

[33] Samkaracarya, Vivekacudamoni, 2nd ed., Tr. P.Samkaranarayanan, (Bombay: Bharatiya Vidya Bhavan, 1979), verse 111.

commentary to Taittiriya Upanishad Acarya says: "Consciousness is the very nature of the Self and inseparable from It."[34]

Consciousness and Causation

Samkaracarya disproves the Samkhyan concept of *Prakrti* as an independent principal, with its theory of Parinamavada. He replaces *Prakrti* by Maya, and deprives *Prakrti* of its independent existence. World is the apparent change or appearance of the unchanging. The causal principle is meaningful only form the empirical standpoint. The *vivartavada* of Advaita is not a theory of causality but is a cancellation of it. Consciousness does not stand in causal relation with the world since world is inseparable form it. Causation is the necessity of thought. Samkaracarya regards causality only as a categorical principle. In tune with this conception, John Hospers says, Causality is "neither true nor false, for it is not a statement (proposition) about the world at all. Rather it expresses a resolve 'Let us find uniformities in the world'. It is sometimes called a leading principle because it leads us, guides us in our empirical invetigaitons."[35]

Advaita contends the notion that Maya is a separate causal power interacting with consciousness, as fallacious. It is with reference to the world that creatorship is given to consciousness. But from the standpoint of the Self it is not even the causal principle. World is but a vivarta, the appearance of consciousness.

---

[34] Karl H. Potter, Gen. Ed. Encyclopedia of Indian Philosophies, vol.III, 1st Ind. Ed., (Delhi: Motilal Banarsidass Publishers, 1981), p.211. Taittiriya Upanishad Samkara Bhasya: 2.10.

[35] John Hospers, An Introduction to Philosophical Analysis, (New Jersey: Prentice Hall Inc., 1964), p.261.

Vedanta Paribhasa says that, it is "... a transformation in relation to nescience and a transfiguration in relation to consciousness."[36] World is the manifestation of consciousness without abandoning its real nature. Consciousness is that "from which occur the birth, continuance and dissolution of the world" (Brahmasutra: I.1.2 – *janmadyasya yatah*) of name and form.

Advaita Vendanta attempts to emphasize the inseparability of consciousness and world. At the same time it explains and includes every piece of experience. Waking, dream and deep sleep states appear and disappear in consciousness. But waking is not present in dream and vice versa. Both waking and dream are not present in deep sleep. The contradictory nature of appearances imply that it has existence only in the time of experience – *pratitikala*.[37] That which has no separate existence seems to be existent in the state of experience. Hence "limitation (*avacceda*) is illusory, but that which appears to be limited (*avaccedyam*) is real" (Drk-drsya-viveka: 33). Therefore to mistake consciousness or the self with something transient is to mistake the absolute – *paramarthika* – for the contingent – *vyavaharika*.

Two major objections are raised against the Advaita concept of Self. The first is that how the Self which is totally unknown can become the substratum of superimposition. And the second objection is regarding the nature of knowledge. If knowledge is opposed to ignorance, then can knowledge be the substratum of ignorance?

---

[36] Dharmaraja Adhvarin, Vedanta Paribhasa, Ed. and Trans. S.S. Suryanarayana Sastri, (Adyar:The Adyar Library, 1942),p.36, verse I.85.

[37] Samkaracarya, Drg-drsya Viveka, Trans. Swami Nikhilananda, 6th ed., (Mysore: Sri Ramakrishna Ashrama, 1976), p.53. verse:39.

Immediacy of Consciousness

Advaita regards consciousness as everybody's Self – sarvasyatma (Brahmasutra-adhyasa-bhasya: *sarvasya atmatvacca brahmastitva prasiddhe)*. It is directly experienced and cannot be grasped as an object. Though Atman is not an object of knowledge – *paroksa* – it is self-evident – *svatasiddha*. It is immediately known as the 'I' or *asmad pratyaya*. The authority of *pramana* is not to reveal an unknown Self, but only to remove superimposition from the self-evident Atman.

The knowledge of the Self is self-established. Self-knowledge finds its consummation in experience, since the "knowledge relates to the reality which is already an existing thing" (Brahmasutra-Samkara-bhasya: 1.1.2). Advaita is a transition from the dividing point of view – *bhedadrsti* – to a unifying point of view – *atmadrsti*. It is a transition from knowing characterized by relations to knowing characterized by immediacy. It is not knowledge as a process in succession but as being instantaneously. Knowledge is not a means to reality, but itself is reality. In Upadesa Sahasri Samkaracarya says: "Awareness (*bodha*) does not require another awareness so that it be known—it is its own nature to illumine just as it is the sun's nature to light itself."[38]

Self-consciousness is not opposed to ignorance or knowledge. Whether one has the cognition that the Self is known or unknown, it does not follow that there is no Self or that the Self is affected thereby. The Self illumines both the valid and

[38] Karl H. Potter, Ed., Encyclopaedia of Indian Philosophies, vol.III, 1st Ind. ed., (Delhi: Motilal Banarsidass Publishers, 1981), p.236, Upadesasahasri: ii.15.41.

the invalid cognition, but is not affected by the merits or demerits of the things superimposed. *Svarupacaitanya* or Self-consciousness is not opposed to *jnanavrtti* or *ajnanavrtti*. Both *ghata ajnana* (ignorance about pot) and *atma ajnana* (ignorance about self) are *vrttis* or modes of mind. It is *jnanavrtti* that is opposed to *atmajnanavrtti*. *Akandakaravrtti* shining in consciousness dispels *atma-ajnanavrtti* and dissolves into consciousness as it cannot exist without its opposite. It is in Self-consciousness both *jnana* and *ajnana vrttis* shine and become known. Bringing the object into the field of perception creates the knowledge of any object. The knowledge of the Self is created not by bringing Self into any filed, but by a process of negation of the superimposition.

Vrttijnana and Svarupajnana

Svarupajnana is consciousness itself while *vrttijnana* is a mode of consciousness. Objects become known when they come in false relation of identification with consciousness. But consciousness to be known does not need anything.

Vrttijnana is of two types – *khandakara vrttijnana* or partite knowledge and *akhandakara vrttijnana* or impartite knowledge. The former can bring about only relative knowledge. It is a blend of the mental modification – *vrtti* – and the reflection of consciousness in the intellect – *cidakasa*. It is an expression of consciousness through a mental mode corresponding to an object. Consciousness is devoid of any relation. It is *asanga*. Therefore any relative knowledge comes in the field of ignorance. It is the impartite consciousness that appears as partite in relational knowledge, as "...content consciousness (*visaya caitanya*), cognitive consciousness (*pramana caitanya*) and cogniser consciousness (*pramatr caitanya*)".[39]

Akhandakara vrttijnana is the impartite knowledge of the Self. The *khandakara vrtti* is sublated by the *akhandakara vrtti*. *Akhandakara vrtti* gives rise to the immediate realization of the Self and dissolves in it. It removes *atma ajnana* – self-ignorance – as well as the effect of Self-ignorance, that is *adhyasa*. And then it perishes because its cause (*avidya*) is destroyed.

Consciousness is Irrefutable

The Self is consciousness and is irrefutable. There cannot be an affirmation or denial without a witnessing consciousness. In all denials, the denial presupposes the unreality of false predication, and is not absolute negation. Consciousness is essentially infinite and unlimited. Hence negation is made of the false categorical distinctions. Consciousness is irrefutable and indubitable since it is the nature of him who attempts the refutation (Brahmasutra-Samkara-bhasya: 3.2.22). Denial or refutation of the multiplicity (*adhyaropa apavada*) is made only to realize the abiding substratum as consciousness. The plurality of objects betokens its basis as consciousness (*arthopalaksita*). Every object or cognition is *sadatmaka* (Vivekacudamoni: 248). The root all existence is consciousness. Negation of the unreal is the affirmation of the real. It is to show that there is nothing other than consciousness. In fact in the attempt to separate the finite, the not-Self from the infinite – the Self – a point will be reached when nothing can be separated as the finite or not-Self –

39 Dharmaraja Adhvarin, Vedanta Paribhasa, Ed. and Trans. S.S. Suryanarayana Sastri, (Adyar: The Adyar Library, 1942), p.22, verse 1.17.

nisedhavadhi. Samkaracarya says in Aparoksa Anubhuti: "Just as a jar is all earth, so also is the body all consciousness. The division, therefore into the Self and not-Self is made by the ignorant to no purpose."[40]

By the *anvaya vyatireka* method, the substratum of the seen or the not-Self is understood as the seer, the Self. The locus of the world of name and form is consciousness. The *drsya* or the seen depends upon *drsta* or the seer. When the seen is there the seer exists as the witnessing consciousness. When the seen is not there also, the seer is there, as Pure Consciousness. When the difference between the seer and the seen is understood there is no seen. Any distinction is a result of the "mixing up of the true and the false" (Brahmasutra-Samkara-bhasya: *satyanrute mithunikritya*) – the real and the unreal. Consciousness is permanent. The witnessed is there only with reference to the witness consciousness. Samkaracarya establishes the relation between the Self and the seen, consciousness and the world as *abheda* or non-separate.

Advaita Vedanta speaks of consciousness as that which is already there. All effort to achieve ones real nature, hence is meaningless, since it stands already achieved (*siddhasya siddhi*). Samkaracarya conveys not the extinction of the ego, but the expansion of the ego from the doer-enjoyer consciousness to Pure Consciousness, "*asanga* and *akhanda*" (Drk-drsya-viveka: 25,28), which one already is.

Advaita theory of consciousness, its identity with the Self, the non-separateness of consciousness and world, are the theories

[40] Samkaracarya, Aparoksanubhuti, 7th imp., Tr. Swami Vimuktananda, (Calcutta: Advaita Ashrama, 1989), p.39, verse 69.

that are criticized by the dualists as solipsistic and world negating. These criticisms emerge from insufficient understanding of the Advaita concepts of *caitanya*, *mithya* and *karma*. Paul Edwards says: "The ambiguous status assigned to Maya is the reason that Samkara regarded it as indefinable or inexpressible (*anirvacaniya*), and it also accounts for the fact that he did not adopt a subjectivist and solipsistic account of appearances."[41]

41 Paul Edwards, Ed. The Encyclopaedia of Philosophy, vol.7, rpt. Ed., (New York: Macmillan Publishing Co. Inc. and the Free Press, 1972), p.282.

5

Consciousness in Bhagavad Gita

nasato vidyate bhavo nabhavo vidhyate satah
ubhayorapi drstontastvanayostattvadarsibhih

The real does not disappear; the unreal does not appear.
The wise see the difference between the two.
Bhagavad Gita 2:16

The Bhagavad Gita gives a wholesome and multiperspectival picture of the concept of consciousness. The Gita presents consciousness not only from the epistemological standpoint but also from the existential and hermeneutic standpoint. The concept of consciousness is given an integral outlook by treating it as an ontological truth than a psychological function.

Consciousness and Existence

The second chapter of the Gita makes an existential statement that the wise do not grieve to give a definition for the Self. "For those who deserve no grief thou hast grieved, and words of wisdom thou speakest. For the living and for the dead the wise grieve not."[1] Wisdom as meant by the word *pandah* is not

[1] Bhagavad Gita: II.11. All verses from Bhagavad Gita and prose from Samkara Bhasya are taken from Alladi Mahadeva Sastri, Tr. The Bhagavad Gita with the commentary of Sri Samkaracarya, corrected rpt., (Madras: Samata Books, 1981).

referred to mean extraneous knowledge. Samkaracarya and other noted commentators on the Gita, like Anandagiri, translate *pandah* as Self-knowledge. Those who have Self-knowledge are the *panditah* or the wise (*atmavisaya buddhih yesam te panditah*). Those who know the real nature of the Self (*atmajnah*) do not grieve. Since the Self as consciousness is known to be eternal, there is no place for grief over death.

The definition for the eternal is that which is always present. The transient is that which has only an intermediate existence. Consciousness is that which is always *is*. Non-existence cannot be attributed to consciousness in terms of the past or the future. Bhagavan says to Arjuna: "Never did I not exist, nor thou, nor these rulers of men; and no one of us will ever hereafter cease to exist" (Bhagavad Gita: II.12). "One is eternally present as identical with the Self" (Gita Samkara Bhashya: II.12). The birth and death of the body is not to be taken as the birth and death of the Self. I as the Self always exist. The Bhasyakara notes: "As the Self, the Atman, we are eternal in all the three periods of time" (Gita Samkara Bhasya: II.12). He interprets the word 'us' (*vayam*) in this verse as to mean bodies that are different and not the plurality of the Self.

According to the Gita the nature of Self is Pure Consciousness. The Self is essentially one and eternal as illustrated in the verse: "Just as in this body the embodied (self) passes into childhood and youth and old age, so does He pass into another body" (Bhagavad Gita: II.13). Childhood, youth and old age are the inevitable and different stages of the *dehi* or one who owns a body. But this does not mean that death occurs to the Self that is Pure Consciousness, at the end of one physical stage and is born when the next stage comes into being. Different stages accrue to the one immutable Self. It is the immutable Self that witnesses the different stages without being touched by any mutation. Logically and experientially if this seems to be correct it can also be understood that it is the immaterial self that passes unchanged onto another body. The Self "is not born, nor does He ever die, after having been, He again ceases not to be; nor the reverse. Unborn, eternal, unchangeable and primeval, He is not slain when the body is slain" (Bhagavad Gita: II.20). This verse rules out the presence of any of the six changes of conditions or *vikaras* to which all beings in the world are subject, in the Self.

Transformations like birth, growth etc. does not happen to the Self, that is consciousness. The final transformation known as destruction is also negated of consciousness. Acarya interprets *kadacit* to mean the negation of all transformations at any time. Consciousness is constant, not subject to the changes of conditions known as decline – *apaksaya*. It does not diminish in its own substance, since it has not parts. As devoid of qualities consciousness does not diminish by the loss of a quality. Consciousness is primeval, since it is not subject to change known as growth – *vrddhi* – as opposed to decline. Growth is increase in size by the accretion of parts. Consciousness that is ever full never grows.

Birth and death never occur to consciousness. In ordinary parlance death is ascribed to that which having once existed ceases to be later – *yo hi bhutva na bhavita sa mriyate iti ucyate*. Consciousness having once existed does not afterwards ceases to be. Having experienced the state of being, it does not again reach the state of non-being. "Hence it does not cease to be" (Samkara Bhasya of Gita: II.20 – *ayam atma bhutva bhavankriyam anubhuya pascat abhavita abhavam ganta na bhuyah punah na mriyate*). Similarly that which having been non-existent when comes into being is said to be born – *yo hi abhutva bhavita sa jayata iti ucyate*. Consciousness does not come into existence like the body, having not existed before. Hence consciousness is not born. Consciousness is *aja* or unborn, *nitya* or eternal, *puranah* or ancient, since it is the primeval Being.

How is the birth and death of the body is to be understood in relation with the imperishable? Bhagavan says that it is to be understood as: "Just as a man casts off worn-out cloths and puts on others which are new, so the embodied (Self) casts off worn-out bodies and enters others which are new" (Bhagavad Gita: II.22). The immaterial Self as consciousness is not affected by the material changes. "It is not affected by the physical elements which ruin one another" (Gita Samkara Bhasya: II.24). Since consciousness is not prone to the mutually destructive elements, it is everlasting – *nityah*. Since it is everlasting, consciousness is also all pervading – *sarvagatah*. Consciousness is stable and firm like a pillar – *achalah* (Gita Samkara Bhasya: II.24). Due to its nature of all-pervasiveness, consciousness present even in stationary objects is "indestructible eternally" (Bhagavad Gita: II.19 – *nayam hanti na hanyamane*).

The Bhasyakara defines eternal as to mean "at all times and in all states" (Gita Samkara Bhasya: II.30 – *nityam sarvada sarva avasthasu*). This definition implies existence holistically. Existence is generally considered as that which is in the past, the present or in the future – the three periods of time. Existence is also taken to be that which is in the three states of waking, dream or deep sleep. The connotation is that consciousness is that which continues to exist at all periods of time and in different states. Hence death, birth etc. which are relative concepts, defined in terms of time and changing states, cannot be introduced in the realm of consciousness which is eternal and immutable. This is the implication of Bhagavan's statement that, "Whoever looks upon Him as the slayer, and whoever looks upon Him as the slain, both these know not aright. He slays not, nor is He slain" (Bhagavad Gita: II.19 – *nayam hanti na hanya mane*). The Self as of the nature of consciousness is not to be misunderstood "... as the agent in the act of slaying', nor, 'as the sufferer in the act of slaying when the body is slain" (Gita Samkara Bhasya: II.30). Bhagavan speaks to Arjuna from his existential situation. Arjuna is reluctant to fight, fearful of causing death. Arjuna takes physical death to be the death of the Self and slaying as done by the Self. Bhagavan extirpates these two misconceptions from a hermeneutic standpoint.

Consciousness is "... unmanifest, unthinkable and unchangeable." Consciousness is unmanifest – *avyakta* – in the sense that it is not accessible to any of the senses. The unmanifest is unthinkable – *acintyam* – too, "Only that which is manifest to the senses can be thought of" (Gita Samkara Bhasya: II.25 – *yat hi indriya gocarah tat cinta visayatvam apadhyate*). Anything to be thought of it must become an object in the tripartite cognitive process, involving the object to be known, the knower and the resultant knowledge. Consciousness is not the object of knowledge, but is the impartite subject that illumines the cognitive process and the factors involved. Hence it cannot become an object of thought. Consciousness is unchangeable – *avikarya* – because it has no parts. Samkaracarya elucidates,

"Whatever has no parts is never found to undergo change" (Gita Samkara Bhasya: II.25).

These descriptions establish that the Self is of the nature of consciousness. The Self as consciousness exists beyond time, at the same time illumines that which is relative to time. Substantiating the identity of Self with consciousness, Sri Aurobindo comments: "... existence is not merely a glorious or a vain, a wonderful or a dismal panorama of a constant mutation of becoming. There is something eternal, immutable, imperishable, a timeless self-existence, that is not affected by the mutations of Nature. It is their impartial witness, neither affecting nor affected, ...but always pure, complete, great and unwounded."[2] The Self as of the nature of consciousness never changes nor perishes, but makes possible all changes knowable.

The Bhagavad Gita appertains eternity and immortality to the nature of the Self. Birth and death are only physical changes, and hence cannot break the continuous existence of the Self as consciousness. Death is not to be lamented upon, for it will not bring about one's non-existence. Identical with consciousness one is immortal. No physical flux can add or take away something from the Self which is Pure Consciousness. On this hermeneutics of the Gita, the noted translator of the Gita, Archie J. Bahm writes: "... he who is interested in immortality as future life become anxious about something which he does not have."[3] If immortality is something to be accomplished in the future time

---

[2] Sri Aurobindo, Essays on the Gita, 8th ed., (Pondicherry; Sri Aurobindo Ashram, 1970), p.289.

[3] Archie J. Bahm, Tr. The Bhagavad Gita, (Bombay: Somaiya Publications Pvt. Ltd., 1970), p.21.

then it is also likely to be lost in a distant future. It is the identity of his Self with consciousness that accounts his immortality for an everlasting present.

Any existential approach distinguishes and demarcates between two kinds of consciousness. Consciousness by being and the intentional consciousness, seem to be two incorrigible extremes in the methodology of 'reduction' and 'bracketing'. This epistemological riddle is solved in the Gita, by the analysis of consciousness from both cognitive and ontological perspectives. A holistic definition of these two kinds of consciousness is made in the second chapter.

"Of the unreal no being there; there is no non-being of the real. Of both these is the truth seen by the seers of the Essence" (Bhagavad Gita: II.16). The Bhasyakara makes a subtle clarification of this profound statement. There is no existence of the unreal. The real on the other hand is never non-existent. The unreal is an effect that is caused and the real is that which is beyond cause-effect relationship. "Heat, cold, etc., and the causes there of, which are...perceived through the organs of perception, are not absolutely real (*vastu-sat*); for they are effects or changes (*vikara*), and every change is temporary. For instance, no objective form, such as an earthen pot, presented to the consciousness by the eye, proves to be real, because it is not perceived apart from clay" (Gita Samkara Bhasya: II.16). All effects are unreal, since they are not perceived as distinct from their causes. "Effects are not perceived apart from their causes" (Gita Samkara Bhasya: II.16). Acarya accounts for the unreal nature of every effect, also because it is not perceived before its production and after its destruction. Effects are transformations. Transformations not being cognizable apart from their causes are unreal. But this does not bring the contingency of an absolute vacuum.

Acarya further elucidates that all our cognitive experiences involve two kinds of cognitions such as the "cognition of the real and the cognition of the unreal" (Gita Samkara Bhasya: II.16 – *sarvatra buddhidvayopalabdheh satbuddhih asat buddhih iti*). The distinction between the real and the unreal depends on our cognitions. "The real is whose cognition is immutable and the unreal is whose cognition is mutable" (Gita Samkara Bhasya: II.16 – *yadvisaya buddhih na vyabicarati tat sat, yadvisaya vyabhicarati tat asat*). Throughout all cognitive experiences two fold cognitions arise with reference to the one and the same substratum. In the cognitive statement 'the pot is', the twofold cognitions are the 'cognition of the pot' and the 'cognition of isness'. Of these the cognition of the pot is mutable, being temporary. It exists only in between the origin and the destruction of the pot.

The object corresponding to the cognition of an effect, in this example, pot, is unreal, its cognition being temporary. But what corresponds to the cognition of the existence is real, its cognition being immutable. The cognition of existence is always present. When a particular objective referent perishes and its cognition proves mutable, the cognition of the real is still available in regard to other objects. The cognition of existence persists forever. Madhusudhana Saraswati supplements this idea in his work Gudartha Dipika: "There is an immutable basis of 'isness' in all experiences, irrespective of the variation of its objects."[4] How the possible doubt is how the real and unreal

[4] Madhusudana Saraswati, Gudartha Dipika, Tr. Sisirkumar Gupta, (Delhi: Motilal Banarsidass Pubs., 1977), p.22.

cognitions rest on the same substratum. This scepticism is ruled out by Acarya by the example of another cognitive statement, 'this is water', with reference to mirage. In this statement the substantive cognition namely water, though absent, along with the attributive cognition refers to an identical substratum.

This exegesis establishes two ontological facts. The caused objects are unreal. The unreal never comes into being. The real is that which continuously exists. It never lapses into non-being. Never ever can the unreal be existent and the real be non-existent. The real is ever existent and the unreal is never existent.

The real always exists. "A real entity like the Self never lapses into non-being, it being present always" (Gita Samkara Bhasya: II.16 – *satah ca atmanah abhavah avidyamanath na vidhyate sarvatra avyabhicarat*). The nature of the Self is consciousness which is "imperishable by which all this is pervaded" (Bhagavad Gita: II.17). The imperishable (*avinasi*) is that which does not habitually perish – *avinasi na vinastum silam asya iti*. The perishable is that which is caused. The perishables are things that have a beginning and an end. In his commentary to the thirteenth chapter, describing the Self as anadi, Acarya explains consciousness as uncaused. *Anadittva* or beginninglessness is the state of what is devoid of cause or beginning" (Gita Samkara Bhasya: II.31 – *anadeh bhava anaditva,adhihkaranam tat yasya nasti tat anadi*). Being uncaused consciousness is that which is real.

The real is imperishable. Bhagavan ascribes tow epithets *avinasi* and *nitya* in describing the imperishable. The Bhasyakara notes that these epithets are not to be taken as tautologies, since they convey two distinct ideas. Two kinds of eternality and perishability are met within our daily experience. The physical body no longer perceptible when reduced to ashes is said to have perished. It is also said to have perished, though existing as such if transformed owing to diseases. The expressions *avinasinah* and *nityasya* imply that consciousness is subject to neither sort of destruction. The eternality of consciousness is hence not misunderstood "to be like that of clay or other material objects" (Gita Samkara Bhasya: II.18).

Consciousness is "… the Real, by which all this world, including the *akasa*, is pervaded, just as pots and other objects are pervaded by the akasa or space" (Gita Samkara Bhasya: II.17). Consciousness being existent does not change. "*Sat* is that which does not change its nature" (Gita Samkara Bhasya: II.17 – *na etat sadakhyam brahma svena rupena iti*). Consciousness does not change its own nature. Since is devoid of properties and is partless, consciousness is immutable. S.H. Jhabwala clarifies Acarya's note: "Samkara defines *Sat* as a condition in regard to which our consciousness never fails, while in the matter of its reverse, viz. Unreal ie. *Asat*, our consciousness fails. Samkara delineates the difference by saying that which the consciousness of objects varies, that of existence with which we are more materially concerned does not. The Changeless Reality is ever manifest to man, and the *Asat* hides the unchanging reality."[5] Acarya generalizes that being immutable, consciousness "neither increases nor decreases" (Gita Samkara Bhasya: II.17 – *upacaya apacayau na yati iti avyayam*). "Moksa consists in the realization of the immutability of one's own Inner Self" (Gita Samkara Bhasya: XVIII.55).

---

[5] S.H. Jhabwala, Gita and its Commentators, (Bombay: Popular Prakashan, Pvt. Ltd., 1991), p.XIV.

Now if consciousness is the only real, how is the seeming existence of the unreal to be understood? As a prologue to this understanding Acarya examines the various theories on the relation between the real and the unreal. The Vaisesika holds that the non-existence comes into existence and the existent lapses into non-existence. This view is in exact contradiction to the view aforesaid by the Gita. The Bhasyakara refutes this theory since it is contrary to all means of right cognition. A.M.Sastri translates Acarya: "If a *dvayanuka* (an aggregate of two atoms) or other substance is absolutely non-existent before its production, and if, remaining for a time after production, it again becomes non-existent, then it follows that what was non-existent becomes existent, and what is existent will become non-existent; that non-entity becomes an entity and an entity becomes non-entity. In that case it must be that a non-entity (*abhava*) which is to become an entity (*bhava*) is like a rabbit's horn before becoming an entity, and that it becomes an entity by the action of the threefold cause, – of the material, the non-material or accidental and the efficient causes.... Now it is not possible to hold (in the present case) that a non-entity is born and needs a cause; for, it does not apply to other non-existence, in also, such as a rabbit's horn" (Gita Samkara Bhasya: XVIII.48). Acarya rejects the Vaisesika version also, that if the non-existent becomes existent, and the existent becomes non-existent, then there can be no certainty as to whatsoever in matters ascertainable by evidence. There can be no certainty that the existent will continue to be existent and the non-existent will continue to be non-existent.

Moreover when Vaisesikas hold that a *dvayanuka* or such other substance is produced as an effect, it is meant to be connected with its cause and as existent. Having been non-existent before production, it by samavaya or intimate relation with the casual relation for the non-existent to have is impossible. Acarya rejects also the Samkhyan theory of transformation, being akin to the Vaisesika theory. Following the process of elimination, he says that the only theory possible is that "... the One Existence, the Sole Reality, is by avidya imagined variously, as so many things undergoing production, destruction and the like changes, like an actor in the stage" (Gita Samkara Bhasya: XVIII.18).

Samkaracarya recognizes an order of the real and the unreal, for clear understanding. The absolutely real or the *Sat* is the *Paramarthika*. *Vyavaharika* and *Pratibhasika*, both are *asat* or unreal, of their non-existence before origin and after dissolution (*prak-pradhvamsa-abhava*). There is another order of the absolutely unreal (*atyantasat* or *tuccam*) to which non-entities like rabbit's horn, sky lotus etc. belong.

Consciousness is the absolutely real. World is not absolutely real, since it has only in between existence. "Beings have their beginning unseen, their middle seen, and their end unseen again" (Bhagavad Gita: II.28). Anandagiri also comments that: "Whatever exists not in the beginning or in the end exists not really in the present."[6] Therefore the world is not absolutely real like Consciousness – the Self. At the same time it is not absolutely unreal lie the rabbit's horn.

Since the beginning and the end of the world are unknown, and it exists only intermediately, it can be said to be neither *sat*,

[6] Alladi Mahadeva Sastri, Tr. The Bhagavad Gita, (Madras: Samata Books, 1981), p.34.

asat (or *atyantasat*). Acarya ascribes world to the order of *sat-asat*. He calls it *mithya*. That which cannot happen or exist seems to have happened or existing in the present. This is *mithya*. "*Mithya* connotes that it depends on the Real" (*mithyayah satyapeksatvam asti*). The absolutely Real is Consciousness of which the world is the manifestation. The theory of manifestation does not mean that consciousness is something less than the world after its manifestation, or the world is separate form consciousness. Edmund Husserl makes a notable comment on the primacy of consciousness: "The consciousness of the world, no doubt is a relation, a factual unity but not a logical necessity in so far as the existence of consciousness is concerned."[7] Consciousness can create out of itself without undergoing any change. If it undergoes change then it becomes unreal. This is against the accepted definition. Hence it can only be said logically as that consciousness appears as the world. In the manifestation or unmanifestation of the world consciousness "does not undergo increase or diminution and is therefore inexhaustible" (Gita Samkara Bhasya: II.17). When the world exists, it does not decrease consciousness by taking off something form consciousness, consciousness does not increase by some kind of addition. Since consciousness is not divided by time, space or substance, it is full. It is purna because it is devoid of any kind of differences. The manifestation and the non-manifestation of the world do not affect consciousness.

[7] Edmund Husserl, Ideas: General Introduction to Pure Phenomenology, Tr. W.R. Royce Gibson, (London: George Allen and Unwin Ltd., 1958), p.112 and p. 151.

Consciousness and Self-knowledge

The Self that is Pure Consciousness is eternal and all-pervasive. It is not that the knowledge of the Self creates or determines the Self. "The Self is Self-established" (Gita Samkara Bhasya: II.18 – *atmanah svadasiddhatvat*). In fact it is only when the Self as the knower is given, it is possible for the seeker, to search for the means of right cognition, with a view to obtain right knowledge. Acarya says that "...without determining the Self – 'I am' – none seeks to determine the knowable objects" (Gita Samkara Bhasya: II.18). "The Self as I is unknown to nobody" (Gita Samkara Bhasya: II.18 – *na hi atma nama kasyacit aprasiddhah bhavati*). It is an apodictic fact. Husserl makes a similar note on the nature of consciousness. He says: "Pure Consciousness is not any particular act of consciousness specifically correlated to any particular object, but the inevitable awareness which world be present in any experience."[8]

The scripture or srutipramana that is the final authority attains its authoritativeness regarding the Self, as serving only to eliminate the superimpositions attributed on the Self and not on revealing what has been altogether unknown. The fiftythird verse of the second chapter hence states: "When one becomes firm and unwavering in concentration he wins the supreme Yoga" (Bhagavad Gita: II.53). The Bhasyakara defines *niscala samadau acala buddhih* as that which is devoid of projections – *viksepa calana varjita*.

The nature of the Self as consciousness is full. It is the ignorance of the Self that projects desire for a want, intended to bring

[8] Edmund Husserl, Ideas: General Introduction to Pure Phenomenology, Tr. W.R. Royce Gibson, (London: George Allen and Unwin Ltd., 1958), p.112.

fulfilment. Throughout its philosophy, the Gita cautions this situation, for a need can be fulfilled, but a desire for fulfilment cannot be fulfilled. It is the Self-ignorance that causes desire. Ignorance of the true nature of the Self causes not only the non-apprehension of the Self as consciousness, but also its misapprehension as something else. Self-ignorance veils the real nature of the Self and projects it as otherwise. Acarya in his commentary to the fourth chapter cites that the ignorant projects two major superimpositions on the Self. He maintains that "I am the agent, this work is mine, its fruits must be reaped by me", and similarly superimposing the cessation from work on the Self maintains, "I do nothing, I rest comfortably" (Gita Samkara Bhasya: IV.18).

Self-knowledge is the one and only means to remove Self-ignorance and superimpositions thereof. Throughout the Gita Bhagavan lauds the inevitability of Self-knowledge. In the fourteenth chapter it is described as "the highest and best knowledge" (Bhagavad Gita: XIV.1 – *jnananam jnanamuttamam*). Acarya notes that it is described as highest – *param* – because its content is the highest reality. Self-knowledge is the best among all forms of knowledge because its fruit is the best, namely liberation. No other form of knowledge tantamount to Self-knowledge, which is ontological in nature. The realized person knows the true nature of the Self as 'I am consciousness'. Self-knowledge is therefore the supreme perfection – *paramsiddhi*. "There is no purifier equal to Self-knowledge" (Bhagavad Gita: IV.38), says Bhagavan in the fourth chapter. For the same reason he upholds the importance of *jñana-yajna* and *jnana-tapas*. Recognizing the importance of Self-knowledge Abraham H. Maslow remarks: "The questions that people ask in the search for identity, real self etc., are very largely 'ought' questions. What ought I to do? What ought I to be? ... what we have learned is that ultimately the best way for a person to discover what he ought to do is to find out who and what he is, because the path to ethical and value decisions to wiser choices, to oughtness, is via 'isness', via the discovery of facts, truth, reality.... The more he knows about his own nature...the more effortless, automatic and epiphenomenal become his value choices... Many problems simply disappears; many others are easily solved by knowing what is in conformity with one's nature, what is suitable and right."[9]

Self-knowledge is not the Intentional Consciousness of the Self

Samkaracarya examines intentionality of consciousness in his commentary to the eighteenth chapter. He analyses a prominent doubt that could emerge in the comparative study of consciousness and Self-knowledge. The objection of the Purvapaksa is that "... knowledge or cognition (*jnana*) is of the form of its object. But it is nowhere admitted that the Self is an object of cognition or has a form" (Gita Samkara Bhasya: XVIII.50). It is generally conceived that consciousness is intentional, that is, it is the consciousness of an object. Therefore consciousness of the Self or Self-knowledge also should correspond to the form of the object namely Self. Referring to the *sastra*, the Purvapaksin's argument is that since the Self is

[9] Abraham H. Maslow, Farther Reaches of Human Nature, (New Jersey: D. Van Nostrand Company, Inc. Princeton, 1962), p.90.

formless, it is to be regarded that Self-knowledge is not possible at all.

Samkaracarya examines the flaws in this conception. The scripture and reason show that the Self is absolutely pure, transparent and subtle. The intellect being pure as the Self, it can put on the semblance of that aspect of the Self and share with it its conscious nature. Similarly mind may reflect or resemble intellect, sense organs may resemble mind and the physical body may resemble the sense organs. Thus according to the level of Self-ignorance and superimposition one may take the Self to be the body, mind or intellect. "It is not that the Self is totally unknown to anybody, at any time and is to be reached or got rid of or acquired" (Gita Samkara Bhasya: XVIII – *na hi atma kasyacit kadacit aprasiddhah, prapyah, hyeyah, adayah va*). But the fact is that the ignorant misses the Self for the not-Self. Highlighting this truth, Lord advices, "Therefore...restrain the senses first.... They say that the senses are superior; superior to the senses is mind; superior to mind is reason; one who is even superior to reason is He" (Bhagavad Gita: III.41-42).

Acarya continues, that it is for the same reason that Carvaka taking consciousness to be an epiphenomenona, regard body as the Self, "Similarly, others again argue that consciousness is a property of the senses; others again argue that consciousness is a property of buddhi" (Gita Samkara Bhasya: XVIII.50). In all theses cases, from the intellect to the body, the cause of illusory identification of each with the Self is the reflection of consciousness in them. Therefore Acarya says that in all these cases it is unnecessary to import the knowledge of the Self. "What is necessary is the mere elimination of the not-Self associated with the Self, – names, forms and the like; but it is unnecessary to try and teach what the consciousness of the Self is like ..." (Gita Samkara Bhasya: XVIII.50). Knowledge does not depend upon an independent means of cognition, for every cognition is self-cognised. "Having abandoned egotism, strength, arrogance, desire, enmity, property, free form the notion of 'mine', and peaceful, he is fit for becoming Brahman" (Bhagavad Gita: XVIII.53). Regarding Self-knowledge, what is to be aimed at is only the elimination of what is falsely ascribed to consciousness, due to Self-ignorance. Since consciousness is absolutely "self-evident, easily knowable, quite near and forming the very self" (Gita Samkara Bhasya: XVIII.50 – *atyantanirmalatvat svacchatvati suksmatvopapatteh atmanah*), no effort is required to know it. For the rendezvous with the reality, Pierre Teilhard De Chardin says: "We have only to get rid our vision of the threefold illusion of smallness, plurality and immobility."[10]

The Bhasyakara at the same time clauses that for one who is caught up in identification with the not-Self, due to non-discrimination, the Self is remote and unattainable. To the deluded, consciousness, "... though effortlessly known, seems hard to know, though the closest being, the very Self, seems alien" (Gita Samkara Bhasya: XVIII.50). But to one who is gifted with subtle discrimination by the grace of the Guru and the *Sastra*, "it is quite impossible to believe in the reality of the dual – the perceiver and the perceived – of our external perception, because they perceive no reality other than the consciousness of the Self" (Gita Samkara Bhasya: XVIII.50). Lord analogizes this

[10] Pierre Teilhard De Chardin, The Phenomenon of Man, (Glasgow: Williams Collins Sons and Co.Ltd, 1959), p.38.

situation to, "What is night to all beings, therein the self-controlled one is awake. Where all beings are awake, that is the night of the sage who sees" (Bhagavad Gita: II.69). Night as such causes confusion of things. Just us what is day to others become night to night-wanderers, likewise to the ignorant, who corresponds to the night-wanderer the reality is dark, like night. "When all beings are said to be awake, that is, when all beings who in reality sleep in the night of ignorance, imbued with the distinct notions of perceiver and things perceived, are as it were mere dreamers in sleep at night, – that state is night in the eye of the sage who knows the Supreme Reality; for, it is nescience itself" (Gita Samkara Bhasya: II.69).

Even though this is the case, Acarya is emphatic in that, even the ignorant, is in search of Self-knowledge, reiterating the fact that the Self is not totally unknown. "Self-knowledge is the aim of all endeavours" (Gita Samkara Bhasya: XVIII.50 – *atma avagatya avasanarthatvaccha sarvavyavaharah*). If the Self is totally unknown, then all undertakings intended for the benefit of oneself would turn out to be meaningless. It is absurd to suppose that they are for the benefit of the body that is inert, and that pleasure and pain subserve themselves. Hence just as there is no need for external evidence by which to know one's own body there is no need for a pramana by which to know consciousness that is far more intimate than the body. "Its apprehension as the Self is immediate" (Bhagavad Ġita: IX.2) – *pratyaksavagamam.*

This apodictic explanation of consciousness bridges the two schismatic statements posited by C.O. Evans in his book "The Subject of Consciousness". Evans considers 'being conscious' and 'consciousness' as distinctively separate. He argues that a meaningful definition for consciousness is possible only if it is interpreted as 'to be conscious' and not in the cognate form of 'self-consciousness'. "To be conscious is to perceive, to feel emotions and sensations, to have images and recollections and to have desires, intentions, and thoughts."[11] According to the Bhasyakara's exposition, to be conscious is not merely to feel or imaging. Because, even while different feelings and imaginations come and go, consciousness remains as the perpetual and immutable witness of all feelings and imaginations. The 'I' always exists as the witness of all thought modulations and acts.

The Bhasyakara supplements his theory of consciousness as an apodictic fact, by upholding the self-revealing nature of consciousness. Consciousness is intentional not because the object is apart from it, but, the object is made knowable by consciousness. There is no need of another functional consciousness to make possible consciousness known, which will then end up in the fallacy of infinite regression. Sir William Hamilton, the noted classical analyst of consciousness, too accepts the self-revealing nature of consciousness. C.O. Evans records Hamilton's view: "Consciousness may be compared to an integral light, by means of which and which alone, what passes into the mind is rendered visible. Consciousness is simple – is not composed of parts, either similar or dissimilar. It always resembles itself...; thus there are not various kinds of consciousness although there are various kinds of mental modes or states, of which wer are conscious."[12]

---

[11] C.O. Evans, The Subject of Consciousness, (London: George Allen and Unwin Ltd., 1970), p.48

[12] C.O. Evans, The Subject of Consciousness, (London: George Allen and Unwin Ltd., 1970), p.39

The cognition of an object or cognitive consciousness is as "immediate like pleasure etc. that is immediately experienced" (Gita Samkara Bhasya: XVIII.50 – *atyanta prasiddham sukhadivat eva iti abhyupagantavyam*). Cognition is not an object to be known like any other object, but is readily apprehend. Just as the cognitive consciousness is self-revealed, the cogniser is also immediately apprehended. In the words of Madhusudhana Saraswati: "The Self is self-luminous consciousness. It needs no light to reveal itself from objects which it reveals."[13] "Therefore', Acarya says, 'it is not for the knowledge (of Self) that any effort is needed; it is needed only to prevent us from regarding the not-Self as the Self" (Gita Samkara Bhasya: XVIII.50). The scriptural exegesis or discipline of knowledge is necessary till the consummation of experience of whatever has been learnt from the sastra, which is no longer exposed to doubts of any kind.

This does not mean that there is a discontinuity between Knowing and Being. Self-knowledge does not add something to the Self, but only takes off the identifications superimposed on the Being due to ignorance. Self-knowledge is therefore in the form of 'I am consciousness' and not 'It is consciousness'. Acarya differentiates Self-knowledge as *asmijnana*, from *astijnana*. In the commentary to the fifteenth chapter he says: "the realized knows the supreme spirit as 'He is I' and [hence] is omniscient" (Gita Samkara Bhasya: XV.19). He is omniscient since he knows his Self as the Self of all. The relation between Self-knowledge and Self-realisation is made clearer in Acarya's commentary to the eighteenth chapter. Acarya elucidates: "By

---

[13] Madhusudhana Saraswati, Gudartha Dipika, Tr. Sisir Kumar Gupta, (Delhi: Motilal Banarsidass Publishers, 1977), p.28.

Bhakti, by the devotion of Knowledge, he knows Me as I am in the diverse manifestations caused by the *Upadhis*. He knows who I am, he knows that I am devoid of all the differences caused by the *upadhis*, that I am the Supreme *Purusa*, that I am like unto *akasa*; he knows Me to be non-dual, the one Consciousness (*caitanya*), pure and simple, unborn, undecaying, undying, fearless, deathless. Thus knowing Me in truth, he enters into Myself immediately after attaining knowledge. It is not meant here that the act of knowledge and the act of entering are two distinct acts – what then is the act of entering? – It is the knowledge itself: for there is nothing to be effected (by knowledge) other than itself, as the Lord as taught. 'Do thou also know Me as *ksetrajna*'" (Gita Samkara Bhasya: XVIII.55 – *brahmavid brahmaivah bhavati*).

Self-knowledge is the final goal. This is established by the Gita in verses like "The Self-knower abides in the Self" (Bhagavad Gita: V.20); "The Supreme Abode, to which having gone none return." (Bhagavad Gita: XV.6 – *yat gatva na nivartande tad dhamam paramam*); "The Goal … whither having gone none return" (Bhagavad Gita: XV.4 – *yasmin gata na nivartanti bhuyah*). Since Self-realization is the realization that 'everything is in consciousness' and 'consciousness is in everything', the realized will not see anything other than consciousness. Hence the knower of consciousness abides in consciousness and there is no return for him. "To one who is content with knowledge and experience" (Bhagavad Gita: VI.8 – *jnanavijnana triptatma*) there remains "nothing more to be known" (Bhagavad Gita: VII.2 – *anyajnatam na avasisyate*).

Consciousness and Epistemic Contradictions

The Gita describes consciousness both in positive and negative terms. In the twelfth chapter it is said that consciousness is "...the imperishable, the indefinable, the Unmanifest, the Omnipresent and the Unthinkable, the Immutable, the Eternal" (Bhagavad Gita: XII.3-4). Consciousness is "... unmanifest, imponderable and immutable" (Bhagavad Gita: II.25). This description does not imply a skepticism about consciousness, but points out that consciousness is not an epistemic construction or function viable to the modulation of thought. Mind can know a thing only by analyzing it into parts. Hence it is structural. Consciousness is that which illumines all possible permutations and combinations of conceptual structural thinking.

Wisdom, according to the Gita, is not a product of structural thinking. Wisdom is the end of structural thinking. Bhagavan says: "Know this: by long prostration, by enquiry, by service, those men of wisdom who have realized the truth will teach thee wisdom" (Bhagavad Gita: IV.34). What is meant is the sensitivity of the whole being, marking the openness of mind. Only an open mind can make effective enquiry into the problematic. Wisdom is not, again, a conclusive answer got for the questioning mind. What the Lord attempts is not giving a conclusive solution for the contradiction, but the dissolution of the contradiction involved itself. "The Perception of the whole is always sudden, not split up in succession."[14] For the dissolution of the contradiction the mind must be open to all possible questions and answers. In the Gita Bhagavan places various

[14] Rohit Mehta, From Mind to Super Mind, (Bombay: P.C. Manaktala and Sons Pvt. Ltd., 1966).p.75.

alternatives before Arjuna and describes the full implication of each alternative, but never gives a conclusive answer. Heidegger compares an open mind to a meditative mind. He stipulates that conclusive thinking which is centered upon an answer, "...Constructs a world of objects understands these objects; but meditative thinking begins with awareness of the field within which these objects are...Meditative thinking is thinking which is open to its content, open to what is given."[15] Heidegger adds, "... Releasement involves openness."[16]

Consciousness is not a transcendent supersensible truth away from thoughts. Lord clarifies consciousness that which is immanent in opposites and contradictions and yet transcendent being untouched by them. "Consciousness is transcendence through and through, not transcendence undergone...but active transcendence."[17] This nature of consciousness is well brought out in its description as "the Being and the Non-Being" (Bhagavad Gita: XI.37 – *satasatparam*), "not said to be *Sat* or *Asat*" (Bhagavad Gita: XIII.12 – *na sattanasaducyate*). Being is the existent and non-being is what engenders the idea of non-existence. Consciousness is that which equally illumines both the 'is' and the 'is not', and yet transcends both. Merleau-Ponty reflects such an ontology of consciousness when he says: "Consciousness is neither the positing of oneself, nor ignorance of oneself, it is not concealed from itself, which means that there

[15] Martin Heidegger, Discourses on Thinking, Tr. John M. Anderson and E. Hans Freund, (New York: Harper and Row Publishers, 1966), p.24.

[16] Martin Heidegger, Discourses on Thinking, Tr. John M. Anderson and E. Hans Freund, (New York: Harper and Row Publishers, 1966), p.25.

[17] M. Merleau-Ponty, Phenomenology of Perception, Tr. Colin Smith, (London: Routledge and Kegan Paul Ltd., 1962), p.376.

is nothing, in it which does not in some way announce, itself to it, although it does not need to know this explicitly. In Consciousness, appearance is not being, but the phenomenon. This new cogito, because it is anterior to revealed truth and error, makes both possible."[18]

Various verses can be noted in the chapters of the Gita, describing consciousness in contradictory terms. Consciousness is 'knowable' in the sense that whatever seen or known is consciousness. And, since there is neither a knower nor knowledge other than consciousness that is the Self, it is 'unkowable'. Being beyond the range of *Sat*, there can arise the doubt, that the 'knowable' is non-existent. Discarding this doubt Lord figuratively eulogizes the supremacy of consciousness, "With hands and feet everywhere, with eyes and heads and mouths everywhere, with hearing everywhere, That exists enveloping all" (Bhagavad Gita: XIII.13). Consciousness functions through the organs of action and knowledge, but still, is untouched by them. Hence it is "Without and within (all) beings; the unmoving as also the moving. Because subtle, That is incomprehensible; and near and far away is That" (Bhagavad Gita: XIII.15) and "Undivided yet remaining divided as it were in beings" (Bhagavad Gita: XIII.16).

The nature of the intellect is to travel in between extremes. It always tries to understand the one extreme forsaking the other, and ends up in parochial and segmented vision. But if knowledge is only conceptual, "...it is a philosophy, an intellectual construction, not a spiritual knowledge and vision, not a spiritual

---

[18] M. Merleau-Ponty, Phenomenology of Perception, Tr. Colin Smith, (London: Routledge and Kegan Paul Ltd., 1962),p.296.

state of consciousness."[19] Taking this situation into account, Lord explains consciousness in terms of many possible contradictions, for clarity of apprehension. Contradictions are not meant to contradict consciousness, but to introduce a wholesome vision comprehending the polarities. The task of the intellect is to stitch all that which it sees or knows, for "everything is strung like pearls on one consciousness" (Bhagavad Gita: VII.7 – *sutre manigana iva*). Throughout his teaching Lord expounds integration as comprehending the opposites together, and not loosing one for the other. According to Bhagavan, true and clear comprehension les in seeing all the seeming contradictions and factors involved together and not in their compartmentalized judgment. Bhagavan, in his exposition of Purusa and Prakrti, individual and world, individual and God, Work and Meditation, gives in and through the Gita, this methodology for right perception.

[19] Sri Aurobindo, Essays on the Gita, 8th ed., (Pondichery: Sri Aurobindo Ashram, 1970), p.354.

6

Consciousness and Matter

karya karana kartrtve hetu prakrtirucyate
purusa sukhadukhanam bhoktrtve heturucyati

Prakrti is the source of body, senses and mind.
Purusa is the cause of experiencing pleasure and pain.
Bhagavad Gita 13:20

If we consider the various theories put forward to analyze the nature, relationship and interaction of consciousness and matter then we find that a common trend is to present consciousness as an abstract principle of unity and matter as a concrete principle of multiplicity. Such a trend and its developments encourage a conceptual clarification of terms like ego, self, consciousness and matter. The Bhagavad Gita elucidates the implications of these concepts in the light of its psychology and puts forth an integral theory.

The Nature of Purusa

In the Gita the concept of consciousness is not given an abstract meaning but is well-defined with the aid of a classification of philosophical and experiential ideas.

Purusa and *prakrti* are the general terms used in the Gita to indicate consciousness and matter. Darsanas like Samkhya of Kapila interprets *Purusa* as both the passive witness and experiencer of *Prakrti*. The Gita illumines this twilight area by differentiating between *ksara purusa*, *aksara purusa* and *purusottama*. The Gita enumerates: "There are these two beings in the world, the perishable and the imperishable: the perishable comprises all creatures, the immutable is called the imperishable. But distinct is the Highest Spirit spoken of as the Supreme Self, the indestructible Lord who penetrates and sustains the three worlds" (Bhagavad Gita: XV:16-17). The *ksara purusa* and *aksara purusa* represent consciousness from a relative standpoint. The *purusottama* denotes Consciousness in its pure form. Samkaracarya marks the classification of *ksara* and *aksara purusa* as pertaining to the world of change or categories – *samsara*. A.M. Sastri translates the Bhasya of Acarya: "In *samsara*, there are two categories, we see, arranged in two separate groups of beings, spoken of as '*purusas*'" (Gita Samkara Bhasya: XV.16).

The perishable manifested state of consciousness is included under the *ksara purusa* that comprises all that which is perished – *ksara* – and is destroyed in time – *vinasi*. It consists of the entire physical body prone to the six kinds of transformations influenced by temporal and spatial modalities. *Aksara purusa* is the imperishable unmanifested state of consciousness, which is described by Bhagavan as *kutastha*. The description of *aksara purusa* as *kutastha* can be understood in two ways. The first meaning is "that which remains immovable like a heap" (Gita Samkara Bhasya: XV.16 – *kutarasiriva sthitah*). *Kuta* can also mean illusion. Hence the second meaning of *kutastha* is "that which manifests itself in various forms of illusion and deception" (Gita Samkara Bhasya: XV.16 – *anekaymaya vancanadi prakarena sthitah kutasthah*). *Aksara purusa* is unmanifest, holding all the latent impressions or potencies of the perishable. The *Aksara purusa* includes both the 'personal unconscious' and the 'collective unconscious' referred to by C.G. Jung. The unmanifest is the beholder of the 'archetypes' – *gunas* – in their equilibrial state. Acarya comments that *Aksara purusa* is imperishable since the seed for transmigratory life is inexhaustible – "*samsarabijanantyat*" (Gita Samkara Bhasya: XV.16). Elucidating the concepts of *ksara* and *aksara purusa*, Annie Besant writes, "In the All everything is always; all that has been, all that now is manifest, all that will be, all that can be, all possibilities as well as all actualities, are even in being in the All. That which is outwards, the forthgoing existence, the unfolded, is the manifested universe. But the Within, the Unmanifested, is as real as the Without, the Manifested."[1]

Acarya denotes *uttama purusa* as the other – *anya* – and distinct – *vilaksana* – from the relative representations of consciousness such as *Ksara* and *aksara purusa*. The adjectives *anya* and *vilaksana* are used to establish the profound nature of consciousness which is supreme – "*uttamah purusastvanyah*" (Bhagavad Gita: XV.17). It is *anya* because it is the other which surmounts the aforementioned categorical realm and is altogether different form the first two – *ksara purusa* – and *aksara purusa*. It is *vilaksana* since its nature is to be distinctively defined. *Uttama purusa* is untouched by the taints of the adjuncts of *ksara* and *aksara*

[1] Annie Besant, A study in Karma, (Adyar : The Theosophical Publishing House, 1975), p.9.

Purusa. The Gita describes: "...That other eternal Unmanifested Being distinct from this Unmanifested (*avyakta*), ... does not perish when all creatures perish" (Bhagavad Gita: VIII.20). It is imperishable being the self-consciousness in every being – "*sarvabhutanam pratykcetanah ityatah paramatma*" (Gita Samkara Bhasya: XV.17).

Though distinct from the *Avyakta*, it may be misunderstood that *Uttama purusa* is of the same nature as the *avyakta*. "To remove this impression, the Lord qualifies Him [*uttama purusa*] by 'other' meaning thereby that He is of a different nature form the *avyakta*" (Gita Samkara Bhasya: VIII.20). *Uttama purusa* is unmanifest in the sense it is imperceptible to the cognitive organs, being the illuminator of cognitions. From the perspective of the world, He is the omniscient Lord, who by His presence, by virtue of His potency – *caitanyabala* – and strength – *saktiya* – upholds the entire universe. Anandagiri gives a notable translation for Acarya's description of Lord's *caitanyabalasakti*, as "*Bala* means energy, the energy of Consciousness or sentience (*caitanya*), and '*Sakti*' means *Maya* which lies therin."[2] Thus from the perspective of the world *uttama purusa* is the Lord of the universe and from the perspective of the individual He is the inner Self of all beings.

Ksara purusa, *aksara purusa* and *uttama purusa* are not to be taken as separate, different kinds of consciousness. Lord says: "Because I transcend the perishable and am even higher than the imperishable, therefore I am known in the world and in the Veda as '*Purusottama*', the Highest Spirit" (Bhagavad Gita:

---

[2] Alladi Mahadeva Sastri, The Bhagavad Gita (Madras: Ṣamata Books, 1981), p.411.

XV.18). Etymologizing the name, Lord reveals that He is of the nature of Pure Consciousness that is highest to His lower natures – "*uttamah utkrstatamah purusa*" (Gita Samkara Bhasya: XV.17). The superlative degree *uttama* implies the transcendental nature of consciousness. Annie Besant notes: "The individual consciousness appears to be a complexity instead of a unity when its manifestations are concerned, and modern psychology speaks of dual and trible and multiple personality, losing sight of the fundamental unity among the confusion of the manifold. Yet truly is our consciousness a Unit, and the variety is due to the materials in which it is working."[3]

The Nature of Prakrti

Prakrti is the general word used by the the Gita for matter. The *ksara purusa* and *aksara purusa* correspond to the lower and higher *prakrti* (*ksetra*). *prakrti* includes all that which is material. With regard to *ksara purusa*, *prakrti* has a manifest state which is perishable. With regard to *aksara purusa prakrti* has an unmanifest state which is imperishable. The terms *purusa* and *prakrti* are used to indicate their respective functions and not to designate them as two independent realities. *Purusa* is the ultimate reality and *prakrti* is described as the creative energy of *purusa*. S. Radhakrishnan notes: "The Gita does not look upon *prakrti* and *purusa* as two independent elements as the Samkhya does but looks upon them as the inferior and superior forms of the one and the same Supreme."[4]

[3] Annie Besant, A Study in Consciousness, (Adyar : The Theosophical Publishing House, 1980), p.106.

[4] S.Radhakrishnan, The Bhagavad Gita, 6th Ind. rpt., (Bombay : Blackie and Son (India) Ltd., 1977), p.308.

On the concept of unmanifest *prakṛti*, Rene Guenon says, ".... there cannot in truth be any other principle than the supreme principle, except in a relative sense; but once we are dealing, even principally, with manifestations, we are already in the realm of relativity. The correlative of *purusa* is then *prakrti*, the undifferentiated primordial substance."[5] Acarya's definition of *purusa* gives a better understanding of *prakrti*. "*Purusa* is literally, that by which everything is filled, (*pri* means to fill) or that which lies in the body (*pur*)..." (Gita Samkara Bhasya: VIII.4). Consciousness is that which fills everything, in the sense, there is nothing other than consciousness. *Purusa* is that which lies in the body in the sense it is that which enlivens the body as the Self.

In the thirteenth chapter Bhagavan gives a description of the gross manifest form and the subtle unmanifest form of *prakrti*. "The Great Elements, Egoism, Reason, as also the Unmanifested, the ten senses and one, and the five objects of the senses: Desire, hatred, pleasure, pain, the aggregate, intelligence, courage – the *ksetra* has been thus briefly described with its modifications" (Bhagavad Gita: XIII.5-6). Under a broader category of *ksetra* Bhagavan includes the unmanifest material world. The great elements refer to the subtle elements "that pervade all *vikaras*, all modifications of matter" (Gita Samkara Bhasya: XIII.5). Apart from the subtle elements, the manifest *prakrti* is comprised of the five gross elements, eleven sense organs including the mind, intellect and ego. It is notable that Bhagavan designates the mind, intellect and ego also as material. The consciousness about which

[5] Rene Guenon, Man and His Becoming, Tr. Richard C. Nicholson, (London: Luzac and Co., 1945), p.46.

the Gita speaks of is not a mental function or a state of non-ego. Consciousness cannot be defined relating to the mind or ego. Defining the nature of the mind and intellect, the Bhasyakara notes that mind is that which conceives or imagines – "*samkalpahadhyatmakam manah*" (Gita Samkara Bhasya: XIII.5). – and intellect is that which decides – "*buddhih adhyavasayalaksana*" (Gita Samkara Bhasya: XIII.5). Consciousness is that which illumines all imaginations and decisions and hence cannot be conceptualized in relative terms of mind or intellect. "The body, the forms of sense with which we identify the subject belong to the object side. The ego is an artificial construction obtained by abstraction from conscious experience. The witnessing consciousness is the same whether it lights up the blue sky or a red flower. Though the field which are lit up may be different, the light which illumines them is the same."[6]

According to the Gita the *prakrti* or the nature of an individual is determined by the *gunas* such as *satva*, *rajas* and *tamas*. S. Radhakrishnan elucidates: "The *gunas* are the three tendencies of *Prakrti* or the three strands making up the twisted rope of nature. *Satva* reflects the light of consciousness and is irradiated by it, and so has the quality of radiance (*prakasa*). *Rajas* has an outward movement (*pravrtti*) and *tamas* is characterized by inertia (*apravrtti*) and heedless indifference (*pramada*)."[7] By presenting the theory of three-fold *guna*, the *Gita* defines the difference in

[6] S. Radhadrishnan, The Bhagavad Gita, 6th Ind. rpt., (Bombay : Blackie and Son (India) Ltd., 1977), p.303

[7] S. Radhadrishnan, The Bhagavad Gita, 6th Ind. rpt., (Bombay : Blackie and Son (India) Ltd., 1977), p.317.

the psychological disposition of different individuals. Roger Marcaurelle in his article, *Sankara's Hermeneutics on Renunciation in the Gita*, compares *guna* with the awareness of the individual. He writes: "This ordering... presents a hierarchy based on a qualitative dimension of awareness."[8] Annie Besant describes *gunas* as the expressive modes of consciousness. She describes, "... matter has three fundamental qualities responsive severally to these modes of consciousness and without these it could no more be manifested than consciousness could express itself without its modes. It has inertia (*tamas*), the very foundation of all, the stability necessary to existence, the quality which answers to Will. It has mobility *(rajas)*, the capacity to be moved, answering to Activity. It has rhythm (*satva*), the equalizer of movement (without which movement would be chaotic, destructive), answering to Cognition."[9] The Gita develops the theory of *gunas* along with the theory of Self. The *guna* or the mental nature of an individual can function leading to Self-realization. *Guna prakrti* does not bind him but is a means to Self-actualization. Establishing this feature, William Beidler exhorts, "The Gita is not claiming that the *gunas* fully represent a closed system but that there is a higher order of activity of the *paraprakrti* beyond the *gunas*. So as long as we are unaware of the higher *Prakrti*, we are like the behaviorist's man driven by the unconscious muscular activity ..."[10]

---

[8] Roger Marcaurelle, Sankara's Hermeneutics on Renunciation in the Gita, Ed. Arvind Sharma, New Essays in the Bhagavad Gita, (Bombay : Books and Books, 1987), p.100.

[9] Annie Besant, A Study in Karma, 6th ed., (Adyar : The Theosophical Publishing House, 1975), p.33.

[10] William Beidler, The Vision of Self in Early Vedanta, (Delhi: Motilal Baharsidass Publishers, 1975), p.149.

Ksetra, Ksetrajna and Ego

According to the Gita semantics, *ksetra* pertains to the physical body or that which is known and *ksetrajna* corresponds to the Self or consciousness which is the knower. The Gita uses the noun *idam* to denote *ksetra*. *Ksetra* constitutes all that which falls in the field of consciousness. It is the knowable. Annie Besant writes, "All that is in our consciousness, affecting the environment, and all the environment affected by our consciousness, make up our world."[11] John Davies translates *ksetra*: "... a plain, a field; and hence matter, as that which is objective to the soul."[12] *Ksetrajna* is consciousness that which illumines the material field, that which makes it knowable. Substantiating this feature S. Radhakrishnan says: "*Ksetrajna* is the light of awareness, the knower of all objects. The witness is not the individual embodied mind, but the cosmic consciousness for which the whole cosmos is the object."[13]

The Gita explains ego as a fictitious product of the union of *ksetra* and *ksetrajna*. At the same time consciousness cannot be described as merely a non-ego state. Consciousness is that which transcends or illumines the non-ego. The *ksetra* includes the non-ego also, it being an epistemic concept. Acarya defines, "egoism is the conceit of Self in the complex of effects and instruments—the body and sense organs" (Gita Samkara Bhasya: III.27). Ego and non-ego have no separate existence severed form

[11] Annie Besant, A Study in Karma, 6th ed., (Adyar : The Theosophical Publishing House, 1975), p.33.

[12] John Davies, The Bhagavad Gita, (New Delhi : Ess Ess Publications, 1983), p.141.

[13] S.Radhakrishnan, The Bhagavad Gita, 6th Ind. rpt., (New Delhi : Blackie and Son (India) Ltd., 1977), p.301.

consciousness. Consciousness is not to be confused for a state of ego or non-ego. For an exegesis of consciousness, Rene Guenon says: "... From the start, as clearly as possible, the fundamental distinction between the 'Self' which is the very principle of the being, and the individual ego ..."[14] is to be made.

In order to bring ego also in the category of knowables, Bhagavan classifies it under *ksetra*. Those attributes that the Vaisesikas speak as that of the Self, are the attributes of ego and thereby comes under *ksetra*. Inordet to ascertain this fact, Bhagavan ascribes desire, pleasure etc. to the *ksetra*. Desire, hatred pleasure, pain, intelligence and courage are knowables which falls in the field of consciousness. Regarding the nature of all modifications of *ksetra*, they by nature appear and disappear and hence are transient – "*agamopayinah anityah*" (Gita Samkara Bhasya: II.14). The cause of the cosmic manifestation is the subtle unmanifest energy – *Maya* – which is the creative power of consciousness as creator – *Isvara*.

Though the Gita uses the term '*purusa*' in describing the experiencer, it is to be understood as corresponding to the ego, according to the context. "All forms and qualities are born of *prakrti*" (Gita Samkara Bhasya: XIII.9 – *vikaran ca gunan ca prakrtisambhavam*). "As the producer of the effect and the instruments, *prakrti* is said to be the cause; as experiencing pleasure and pain, *purusa* is said to be the cause" (Bhagavad Gita: XIII.20). In this verse *purusa* refers to ego. As producing the physical body and the sense organs, *prakrti* is the cause. Elucidating this Acarya comments, "The effect (*karya*) is the physical body, and the

[14] Rene Guenon, Man and His Becoming, Tr. Richard C. Nicholson, (London: Luzac and Co., 1945), p.27.

instruments (*karanas*) are the thirteen located in the body. The five elements (*bhutas*) which build up the body and the five sense-objects which are the emanations of *prakrti* ... included under the term 'effect'; and all qualities such as pleasure, pain and delusion, which are born of *prakrti* are included under the term 'instruments' ..." (Gita Samkara Bhasya: XIII.20). As producing the physical body and the senses, *prakrti* is the cause of the material world. *Purusa* is the cause as perceiving pleasure, pain and other objects of experience.

The *purusa* who experiences pleasure, pain etc. is the ego or *jiva*. It is the ego that which is described as "The ear, the eye and the touch, the taste and the smell, using these and the *manas*, he enjoys the sense objects" (Bhagavad Gita: XV.9). *Jiva* is then the "*prakrtisthapurusa*" (Bhagavad Gita: XIII.21) – the experiencer identified with the body and senses that are the emanations of *prakrti*. He is the "*Samsarin* ... the experiencer of pleasure and pain" (Gita Samkara Bhasya: XIII.20), *samsara* being the experience of pleasure and pain. In this context Anandagiri says: "... while experiencing pleasure or pain, the Self, the experiencer, remains quite unchanged. It is this experience (*bhoga*) which constitutes His *samsara* and which makes him a *samsarin*."[15]

Identified with the body, he thinks 'I am happy, I am miserable, I am deluded, I am wise', and is thus conditioned by delusion. Maintaining that 'I am the doer, I am the enjoyer' *jiva* is swayed by the *samsara*. As explained in the fifteenth chapter transmigration is ordained to this jiva of deluded consciousness, which "... follows the principle of selection and finite

[15] Alladi Mahadeva Sastri, The Bhagavad Gita, (Madras: Samata Books, 1981), p.538.

determination."[16] Not having the discriminative knowledge of *ksetra* and *ksetrajna* he is subjected to birth and death. Sri Aurobindo says: " ... subject to Nature, ... when the self awareness in the mind-consciousness identifies itself with the ego, it creates appearance of a lower self, an ego-self.... The impure natural consciousness over clouds the pure soul Consciousness; the mind forgets the Person in the ego and the personality."[17] Determined by nature, *jiva* works according to the quality of its psychological nature or the three-fold *guna*.

Jiva or ego is 'empirical', for it is the *samsarin*. It can be compared to the 'empirical ego' in Husserlian phenomenology. But, since ego is a non-entity, a fictitious product, it cannot be called transcendent. It is not the ego that transcends, but consciousness is that which transcends. Consciousness transcends in the sense it is immanent in the ego and is still untouched by the ego. Transcendence and Purity that Husserl attributes to ego, belong to consciousness. Further, when Sartre speaks of egoless consciousness as empty or contentless, the Gita speaks of consciousness that is the content of everything and at the same time containing everything. According to the Gita version, consciousness is not affected by the presence or absence of ego, ego being non-existent. The transcendental ego which is described as that which "...bracket the world and conceive of himself as a function of consciousness to which the world is given"[18]

---

[16] Sri Aurobindo, Essays on the Gita, 8th ed., (Pondicherry: Sri Aurobindo Ashram, 970), p.357

[17] Sri Aurobindo, Essays on the Gita, 8th ed., (Pondicherry: Sri Aurobindo Ashram, 970), pp.205-206.

[18] Pratima Bowes, Consciousness and Freedom, (London: Methuen and Co.I.td., 1971), p.125.

corresponds to the witnessing nature of consciousness. In fact consciousness is not even a witness, in the sense there is nothing outside it or other than it for it to witness. But then it is not the ego that is transcendent, but consciousness, of which transcendence is the nature. Hence consciousness cannot be translated as 'transcendent ego' or 'pure ego', for when the ego is transcendent or pure, there is no more the ego.

Relation between Pure Consciousness, Isvara, Jagat, and Jiva

With reference to Pure Consciousness the Gita explains the nature of *jiva* – the psychophysical organism – ,*jagat* – the world of experience and *isvara* – the Lord of creation. Is the Pure Consciousness posited as a reference, and *jiva, jagat* and *isvara* mentioned are distinct states of consciousness? The discrete explanation of *jiva, jagat* and *isvara* by a hierarchical account of consciousness is made, first of all to establish their existence as non-separate from Pure Consciousness. Finally this kind of explanation reveals the essential oneness of consciousness.

From the perspective of the psychophysical organism consciousness is the inner Self of all beings. S.Radhakrishnan explains: "*Purusa* or *ksetrajna* cannot be recognized as an object among other objects or as a substance. He can only be recognized as subject, in which is hidden the secret of existence, a complete universe in an individual form. He is not therefore a part of the world or of any other whole.... As a subject he enters into infinity and infinity into him. *Ksetrajna* is the universal in an individually unrepeatable form."[19] From the perspective of the

[19] S.Radhakrishnan, The Bhagavad Gita, 6th Ind. rpt., (Bombay: Blackie and Son (India) Ltd., 1977), p.301.

objective world consciousness can be known as the Lord of the universe. Reflecting this idea Bhagavan says He is to be known as the "*Ksetrajna* in all *Ksetras*" (Bhagavad Gita: XIII.2 – *ksetrajnamcapi mam viddhi sarvaksetresu bharata*). He is the "Self … seated in all beings" (Bhagavad Gita: X.20 – *ahamatma … sarva bhutasya sthitah*). Bhagavan reveals the non-separateness of *ksetrajna* and *Isvara* when He says "The Lord dwells in the heart of all beings" (Bhagavad Gita: XVIII.61 – *isvara sarvabhutanam hrdesa arjuna tistati*) and controls them by his creative power – *Maya*. Radhakrishnan clarifies: " … the Supreme Self is different from the psycho-physical individual who becomes the immortal Self by transcending the separatist consciousness, due to entanglement in the activities of *prakrti*. In the Gita, no distinction is made between the knower of the field and *Isvara* the Supreme Lord."[20] To one who is less competent to know the oneness of the Self and Isvara Bhagavan exhorts to know Him as the cause of the world, "I am the beginning, and the middle, as also the end, of all beings" (Bhagavad Gita: X.20). All beings have their birth from consciousness, unto consciousness do they dissolve and in the in between life also they exist in consciousness. Consciousness is the seed of all beings. Nothing can exist without consciousness, because "anything into which", consciousness have not entered, "would be without Self (would not exist) and would be void (*sunya*)" (Gita Samkara Bhasya: X.39). Hence consciousness is the essence of all existence.

In the thirteenth chapter of the Gita it is said that consciousness is knowable as *bhuta-bartr*. It is knowable as that which sustains

[20] S. Radhakrishnan, The Bhagavad Gita, 6th Ind. rpt., (Bombay : Blackie and Son (India) Ltd., 1977), p.309.

beings during their existence. The Lord Himself is Consciousness unto which the world is dissolved at the time of dissolution, and which manifests world at the time of creation. Consciousness itself is *Param Brahma*, *Adideva*, *Sasvatam Purusa* and *Param Dama*. Arjuna lauds: "Thou art the Supreme *Brahman*, the Supreme Abode and the Supreme Purifier, the Eternal, Divine Person, the First of the gods, the Unborn, the All-pervading."[21]

According to the Gita Pure Consciousness is that which encompasses and enlivens everything. The thirteenth chapter describes *Parah Purusa* – the Supreme Consciousness as *upadrsta*, *anumanta*, *bharta*, *bhokta*, *mahesvara* and the Self, in the twenty-second verse. Referring to this verse Robert Minor, in his exegetical commentary on the Gita, opines that the '*Purusa*' referred to in this verse "... is not the pure consciousness of Samkara's thought, though it is not attached to the activity of *Prakrti*."[22] This observation seems to be incongruous with Samkaracarya's commentary to the same verse. The examination of Acarya's *bhasya* reveals a different picture concerning Minor's version.

Purusa is not an abstract content of consciousness but is the Self which runs in and through everything. *Purusa* is Pure Consciousness itself. "Spectator and Permitter, Supporter, Enjoyer, the Great Lord, and also spoken of as the Supreme Self [is] the *Purusa* Supreme in this body" (Bhagavad Gita: XIII.22). Consciousness is described as *upadrsta* – the closest observer. Acarya defines it as "... a bystander and a witness, Himself not

[21] S. Radhakrishnan, The Bhagavad Gita, 6th Ind. rpt., (Bombay : Blackie and Son (India) Ltd., 1977), p.260.

[22] Robert N.Minor, Bhagavad-Gita — An Exegetical Commentary, (New Delhi: Hertiage Publishers, 1982), p.394.

acting" (Gita Samkara Bhasya: XIII.22). Though by itself inactive the Supreme *Purusa* observes the activities of the body and mind standing close by. The suffix '*upa*' is used not to say that, in succession consciousness is next to the observed but to figuratively indicate its essential presence. Acarya explains: "The body, the sense of sight, *manas*, *buddhi*, and the Self are the seers. Of these the body is the most external seer; and viewed from the body inwards, the Self is the innermost and nearest seer, and beyond Him there is no seer in the interior" (Gita Samkara Bhasya: XIII.22). Consciousness as the Self is *upadrsta* being the closest and innermost observer than the body, mind and intellect.

Consciousness is *anumanta*, for though not engaged in the activities of the body and mind, it seems to promote them. Or "being their witness, it never stands in the way of those that are engaged in their respective activities" (Gita Samkara Bhasya: XIII.22) and hence is the sanctioner. Consciousness is called *bharta*, the supporter, "because the body, senses, manas and buddhi – which aggregate together to serve the purposes of someone close, such as, the Intelligent Self, and which are, or which convey, mere reflections of that Intelligent Self" (Gita Samkara Bhasya: XIII.22). Consciousness is *bhokta* – the experiencer – since it is that which makes possible the apprehension of mental modifications like pleasure, pain etc. As "one with the whole universe and independent of all" (Gita Samkara Bhasya: XIII.22 – *sarvatmatvat svatantratvaca mahamsca...mahesvarah*) consciousness is *Mahesvara*, the Great Lord. Consciousness that has been defined as the closest observer etc. is *parah* – Supreme – because it is superior to everything beginning "from the physical body up to the Avyakta" (Gita Samkara Bhasya: XIII.22) which is mistaken for the Self, owing to ignorance. Hence consciousness is spoken of as *Paramatma* or Supreme Self.

Matter is Not the Becoming of Consciousness

Amongst theories on the relation between matter and consciousness, and on the origin of matter, the prominent one is that matter is a change, a modification, a becoming of consciousness. This theory has its own inherent difficulties. Another theory that holds that matter itself is consciousness also projects certain discrepancies. The very same theories demand an explanation of the nature of the union of consciousness and matter.

The union of consciousness and matter is of the nature of ignorance. The eighteenth chapter of the Gita describes it as *maya* or cosmic illusion. Due to delusion "*Purusa* becomes seated in *prakrti* and experience the qualities born of *prakrti*" (Gita Samkara Bhasya: XIII.21). As a result of this union due to ignorance two kinds of superimposition are made. The existent nature of consciousness is superimposed on *prakrti* and the inert limited nature of *prakrti* is superimposed on consciousness. Henceforth the unreal body born of *prakrti* is taken as the Self, and the Self is relegated as the enjoyer of the unreal *prakrti*. A mutual superimposition of the real and the unreal is made. "Thus the deluded takes the world as the field for experiencing pleasure and pain and suffers transmigration" (Bhagavad Gita: XIII.20). Dr. Radhakrishnan elucidates: "All life is a commerce between Self and not-Self ... the union of the two is of the nature of *adhyasa*, which consists in confounding the one with the other. When the confusion is cleared, bondage terminates".[23]

Since the nature of the union of consciousness and matter is self-ignorance, it can be contended that consciousness is not affected by its union with matter "just as the sky is not dirtied by the superimposition of impurities on it by the ignorant' or just as 'the water of the mirage does not wet the saline soil" (Gita Samkara Bhasya: XIII.2). In actual life also "no advantage or disadvantage accrues to an entity by means of a feature ignorantly superimposed upon it" (Gita Samkara Bhasya: XIII.2). Ignorance is not a real entity. It is an absence. Like darkness it can only obscure or veil the real until the dawn of light. Consciousness is defined by Acarya as "*nitya suddha buddha mukta svarupa*" (Gita Samkara Bhasya: XV.16), in his commentary to the fifteenth chapter. "Other than these two, the perishable and the imperishable, untouched, by the taints of these two groups of adjuncts, and eternally pure, awake, and free is the Supreme Spirit."[24] The non-existent in no way can taint the existent – *nitya*. Being untouched by matter consciousness is immaculate – *suddha*. There is nothing that transgresses the purview of consciousness. Hence it is awake – *buddha*. Consciousness pervades everything and is not limited by anything and hence is free – *mukta*. The Self – *svarupa* – that is of the nature of consciousness is not affected by ignorance.

Ignorance is not to be taken as an attribute of the cognizer.

---

[23] S. Radhkrishnan, The Bhagavad Gita, 6th Ind. rpt., (Bombay: Blackie and Son (India Ltd., 1977), p.310.

[24] A.G. Krishna Warrier, Srimad Bhagavad Gita Bhasya of Sri Samkaracarya, (Madras: Sri Ramakrishna Math, 1983), p. 506.

Acarya elaborates, that just as defects like blindness pertain to the eye, the cognizer's instrument of cognition and not to the cognizer, "non-perception, false perception and doubt, as well as their cause, properly pertain to the instrument, to one or another sense-organ, but not to the *ksetrajna*, the cognizer" (Gita Samkara Bhasya: XIII.2). Also being knowable or pertaining to the field of consciousness, these defects have to be cognized by a principle other than them. Ignorance though is beginningless – *anadi* – has an end – *santam*. Just as the end of darkness is marked by light, the end of Self-ignorance is marked by Self-knowledge.

If consciousness does not become matter then how is the relation between consciousness and matter is explained? World is not the becoming of consciousness. If it is a becoming, then the definition of the real as immutable will be violated, creating an unexplainable gap between being and becoming. Further, it is illogical to contend that the real existent consciousness modifies to become the unreal inert matter. The material world can be understood only as a manifestation of consciousness. World has no severed or separate existence but is non-separate from Consciousness. The Gita contends material world to be the expression of the creative energy of consciousness. Hence any attempt to see Consciousness and World as dual is as futile as attempting to separately view heat from fire or motion from the mover.

Is the psychophysical problem a fictitious and enigmatic one? G.F. Stout opines: "The psycho-physical problem is a strange and troublesome intruder from outside. It emerges only with the reflection that physical science, even if it completely realized its ideal, would not cover the whole field. There is a residuum that cannot be denied or explained away. The man of science cannot deny his own existence ... He is thus bound to recognize that in self-consciousness there is revealed something which falls outside the range of physical science."[25] Sarvepalli Radhakrishnan writes in his commentary to the Gita. "The fundamental dualism is that of spirit and nature and not of soul and body. It is the distinction between the subject and the object. Nature is the world of objectivization, of alienation, of determinability. There we have, the distinction of minerals, plants and animals and men, but they all have an inner non-objective existence. The subject, Reality, dwells in all of them. This affirmation of basic identity is not inconsistent with the empirical variety."[26]

Consciousness is that "in which all beings dwell and by which the whole world is pervaded" (Bhagavad Gita: VIII.22). Bhagavan emphasizes idea when He says: "By Me all this world is pervaded, My form unmanifested. All beings dwell in Me; and I do not dwell in them. Nor do those beings dwell n Me; behold my divine Yoga! Sustaining all the beings, but not dwelling in them, is My Self, the cause of beings" (Bhagavad Gita: IX.4-5). "A ray of Myself, the eternal *jiva* in the world of Jivas, attracts the senses, with *manas* the sixth, abiding in *prakrti*" (Bhagavad Gita: XV.7). In these verses Bhagavan rules out any disconnected vision of Consciousness and the World. Guenon says, "The 'Self' is as such is never individualized and cannot become so, for since it must always be considered under the aspect of the eternity and

[25] G.F. Stout, Mind and Matter, Ed. G.N.A. Vesey, Body and Mind-Readings in Philosophy, (London: George Allen and Unwin Ltd., (1964), p.258.

[26] S.Radhakrishnan, The Bhagavad Gita, 6th Ind. rpt., (Bombay: Blackie and Son (India) Ltd., 1977), pp.181-182.

immutability."[27] Division and separation are illusory. The entire world of beings exists in consciousness, for "no being devoid of Self can empirically exist" (Gita Samkara Bhasya: IX.4 – *na hi niratmakam kimcit bhutam vyavaharaya avakalpate*). But this does not mean that beings exist in consciousness like something contained in the container. Hence Bhagavan says: 'no beings dwell in Me'. The relationship between consciousness, and world is not a cause-effect relationship. World is not a product of consciousness. Consciousness does not change into matter. There is no real contact or relation between consciousness and matter. Because, there should be a prior separation for any contact or relation to happen. Since world is non-separate from consciousness there is no contact between them. It can only be said that consciousness and the material world are non-separately related.

World is not a phenomenal process of consciousness. Bhagavan says: "As the mighty wind moving everywhere rests ever in the *akasa*, so, know thou, do all beings, rest in Me" (Bhagavad Gita: IX.6). Acarya explains this by the eulogies of the reflected image of sun, and pot-space. When the sun is reflected in water in a container, and later when water is removed, it cannot be said that at first sun entered the water and existed as the reflection and later it returned back. Similarly, the pot-space is never limited or separated from cosmic space. But space exists in and through the pot. Pot-space is nothing else, but is to be understood as all-pervading space. The creation and destruction of the pot never affects space. In fact there is nothing called pot, but what is, is only space.

---

[27] Rene Guenon, Man and His Becoming, Tr. Richard C. Nicholson, (London: Luzac and Co., 1945), p.29.

The theory that world is a manifestation of consciousness cannot be objected by the argument that consciousness is constrained to manifest, or is exhausted in its manifestation. Since the extent of consciousness is not limited, it exceeds ever its manifestation. It is not exhausted in creation since it transcends its own manifestation. Manifestation has no real existence. Therefore Lord says: "I stand sustaining this whole world by one part (of Myself)" (Bhagavad Gita: X.42). Consciousness being omnipotent can create out of itself without undergoing any change or diminution. Epistemologically explained consciousness appears as undergoing change. The change is not real but is only apparent. Creation and dissolution of the world does not affect consciousness since consciousness is always full. "The radical novelty of each moment of evolution in time is not inconsistent with Divine Eternity."[28]

The limitless extent of consciousness is reflected when the Gita holds that one really knows the Lord when he comprehends the extend of the Lord. It is he who knows Him in truth – *tatvatah*. Consciousness is "that which stands encompassing all beings" (Bhagavad Gita: XIII.13 – *sarvamavritya tistati*), "apparently possessing all sense-organs and their properties, but in truth devoid of them, unattached, sustaining all, but beyond the constituents exists as if experiencing them" (Bhagavad Gita: XIII.14).

It is the existential vision of this metaphysical truth that is presented in the Gita, in the chapters on *Vibhutiyoga* and *Visvadarupadarsanayoga*. *Vibhutiyoga* presents the ontological

[28] S.Radhkrishnan, The Bhagavad Gita, 6th Ind. rpt., (Bombay: Blackie and son (India) Ltd., 1977), p.281.

understanding – *jnana* – that consciousness exists in everything. *Visvarupadarsanayoga* is the axiological vision through surrender – *bhakti* – that everything exists in consciousness. *Vibhutiyoga* presents the revelation that consciousness exists in all material configurations. *Visvarupadarsanayoga* presents the revelation that consciousness manifest as all material configurations. The former indicates the method of *vyatireka* – exclusion. And the latter indicates the method of *anvaya* – inclusion "The knowledge that everything is enlivened by consciousness will destroy the ego and bless the knower with the eye to see the supreme – *jnanacaksuh* – which empowers her to experience the material world subsumed in the spirit. That is the highest value. Therefore it is axiological."[29] In the ninth chapter the Lord declares His Supreme nature: "I am the Goal, the Sustainer, the Lord, the Witness, the Abode, the Shelter and the Friend, the Origin, Dissolution and Stay, the Treasure-house, the Seed imperishable" (Bhagavad Gita: IX.18).

Liberation consists in knowing *prakrti* and *purusa*, *ksetra* and *ksetrajna*, matter and consciousness together. It is the One Pure Consciousness that exists in and through the principles of *prakrti*. Hence the liberative knowledge is "the knowledge of the field and the field-knower" (Bhagavad Gita: XIII.2 – *ksetra ksetrajnayor jnanam yat tat jnanam*). And, "He who thus knows *purusa* and *prakrti* with qualities ... he is not born again" (Bhagavad Gita: XIII.23). Sri Aurobindo notes in his commentary: " ... man must know and must embrace both and learn of the Supreme in His eternity ... in order to enjoy

[29] Swami Bodhananda, in a discussion with the author in November 1995.

immortality and live in the Eternal."[30] "In the spiritual vision we find not that all this does not really exist, but rather that all is, but with a sense quite other than its present mistaken significance."[31] "The unity is the greater truth, the multiplicity is the lesser truth, though both are a truth and neither of them is an illusion."[32]

According to the Lord, Self-realization is not localized knowledge, but is a vision that strings the apparent contradictions. To understand the transcendent nature of consciousness, its immanence is to be seen. "Understanding transcendence or transcendent', in the words of Alan M. Olson, is 'understanding the nature and operations of Consciousness."[33]

Understanding the transcendent nature of consciousness lies in knowing the non-separateness of consciousness and matter. To understand the non-separateness, at first, the discrimination between *prakrti* and *purusa* is to be made. The Lord says, "They who by the eye of wisdom perceive the distinction between *ksetra* and *ksetrajna* and dissolution of the cause of beings, – they go to the Supreme" (Bhagavad Gita: XIII.34).

It is notable that even when referring to the manifest and unmanifest matter – *ksara* and *aksara* – Bhagavan designates

[30] Sri Aurobindo, Essays on the Gita, 8th ed., (Pondicherry: Sri Aurobindo Ashram, 1970), p.424; p.426;p258.

[31] Sri Aurobindo, Essays on the Gita, 8th ed., (Pondicherry: Sri Aurobindo Ashram, 1970), p.424; p.426;p258.

[32] Sri Aurobindo, Essays on the Gita, 8th ed., (Pondicherry: Sri Aurobindo Ashram, 1970), p.424; p.426;p258.

[33] Alan M. Olson, Transcendence and Hermeneutics — An Interpretation of the Philosophy of Karl Jaspers, (Hague: Martinus Nijhoff Publishers, 1979), p.XVIII.

them as *ksara* and *aksara purusa*. *Prakrti* is not to be seen apart form *purusa*. In fact Bhagavan introduces the concept of *prakrti* or *ksara* and *aksara purusa*, for a better understanding. The Self-knower does not see the world. To him the world or *prakrti* does not exist, for he sees only Consciousness. Though he dwells in the body "... he neither acts nor is tainted" (Bhagavad Gita: XIII.31 – *sarirasthapi ... na karoti na lipyate*). "Renouncing all actions by thought, and self-controlled, he rests happily in the nine-gated city, neither at all acting nor causing to act" (Bhagavad Gita: V.13). To him the material body is not an obstacle for liberation. The manifestation or non-manifestation of the world does not affect his consciousness.

7

Consciousness and Karma

karmani akarma ya pasyetakarmani ca karma yah
sa buddhiman manusyesu sa yuktah krtsnakarmakrt

He who can see inaction in action, who can also see action in inaction, he is wise among humans, he is well integrated, he is the performer of all actions.

Bhagavad Gita 6:18

The theory of *karma* (action) according to the Gita is best understood in conjunction with its theory of the identity of the Self and Consciousness. As per the psychology of the Gita, activity is not merely a pragmatic notion, but is a definite ontological concept. There is an inalienable relationship between action and human consciousness. Therefore an attempt to study the concept of consciousness demands a comprehensive analysis of action. The ontological pragmatism of the Gita extends the limits of the concept of action, by examining it from the psychology of the individual and the ontology of the Self. This examination clarifies the appended suffixes of action like, inaction – *akarma* – non-action – *naiskarmya* – agency, object of action, intention of action etc.

Karma and Agency

The first question pertaining to the nature of work is who does the work – *prakrti* – or the Self, which is Pure consciousness. All forms of actions, secular and scriptural, are engaged in by the *prakrti* using its effects – sense objects, and instruments – sense organs and organs of action. "Actions are wrought in all cases by the energies of nature" (Bhagavad Gita: III.27). "It is the nature that acts" (Bhagavad Gita: V.14 – *svabhavastu pravartate*). It is ones nature – *guna prakrti* – that operates both as the direct and causal agent.

All works are accomplished by five causes. "The seat and actor and the various organs, and the several functions of various sorts and the Divinity also, the fifth among these. Whatever action man does by the body, speech and mind, right or the opposite, these five are its causes" (Bhagavad Gita: XVIII.14). The ground or seat of any action is the body. The agent is the enjoyer who takes the body to be the Self. The instruments for action are the sense organs. The manifold functions refer to the movement of vital airs. Divinity is the supernatural element that superintends the functions of the sense organs. Any work is done with the conjunction of these five causal factors.

Agency cannot be attributed to the Self. Since Self, which is consciousness, is immutable, "It is neither the agent nor the object of action" (Gita Samkara Bhasya: II.19 – *avikriyatvat ayam atma na karta karma na bhavati*). It is due to indiscrimination born of delusion, that one ascribes agency and enjoyership to the Self. "Those deluded by the energies of nature are attached to the functions of the energies" (Bhagavad Gita: III.29). "He like a silk-worm, caught in its won creation, will get bound by his works" (Gita Samkara Bhasya: IX.9 – *karmabhih badhyate mudah kosakaravat*) But one who realizes the distinction between constituents of *prakrti* (*guna*) and their operations (*karma*) do not attach himself to work.

The Gita is emphatic in that a person of deluded intelligence, who mistakes the Self to be the agent and the enjoyer, understands the truth of neither the Self nor of the action. "He who is untrained in understanding, looks on the pure Self as the agent, that man of perverted intelligence sees not" (Bhagavad Gita: XVIII.16). He becomes bound by "the threefold fruit of action – evil, good and mixed" (Bhagavad Gita: XVIII.12). But he whose understanding is untainted and attitude is selfless, though he works is not bound by his work. "He who is free from egoistic notion, whose mind is not tainted.... He is not bound" (Bhagavad Gita: XVIII.17). To him work is a medium for creative expression.

The Mimamsakas uphold *jnana-karma-samuccaya* as the means to liberation. But when the Gita talks about *karma* it is not as a supplementary factor to Self-knowledge to bring about realization. The Gita explains activity itself as an expression of liberated consciousness. Self-knowledge need not be combined with activity, for the Self is not something to be acquired or reached. The major argument raised by the Purvapaksa on the treatise of *karma* is that the Self is the agent and the enjoyer of activity. Acarya presents the argument of the Purvapaksa and his answer refuting the argument, in his commentary to the eighteenth chapter. The Purvapaksin's argument is: "Though not directly engaged in action, the Self does act by mere presence. This by itself constitutes the real agency of the Self. A king, for instance, though himself not acting, is said to fight when his soldiers fight, in virtue of his mere presence, and he is said to be victorious or defeated ... So the acts of the body, etc., we may hold, are done by the Self, in as much as their results accrue to the Self.... Real agency may rest with what is not actually engaged in an act. And so also in the case of the Self" (Gita Samkara Bhasya: XVIII.66). Acarya refutes this contention: "... we find that the king, etc., (as instanced above) are direct agents also.... Agency by mere presence is merely a *gauna* or figurative agency. Such being the case, even the connection with results can only be *gauna* or unreal. By a *gauna* or figurative agent no real action is performed" (Gita Samkara Bhasya: XVIII.66).

Action and Renunciation

According to the transpersonal psychology of the Gita action and renunciation are not two antithetical processes. By action it is not meant the mere movement of the body. Neither renunciation is the abstention from action. In the Gita Lord inspires for a vision of action from a wider and deeper consciousness. Action is not solely an ethical concept but has profound psychological significance. The exact nature of action can be understood only in relation with renunciation. Renunciation is not the physical giving up of work but is the essential attitude for the performance of work. It is the subtle awareness that springs form the discrimination of the Self and the not-Self. Renunciation is the quality of mind that promotes true action. In the words of Dr. S.Radhakrishnan: "Inertia is not freedom. Again, the binding quality of an action does not lie in its mere performance but in the motive or desire that prompts it. Renunciation refers, not to the act itself but to the frame of mind behind the act. Renunciation means absence of desire. So long as action is based on false premises, it binds the individual soul. If our life is based on self-ignorance however altruistic our conduct may be, it will be binding. The Gita advocates detachment form desires and not cessation from work."[1]

By the mere abstention from work one does not achieve freedom. The Gita notes: "Not by abstaining from action does man win actionlessness, nor by renunciation does he attain perfection" (Bhagavad Gita: III.4). And also, "None, verily, even for an instant, remains doing no action; for everyone is driven helpless to action by the energies born of Nature" (Bhagavad Gita: III.5). Radhakrishnan emphasizes: "Nature is ever at work and we are deluded if we fancy that its process can be held up."[2] Hence even if one wishes to non-initiate any work he will be helplessly forced to do by his very nature. When Bhagavan speaks about freedom, it is not the freedom form action by its non-doing, but freedom in action. Freedom is the very essence of the Self.

Renunciation is the knowledge of the Self as Pure Consciousness. "Renunciation in its final meaning ... is nothing but Self-knowledge"[3], writes Kapil N. Tiwari quoting Samkaracarya's exposition. Renunciation is the discarding of the false notion that 'I am the doer, I am the enjoyer'. It is not

[1] S. Radhakrishnan, The Bhagavad Gita, 6th Ind. rpt., (Bombay: Blackie and Son (India) Ltd., 1977), pp.67.

[2] S. Radhakrishnan, The Bhagavad Gita, 6th Ind. rpt., (Bombay: Blackie and Son (India) Ltd., 1977), pp.68.

[3] Kapil N. Tiwari, Dimensions of Renunciation in Advaita, (Delhi: Motilal Banarsidass Pubs.,1977), p.105.

action that is to be renounced, but the false notion polluting its quality. The Mimamsaka as well as the Self-knower takes up work. But, when the Mimamsaka works with attachment to the results, prompted by desire, the intelligent works detached, for world's integration. "As ignorant men act attached to work ... the wise men act, unattached from a wish to protect the masses" (Bhagavad Gita: III.25). The former acts from a consciousness veiled by desire and the latter renounces the agency of action, from Supreme Consciousness. Renunciation is not another action of giving up the work, but is detachment to the results of the work. Renunciation of attachments is not the physical renunciation of them successively, but by being aware of it. According to the Lord, Awareness is Renunciation. Hence. "He whose engagements are all devoid of desires and imaginations, and whose actions have been burnt by the fire of wisdom, him the wise call a sage" (Bhagavad Gita: IV.19).

The Gita enunciates *karma yoga* and *sanyasa yoga*. *Karma yoga* endows the agent with the fitness for renunciation. It is not to be considered that action and renunciation are two different techniques yielding antagonistic and varied fruits. Bhagavan says, "He who is rightly devoted to even one obtains the fruits of both" (Bhagavad Gita: V.4). "There is one thought of a resolute nature" (Bhagavad Gita: II.41 – *vyavasayatmika buddhih ekeha kurunandanah*), as regards the two fold *yoga*. *Karma yoga* is the performance of work with evenness of mind. *Sanyasa* is the renunciation of the false notion of ascribing agency and enjoyership to the Self. It is the relinquishment of desire-prompted works – "*kamyanam karmanan nyasam*" (Bhagavad Gita: XVIII.2). Both *karma yoga* and *sanyasa* can be defined as non-expectation – *niskāma*. A *Yogi* or *Sanyasi* in Lord's words is "He who, without depending on the fruits of action, performs his bounden duty, he is a *Sanyasin* and a *Yogin*: not he who is without fire and without action" (Bhagavad Gita: VI.1). Therefore Lord says that what is called *sanyasa* is *yoga*. "…Know *Yoga* to be that which they call renunciation" (Bhagavad Gita: VI.2). Renunciation of attachment is absolute transparence to the Self. *Sanyasa* is *yoga* since it brings about the natural discovery of the Self as consciousness. If *sanyasa* is taken as the end then *Karma Yoga* becomes a means to realize it. If *sanyasa* is taken as a means, then *yoga* becomes equivalent to it. *Yoga* and *sanyasa* are not antitheses but are like two sides of a coin. In analyzing action and renunciation, Archie J. Bahm holds, "*Yoga* is enjoying work as an end in itself."[4] In Feurstein's observation "*Yoga* comprises three great approaches which bring together and cultivate combinedly the conative, cognitive and affective aspects of human Nature."[5]

To be a *Yogi* or a *Sanyasin*, according to the Lord, one has to renounce his mental constructions – "*sanyastha samkalpah*" (Bhagavad Gita: VI.2). For a balanced mind devoid of imaginations, conscientious performance of *karma* is the means. Through *karma yoga* one becomes fit for *sanyasa* or meditation. And through *sanyasa* he reaches *karma-sanyasa yoga*, "When a man, renouncing all thoughts is not attached to sense-objects and actions, then he is said to have attained to *yoga*" (Bhagavad

---

[4] Archie J. Bahm, Tr. The Bhagavad Gita, (Bombay: Somaiya Publications Pvt. Ltd., 1970), p.28.

[5] George Feurstein, Tr. The Bhagavad Gita, (New Delhi: Arnold – Heinemann (India) Pvt. Ltd., 1980), p.42.

Gita: VI.4). Renunciation of imaginations is the quality of a free mind. A free mind is a pure mind that is not swayed by dualities. In the words of S.Radhakrishnan: "...When the mind becomes free and disinterested and sinks into that secret serenity. When its consciousness becomes illumined, it gladly accepts whatever happens, knowing fully well that these contacts come and go and are not itself, though they happen to it."[6]

Work and Mental Purity

Action according to Bhagavan can bind the individual consciousness or can be a means to liberation. When the ignorant works, being deluded by indiscrimination, he superimposes upon his Self, the agency of action and the enjoyership of results. His mind is constantly swayed either by attachment – *raga* – or aversion – *dvesa* – to the result of work. To him the discrimination between the Self and the not-Self is difficult, whereas the wise with the evenness of mind becomes fit for the discriminative knowledge. Therefore Bhagavan gives two-fold discipline for the two classes of people – "the discipline of knowledge for the Samkhya and that of work for the *Yogins*" (Bhagavad Gita: III.3). For an *aruruksu* – one who wishes to master *yoga*, conscientious performance of duty without attachment to the results, is the means – *karmakarana* – to be equipped with an even mind. And to a *yogarudah* – one who has mastered *Yoga* and whose mind is purified – that peace of mind (*sama*) is the means for meditation.

---

[6] S. Radhakrishnan, The Bhagavad The Gita, 6th Ind. rpt., (Bombay: Blackie and Son (India) Ltd., 1977), pp.105.

The unintegrated mind – *ayukta*, Lord says, has no knowledge of the true nature of the Self, nor is such a mind fit for meditation. Meditation or renunciation of thoughts is difficult for a reacting and uncontrolled mind. The fifth chapter, therefore, says: "Renunciation…is hard to attain except by *Yoga*" (Bhagavad Gita: V.6). Lord reiterates the importance of mental integration as the only means to win the meditative quality of mind. Hence any attempt :o gain sense-control without the necessary thought-control can be labeled only as hypocrisy. "He who restraining the organs of action, sits thinking in his mind of the objects of the senses, self-deluded, he is said to be one of false conduct" (Bhagavad Gita: III.6). On the other hand, "all actions, without exception', executed with an even mind, 'is comprehended in wisdom (Bhagavad Gita: IV.33)".

The given nature of mind is to initiate action motivated by a desire, and to be perturbed by the results. The root of desire is the attachment of mind to objects in the form of expectation for happiness or contentment. Attachment to objects marks a chain of psychological mishaps. The Gita cautions: "when a man think of objects, attachment for them arises. From attachment arises desire; from desire arises wrath. From wrath arises delusion. From delusion, failure of memory; from failure of memory, loss of conscience; from loss of conscience he is utterly ruined" (Bhagavad Gita: II.62-63). Attachment to objects is the product of the ignorance of the nature of Self as Pure Consciousness. One who is ignorant of the true nature of his Self, work either to won something – *pravrtti* – or to discard something – *nivrtti*. "From the delusion of pairs caused by desire and aversion … all beings are subject to illusion" (Bhagavad Gita: VII.27). Work prompted by desire for happiness obscures the Self which is Pure Consciousness, just "as fire is obscured by smoke, as a mirror by rust, as the fetus is enclosed in the womb…."(Bhagavad Gita: III.38). To such a person the required mental quality of quiescence can be got only by performing work without attachment to the results. Action is the only means to restore mental purity. Bhagavan cites, "Serenity of mind, good-heartedness, silence, Self-control, purity of nature…"(Bhagavad Gita: XVII.16), as constituting the penance of mind – *manasam tapah*.

The course of action and its result are determined by five factors. As the first lesson to a person of action Lord says: "Thy concern is with action alone, never with results. Let not the fruit of action be thy motive, nor let thy attachment be for inaction" (Bhagavad Gita: II.47). The immediate tendency of a deluded mind is to initiate a work expecting a pleasant result. It may also abstain from initiating work presupposing a disagreeable result. According to the Gita these two tendencies are to be curbed. Three reasons can be traced behind Bhagavan's exhortation to work without attachment. If work is done with an expectation for agreeable result, the mind will be unable to focus its energy towards the performance of work. It is dissipated in pondering about the results. Work done without concentration can emerge only handicapped. This is the first reason. Som P. Ranchan substantiates this situation when he remarks: "When the doer is fully in the deed he is not creating residues which clog consciousness."[7] The second reason is that, since action is operated by the factors of *prakrti*, the course of results may not be apprehensible to the doer. However agreeable

[7] Som P. Ranchan, Revisioning Gita, (Delhi: Konarak Publishers, 1991), p.19.

the result of a work, that may not give contentment and happiness. This is the third reason for the profound lesson on action given by the Lord.

If work, impelled by desire is not to be performed, then how it is to be performed? The Gita advises that reducing attachment and aversion – "*sangam tyaktva*" (Bhagavad Gita: II.48) – one should perform his duty with evenness of mind in success and failure. Work is to be done for the purity of mind – *atmasuddhi*. Mental purity is the quiescence of mind won by the curbing of its movement in terms of attachment and aversion. A pure mind is an alert mind. Peace and subtle sensitivity is the nature of an alert mind. Alertness of mind can be gained by *abhyasa* – practice – and *vairagya* – detachment. *Abhyasa* implies the practicing of evenness of mind and *vairagya* denotes "freedom from desire for covetable experiences in the plane of the seen and the unseen" (Gita Samkara Bhasya: VI.35 – *drastadrsta bhogesu dosadarsanabhyasat vaitrsnyam*) through discrimination. "Freedom from desire which is otherwise difficult is won by Self-knowledge" (Gita Samkara Bhasya: III.43). Desire is the urge to be happy or fulfilled. It can be destroyed only by the knowledge of ones Being as happiness or fulfillment. Desire is therefore an estrangement from ones original nature. Annie Besant cautions: "Never let us forget that objects are desireable because of the immanence of God."[8]

Swami Bodhananda elaborates two statements concerning happiness that are both transpersonal and transcendental in

[8] Annie Besant, A Study in Karma, (Adyar: Theosophical Publishing House,1975), p.43.

nature.[9] These are (i) All desires are for happiness. Why? Through all objects we expect happiness. (ii) At the same time, desire is the denial of happiness. Why? The different objects through which we expect and experience happiness keep changing. The same object cannot make us happy all the time and in all places. They need not be individually necessary for us to be happy. Therefore desire is always for happiness, through the fulfillment of objects. Also, happiness brought out by the object eliminates the desire for the object. Therefore a happy state is a desireless state. How is that desire the denial of happiness? There can be two reasons: (i) Desire is seeking happiness in the object. Happiness is not a property of objects. Objects include mind, body etc. Desire is extrovertedness of mind. If happiness is not the property of objects then whose property is it? It must be the property of the subject. If happiness is the property of the subject then desire is the expression of subjective ignorance. That means, desire is the denial (missing) of happiness. It is not a conscious act of denial. But we are ignorant of the fact that our nature is happiness. (ii) One who desires happiness has to be unhappy. An unhappy person's nature has to be unhappiness. What is the substratum of unhappiness? The unhappy person is the substratum of unhappiness. Therefore unhappiness becomes her nature. But, if unhappiness is her nature then she will not desire unhappiness. Since she desires happiness, her nature has to be happiness. Still she seeks happiness shows that she is ignorant of her true nature. Self-ignorance is ignoring her being happy.

[9] Swami Bodhananda in a discussion with the author in 1995. Also See Swami Bodhananda, Happiness Unlimited: Self-unfoldment in an interactive world, (Delhi: BlueJay Books, 2003).

Desirelessness is happiness. Therefore desire is the denial of desirelessness or happiness.

By giving up the fruits of work a *Yogi* attains disciplined peace – "*naistikam santi.*" (Bhagavad Gita: V.12). He is free from craving and accepts dualities equally. Mental purity, according to the Gita, is the equal acceptance of dualities. Lord says: "... to whom pleasure and pain are same, he for immortality is fit" (Bhagavad Gita: II.15). Acceptance marks the transcendence of the dual. The individual whose mind is receptive and not selective is truly integrated – *yuktah*. He will not react to a situation but will respond spontaneously. Mind alone is the reason for one's bondage and liberation. Hence Lord advises: "Let a man raise himself by himself, let him not lower himself; for he alone is the friend of himself, he alone is the enemy of himself" (Bhagavad Gita: VI.5). The steady-minded – *sthirabuddhih* – neither elates on the gain of the pleasant, nor grieves on meeting with the unpleasant. He "...self-controlled approaches objects with the senses devoid of love and hatred ..." (Bhagavad Gita: II.64). His intellect is even – *samabuddhih* – in respect of 'clod, stone and gold, good men, friends, foes, indifferent persons, neutral, antagonists, relatives, the righteous and the unrighteous'. He has given of both the good and the evil – *subhasubhaparityagi* – and is silent – *mauni*. He treats praise and contempt alike – *tulyanintastutih* – and is content with whatever accrues to him – "*santustoyenakenacit*" (Bhagavad Gita: XII.19). Having the senses under control as a result of evenness of mind he "engages in *karma yoga*, unattached, with the organs of action" (Bhagavad Gita: III.7).

The concept of *yajna* or sacrifice is introduced by the Lord, in his exposition of the technique for performing work efficiently. *Yajna* is the law of life. Through *yajna* the individual consciousness is brought towards a collective consciousness through active participation. The Gita holds, "Except in the case of action for sacrifice's sake, this world is action-bound" (Bhagavad Gita: III.9). Through the *yajna* concept, the participatory consciousness underlying the Vedic ritual is brought to bear in all action. Bhagavan calls for the efficient performance of action – *samacara* – free from attachment – *asakta* – as a sacrifice. Work done as a sacrifice will not leave a binding effect since it plants a seed in the unconscious for "wisdom of fire reduces all actions to ashes" (Bhagavad Gita: IV.37). "Of the man whose attachment is gone, who is liberated, whose mind is established in knowledge, who acts for the sake of sacrifice—his whole action melts away" (Bhagavad Gita: IV.23). Translating *yajna* as "the principle of reciprocity"[10], Bahm comments: "…The Gita not only recognizes *yajna* as a sacrificial ceremony but also allegorically extends the idea involved to the business of living as a whole."[11] In Sarvepalli Radhakrishnan's point of view, "Sacrifice is a making sacred to the Divine. It is not deprivation or self-immolation but a spontaneous self-giving, a surrender to a greater consciousness … By such a surrender, the mind becomes purified of its impurities and shares the power and knowledge of the Divine."[12]

---

[10] Archie J. Bahm, Tr. The Bhagavad Gita, (Bombay: Somaiya Publications Pvt. Ltd., 1970), p.43;p.70.

[11] Archie J. Bahm, Tr. The Bhagavad Gita, (Bombay: Somaiya Publications Pvt. Ltd., 1970), p.43;p.70.

[12] S.Radhakrishnan, The Bhagavad Gita, 6th Ind. rpt., (Bombay: Blackie and Son (India) Ltd., 1977), pp.70.

Apart from the *yajna* concept of participation, Lord speaks also about the nature of a surrendered mind. A mind that is able to surrender or dedicate towards a higher consciousness is a free mind. Only a free mind can make work creative. Therefore Bhagavan advises: "Whatever thou doest, whatever thou eatest, what thou sacrificest, whatever thou givest, in whatever activity thou engagest, do it is an offering to Me. Thus shalt thou be liberated from the bonds of action which are productive of good and evil results" (Bhagavad Gita: IX.27). Acarya expresses Bhagavan's works in his commentary: "Seek Me thy sole Refuge in the belief 'I myself am that *Isvara*'; ie., do thou understand that there is naught else except Me. When thou art firm in the faith, I shall liberate thee from all sin's, from all kinds of *dharma* and *a-dharma*, by manifesting Myself as thy own Self" (Gita Samkara Bhaśya: XVIII.66). Through *bhakti* or devoted work mind merges with Supreme Consciousness. The Gita concept of *bhakti* brings forth a Divine altar that is Pure Consciousness, where all imaginations and premonitions of the mind can be dedicated. According to the Gita a free and creative mind is a mind that does everything as a dedication. Through surrendered work one gains "clear freedom from every disguise of the insistent ego."[13] Sri Aurobindo adds: "...he rises ... to that highest Numen by his soul's love and joy in God and the adoration of the will in him for the Master of its works."[14] *Bhakti* and *jnana* are the two concepts, for which the Gita gives an integral

[13] Sri Aurobindo, Essays on the Gita, 8th ed., (Pondicherry: Sri Aurobindo Ashram, 1970), p.443.

[14] Sri Aurobindo, Essays on the Gita, 8th ed., (Pondicherry: Sri Aurobindo Ashram, 1970), p.455.

meaning. In Lord's opinion, a *jnani* is a *bhakta* and a *bhakta* is a *jnani*. Only one who has surrendered his thoughts and actions can be a *jnani*. Only one who knows and abides in the intimate relationship of his Self and Supreme Consciousness is a *bhakta*. Lord says: "... the wise man, ever steadfast and devoted to the One, excels; for, exclusively dear am I to the wise, and he is dear to Me" (Bhagavad Gita: VII.17).

Commenting on Bhagavan's description for the devotee dear to Him Acarya translates: "This Sannyasin has directed to Me exclusively his Manas – purposes and thoughts – as well as his Buddhi – the faculty of determining. Such a devotee is dear to Me" (Gita Samkara Bhasya: XII.14). "... the wise man, as knowing the truth, is ever steadfast, and devoted to the One" (Gita Samkara Bhasya: VII.17). The Gita recognizes devotion as the realization of ones Self as Pure consciousness. Devotion is the renunciation of all identifications. In the words of Sri Aurobindo, "The spiritual transference of all our works to the Master and his *Shakti* is the real *Sanyasa* in the teaching of the Gita."[15]

Work is Meditation

A major postulate that is brought out by the Gita is that work and meditation are complementary to each other. True work can be executed only by a meditative mind. One can meditate only if he has gained the evenness of mind through non-reactive performance of work. Hence in order to work one has to meditate and in order to meditate one has to work. Krishna Caitanya

[15] Sri Aurobindo, Essays on the Gita, 8th ed., (Pondicherry: Sri Aurobindo Ashram, 1970), p.478.

proclaims: "Self-awareness and action ... seem essential ... for the transition from the unconscious symmetries of natural existence to the achieved harmonies of man's coexistence with themselves and with the world."[16]

What the Gita indicates by its theory of meditation is a deepening and broadening of consciousness beholding all beings in consciousness and consciousness in al beings. "The Self abiding in all beings, and all beings (abiding) in the Self..."(Bhagavad Gita: VI.29 – *sarvabhutastham atmanam sarvabhutani ca atmani*) is the vision revealed by the Gita. In this context an examination of Merleau-Ponty's view on the phenomenology of perception seems to be relevant. Merleau-Ponty says in "Phenomenology of Perception": "Analytical reflection starts from our experience of the world and goes back to the subject as to a condition of possibility distinct from that experience, revealing the all-embracing synthesis as that without which there would be no world."[17] Ponty defines such an all-embracing synthesis as the "deep-seated momentum of transcendence', where there is the, 'simultaneous contact with one's own being and the world's being."[18]

To one who has not inculcated the inclusive nature of work, renunciation and meditation, Bhagavan gives a hierarchical account for better understanding. Hence to Arjuna's question on the superiority of the *Yoga*s, Bhagavan replies,

---

[16] Krishna Chaitanya, Freedom and Transcendence, (New Delhi: Manohar Publications, 1982), p.332.

[17] M. Merleau-Ponty, Phenomenology of Perception, Trans. Colin Smith, (London: Routledge and Kegan Paul Ltd., 1962), p.IX.

[18] M. Merleau-Ponty, Phenomenology of Perception, Trans. Colin Smith, (London: Routledge and Kegan Paul Ltd., 1962), p.377.

"Renunciation and *Yoga* through action both lead to the highest bliss: but, of the two, *Yoga* through action is esteemed more that renunciation of action" (Bhagavad Gita: V.2). "Because ... renunciation ... is hard to win without Karma Yoga" (Bhagavad Gita: V.6). Also "greater is their trouble whose thoughts are set on the Unmanifest" (Bhagavad Gita: XII.V). Renunciation of desire and agency imposed on the Self is possible only for a mind that can endure the dualities equanimously. Renunciation is the natural state of a *karmayogi*. A *Yogi* who neither takes up any undertakings – "*sarvarambha parityagi*" (Bhagavad Gita: II.16). – nor abstains from any work is a perpetual renouncer – "*nitya sannyasi*" (Bhagavad Gita: V.3) – abiding all the time in the Self. The meditative nature of his mind is not affected, no matter he is engaged in work or not. He is "not moved even by a great pain" (Bhagavad Gita: VI.22), having gained the Supreme. If work, renunciation and meditation are seen as separate disciplines, detached work is superior to renunciation and meditation. "Better indeed is knowledge than practice; than knowledge is meditation more esteemed; than meditation the abandonment of the fruits of actions; on abandonment, peace follows immediately" (Bhagavad Gita: XII.12). Detached work is indispensable for one to sit in the seat of meditation. One should not abstain from work to meditate. Only a *karmayogi* can take up the practical lessons for meditation. Self-knowledge is more important than deliberate practices for meditation. If Self-realization is taken as the goal, meditation is more important than scriptural knowledge. If meditation is taken as a discipline, detached work is more important. According to the Gita, a renouncing mind is a meditative mind, which always abides in Supreme Consciousness.

A *Yogi* is one who engages in work with a meditative mind. Therefore Lord marks, "... those who worship Me, renouncing all actins in Me, regarding Me Supreme, meditating on Me with exclusive devotion (*yoga*); for them whose thought is fixed on Me, I become ere long, ... the deliverer out of the ocean of the mortal *samsara*" (Bhagavad Gita: XII.6-7). Such a *Yogi* is in meditation or non-separate union with the Self – *ananya yoga* – even while he is engaged in work.

In order to bring out the identity of Consciousness and Activity or Meditation and Work, Bhagavan examines the integral nature of action, inaction and bad action – *karma*, *akarma* and *vikarma*. In common experience *karma* is considered to be the voluntary movement of the body – willed action – and *akarma* or inaction as the abstention from immoral actions. Any willed action or cessation form actions presuppose an agent, prompted by desire, being ignorant of the real nature of the Self. Hence, even when one abstains from action, that is not inaction, but only another form of action. It is due to Self-ignorance that one superimposes agentship and cessation of work of person on the Self. As to correct the contrary perception of action and inaction, the Lord reveals the veridical perception: "He who can see inaction in action, who can also see action in inaction, he is wise among men, he is integrated; he is the performer of all action" (Bhagavad Gita: IV.18). "Seeing what *is* and what *is not* is meditation.... Experiencing the whole world integrally is meditation.... Meditation is freedom in action, not freedom from action."[19]

[19] Swami Bodhananda, Meditations, (New Delhi: Sambodh Foundation, 1991), p.8.

In the analysis given by the Gita, the vision of inaction in action is the vision of the Self. The knower of the Self even while engaged in action, is not caught up in the agency and the fruits of action. When he sees, hears, touches, smells, eats, walks, sleeps, breaths, talks etc., he knows the truth that he does not work at all – *aham na karmakaromi*. He understands that it is the interaction of senses with their objects – "*indriyani indriyarthesu vartanta*" (Bhagavad Gita: V.9). Action pertains to the operation of sense organs on their respective objects – "*gunagunesu vartante*" (Bhagavad Gita: III.28). A *Yogi* acts from the discriminative knowledge: "Neither agency nor objects does the Lord create for the world, nor union with the fruits of actions. But it is the nature that acts" (Bhagavad Gita: V.14).

Work does not add something to the *Yogi's* consciousness, nor it reduces his inner contentment. Hence whatever action he does, he experiences essential inaction. Inaction is the nature of the Self. Action is the creative urge of the individual. The Self-knower is always in inaction or Supreme consciousness, even while he is engaged in works. He acts not for fulfillment but out of his fullness. Work becomes a constant source of inspiration for him. Since he never reacts, he responds spontaneously to a situation. Since he never impedes work with past imaginations or future expectations he experiences timelessness in the present. To him work is meditation. His consciousness is ever fresh and creative. "Having abandoned attachment for th fruits of action, ever content, dependent on none, though engaged in actions, nothing at all does he do" (Bhagavad Gita: IV.20). Som P. Ranchan explains inaction: " ... being established in transcendence, yet not off from the dynamism of the Mysterium tremendum of the Numinosum."[20]

Work is extolled to the supreme status by the Lord to establish the integral nature of consciousness. In many verses Bhagavan repeats not to mistake the abandonment of action to be inaction. "The duty born with oneself ... one ought not to abandon ..." (Bhagava l Gita: XVIII.48). To the activist who takes inaction to be the cessation of action, Bhagavan advises: "Do thou perform (thy) bounden duty; for action is superior to inaction. And even the maintenance of the body would not be possible for thee by inaction" (Bhagavad Gita: III.8). Inaction is not *naiskarmyam* – not doing anything – but *nishkamakarma* – working without expectation. Hence Bhagavan adds: "Therefore without attachment, constantly perform the action which should be done; for performing action without attachment; man reaches the Supreme" (Bhagavad Gita: III.19). Samkaracarya comments on the exhortation of the Lord: "... do not sit quite, nor renounce action. If thou art ignorant, do thou perform action to purify the Self. If thou art wise and knowest the truth, do thou perform action for the protection of the masses" (Gita Samkara Bhasya: IV.15). From the description of action and meditation the Gita gives, it can be understood that it takes neither of the concepts from a mere moral perspective. In S.Radhakrishnan's analysis: "The man of the world is lost in the varied activities of the world ... The quietist withdraws into the silence of the Absolute (*aksara*) but the ideal man of the Gita goes beyond these two extremes and works like Purusottama who reconciles all possibilities in the world without getting

[20] Som P. Ranchan, Revisioning Gita, (Delhi: Konarak Publishers, 1991), p.19.

involved in it. He is the doer of works who yet is not the doer, *kartaram akartaram*. The Lord is the pattern of an unwearied and active worker who does not, by His work forfeit His integrity of spirit."[21]

Inaction is the perpetual nature of one who knows the nature of his Self as pure Consciousness. To him action is not a process or a phenomenon, but the expression of his creativity and inner solitude. Bhagavan sets Himself as the example when He says: "I have nothing whatsoever to achieve in the three worlds, … nor is there anything unattained that should be attained; yet I engage in action." (Bhagavad Gita: III.22). To the Lord work is a play. He acts in a sportive spirit, as a recreation. Annie Besant elaborates this nature of activity when she contends activity as the mode of Self-expression. Besant writes in A study in *Karma*: "The mode of Self-expression which directly affects the environment, the energy going forth from the Self, is Activity, the action for the Self on the Not-Self. The power of concentrating all energies into one is Will; the power of becoming aware of an external world is Cognition; the power of affecting that outside world is Activity."[22]

Counting the non-separate relationship between Consciousness and Activity, Brahman and Karma, in the Gita Lord introduces the word *yoga* to designate *karma*. The word *yoga* is derived from the root '*yuj*' which means to unite. Sir Monier Williams defines '*yujya*' as "to draw towards one's self,

[21] S. Radhakrishnan, The Bhagavad Gita, 6th Ind. rpt., (Bombay: Blackie and Son (India) Ltd., 1977), p.72.

[22] Annie Besant, A Study in Karma, (Adyar: The Theosophical Publishing House, 1975), p.31

be absorbed in meditation."[23] Brahman and *karma* or Pure Consciousness and its Creative Power are not to be viewed as two separate principles. Hence Bhagavan uses the word *yoga* to mean both work and meditation. Any attempt to separately analyze activity and consciousness will obstruct the truth about both. Activity and meditation according to the Lord are to be realized as one continuous experience. When consciousness is expressed creatively it is work. When work is performed meditatively it is realization of the Self as Pure Consciousness. Activity emerges from consciousness and dissolves into consciousness. Hence engaging in action is meditating on the Self. It is illumining this fact that Bhagavan advises Arjuna to be only an instrument – "*nimittamatrambhava*" (Bhagavad Gita: XI.33). One who employs his psycho-physical setup as an instrument is always in non-separate identity with the Lord who is of the nature of Pure Consciousness. He is described as "*nityasatvastha*" (Bhagavad Gita: II.45) – one who is ever alert. Every instant he experiences *samadhi*. Activity itself is meditation to him – "*brahmakarma samadhi*" (Bhagavad Gita: IV.24).

Apart from the phrase *karmaniakarmadarsanam*, the Lord conveys the essential non-separateness of activity and consciousness by the threefold definition of *yoga*. *Yoga* is defined as *samatvam*, *karmasukausalam* and *dukhasamyogaviyogam*. *Yoga* is the evenness of mind – *samabuddhi* – in terms of dualities. "Steadfast in devotion do thy works, ... casting off attachment, being the same is success and failure. Evenness is called *Yoga*" (Bhagavad Gita: II.48). *Yoga* is seeing the fact as a fact and

[23] Sri Monier Monier-Williams, A Sanskrit – English Dictionary, rpt. new. ed., (New Delhi: Motilal Banarsidass Publishers, 1990), p.853.

accepting the inevitable. Its movement in terms of dualities marks the apparent estrangement of mind from its essential nature of Pure Consciousness. A mind that can endure dualities without elation or depression is a meditative mind, in union with Pure consciousness. A non-reactive mind is a mind that abides in Pure Consciousness. The Gita identifies meditation with a non-reactive mind. Control of thoughts is possible only for a non-reactive mind. "He who is equipped with *Yoga*, whose mind is quite pure, ... whose senses have been subdued, whose Self has become the Self of all beings — though doing, he is not tainted" (Bhagavad Gita: V.7).

Yoga is skillfulness in action, which is described as *karmasukausalam*. It is maintaining the evenness of mind for the efficient performance of work. "He who is endued with wisdom casts off here both good deeds and bad deeds. Wherefore apply thyself to devotion. In regard to actions devotion is power" (Bhagavad Gita: II.50). A.M. Sastri translates the word *kausala* used by Bhagavan as 'power'. Attributing the meaning as 'power' to *kausala* he translates the commentary of Acarya. "... Devotion is a power, – devotion being the equanimity of mind in success and failure on the part of him who is engaged in the performance of his own duties, his mind resting no the *Isvara* all the while. It is indeed a power, because works which are of a binding nature loses that nature when done with evenness of mind" (Gita Samkara Bhasya: II.50). Desire-prompted action is of inferior nature, it being the helpless expression of a mind swayed by dualities. Such a mind is never able to initiate any fresh activity, for all actions are tainted by the past results and future expectations. Activity can only bind and cannot liberate him.

Hence the skillful way of executing work is by maintaining fresh and pure mind. Sir Edwin Arnold says: "The Gita is a comprehensive treatise on *Yoga*', that 'facilitates the passage from the narrow ego of the Self to the transcendental personality."[24]

Yoga is disjunction from unhappiness – ***dukhasamyoga viyogam***. "This severance from union with pain, be it known, is called 'union' (*yoga*). That *yoga* must be practiced with determination and with undepressed heart" (Bhagavad Gita: VI.23). *Yoga* is described by the principle of exclusion, using double negatives. This is to show that *yoga* is not a state to be acquired, but which is to be realized by the removal of superimpositions made on the Self. It is the disjunction form the apparent conjunction with unhappiness. This form of disjunction can be brought about only by the knowledge of the Self as of the nature of Pure Consciousness. Acarya comments: "Severance from union with pain is called *yoga* (which means union) by a sort of irony. Having thus concluded speaking of the effect of *yoga*, the Lord again refers to the necessity of it, with a view to show that determination and nón-depression (self-reliance) are necessary means to *yoga*" (Gita Samkara Bhasya: VI.23).

Unhappiness is a false acquisition. It is a presumption. It has no real existence. Happiness or Bliss is the real nature of the Self. Therefore *yoga* is the disunion from the apparent identity with unhappiness. Hence Lord advises that instead of eliminating unhappiness, one should look into it and see that it has no existence. The inquiry into the problematic of pain with alertness,

---

[24] Sir Edwin Arnold, Tr. The Song Celestial, (New Delhi: Interprint, 1978), p.14.

itself reveals that the nature of the inquirer's Self is Happiness. Happiness is another name the Gita assigns to Pure Consciousness.

8

Consciousness and Freedom

ksetraksetrajnayorevamantaram jnanacaksusa
bhutaprakrti moksam ca ye viduryanti te param

They who by the eye of wisdom perceive the distinction between *ksetra* and *ksetrajna* and the dissolution of the *ksetra* in the *ksetrajna*, they go to supreme.

Bhagavad Gita 13:34

Freedom is a concept that is much related to the study of consciousness in its phenomenological and existential analysis. The terms of existential significance like intention, constitution, ego, transcendence, anguish and nothingness are the emergent terms of the comparative study of consciousness and freedom. The Gita allocates a significant place to 'freedom' in its philosophy of consciousness. Though 'freedom' is presented in the background of the conflict situation that Arjuna faced, the Gita's version of freedom is not only existential but also ontological in nature. The ontological nature of freedom is equated with Self-knowledge, Happiness, Peace and Transcendence.

What is Freedom

The Gita names a liberated person variously as *sthitaprajna* – sage of stable wisdom – *nistraiguniah* – one who has transcended the *gunas* – *nityayukta* – one who is ever integrated – *yogi* – the integrated – etc. in the second, twelfth and fourteenth chapters the Gita enlists the characteristics of the liberated. According to the Gita hermeneutics the definitions given to freedom are also the definitions of a liberated individual. Theses definitions reveal the consciousness of a liberated individual as well as imply her experiences and attitudes. A comment made by Fritjof Capra is quotable in this context. He says: "A true science of consciousness … would have to be a new type of science dealing with qualities rather than verifiable measurements. The data of such a science would be patterns of experience that cannot be qualified or analysed."[1]

The characteristic features of freedom promulgated by Bhagavan in the Gita are at once the means demanding efforts on the part of the aspirant, as well as the distinctive marks of the accomplished sage. What is natural to a *siddha* is a *sadhana* for the seeker. It is of distinctive significance that the Gita identifies *freedom* with a *free individual.* Freedom is not an abstract concept or a standard that is to be actualized. The Gita conceives freedom as the essential nature of the individual. This fact is emphasized by Dr. S. Radhakrishnan in his words: "His body, mind and spirit, the conscious, the pre-conscious, and the unconscious … work flawlessly together and attain a rhythm expressed in the ecstasy of joy, the illumination of knowledge and the intensity

[1] Fritjof Capra, Uancommon Wisdom, (London: Century Hutchinson's Ltd., 1988), p.145.

of energy. Liberation is not the isolation of the immortal spirit from the mortal human life but is the transfiguration of the whole man. It is attained not by destroying but by transfiguring the tension of human life. His whole nature is subdued to the universal vision, is wrought to splendor and irradiated by the spiritual light. His body, life and mind are not dissolved but are rendered pure and becomes the means and mould of the Diving Light, and he becomes his own masterpiece. His personality is raised to its fullness, its maximum expression, pure and free, buoyant and unburdened."[2]

The term *sthitaprajna* is not only an adjective qualifying the liberated but is also a noun. A *sthitaprajna* is one who has the assured wisdom born of experience – *aham asmi param brahma* – 'I am supreme consciousness'. He is one who has renounced the desire for happiness – "*prajahati … kaman*' – and rejoices in his Self – '*atmanyevatmanatustah*" (Bhagavad Gita: II.55). "When a man, satisfied in the Self alone by himself, completely casts off all the desires of the mind, then he is said to be one of steady knowledge" (Bhagavad Gita: II.55). Since happiness is one's own nature, the sage never makes it an object of desire. Through subtle discrimination he understands that procrastinating happiness is equivalent to denying happiness. He is ever happy – "*santusta satatam*" (Bhagavad Gita: XII.14). He does not wait for a situation of an object, to be happy. Being a happy person he is not swayed by agreeable or disagreeable situations, but remains steadfast. Acarya comments: "He does not exult in pleasure, nor he is averse to pain that may befall

[2] S. Radhakrishnan, The Bhagavad Gita, 6th Ind. rpt., (New Delhi: Blackie and Son (India) Ltd., 1977), p.76.

him" (Gita Samkara Bhasya: II.57). He is not troubled by the world nor does he trouble the world; "He by whom the world is not afflicted and who is not afflicted by the world, who is free from joy, envy, fear and sorrow ..." (Bhagavad Gita: XII.15). The liberated sage is *anapeksa* – non-demanding, *suci* – pure at mind, *daksa* – determinative, and *gatavyadha* – untroubled.

The Yogi is also called a *nistraiguniah*. Seated as if indifferent – *udasinavadasina* – he is not disturbed by the mutual operation of physical constituents. "He who, seated as a neutral, is not moved by *gunas*; who, thinking that *gunas* act, is firm and moves not ..." (Bhagavad Gita: XIV.23). The *nistraiguniah* transcends the operation of *gunas* by the Yoga of unwavering devotion – "*avyabhicarena bhakti yogena*" (Bhagavad Gita: XIV.26). Such devotion of a Yogi is described by the Lord as *ekabhakti* – exclusive devotion. His devotion is exclusive or one-pointed, since he sees his Lord in everything and everything is his Lord. He is *aniketa* – has no fixed house – since he sees the whole world as the abode of her Lord.

Freedom is Self-Knowledge

In the Gita's perspective freedom is not a quality, but is the essence of an individual. It is not an acquired characteristic, but is the nature of the Self. Hence freedom is Self-knowledge and bondage is Self-ignorance. The Self-knower cuts asunder the transmigratory cycle and enjoys everlasting freedom. "With their consciousness in That, their Self being That, intent on That, with That for their supreme goal, they go never again to return, their sins shaken off by means of wisdom" (Bhagavad Gita: V.17). It is freedom not in the sense of having freedom, but being free due to "*adhyatmajnananityatvam*"

(Bhagavad Gita: XII.11) – constancy in Self-knowledge.

Bondage is identification with the part – the psychophysical complex – forgetting the whole, which is consciousness. Identifications born of ignorance can be removed only by the knowledge of the true nature of the Self. Acarya says: "Pure Self-knowledge alone is the means to the Highest Bliss; for, as removing the notion of variety, it culminates in liberation – *kaivalya*" (Gita Samkara Bhasya: XVIII.66). Acarya dispenses with the notions that activity or knowledge combined with activity can result in liberation. Since freedom is not a product, it is illogical to bold that activity can bring about liberation. Being the real and original nature, freedom cannot be produced by activity. Self-knowledge also does not produce freedom in the sense that freedom or liberation is not an acquisition of something that was yet absent. Acarya comments: "Indeed, the Eternal Reality is not produced either by knowledge or by works" (Gita Samkara Bhasya: XVIII.66 – *na hi nityam vastu karmana jnanena va kriyate*). Self-knowledge is liberation since it dispels ignorance that crates plurality, division and separation. Liberation is the immediate fruit of Self-knowledge. There is no gap between the knowledge of the Self and liberation, for it is the accomplishment of that which is already accomplished. Som P. Ranchan remarks: "What is involved is not merely adaptation to outer reality, understanding of ones script, complexes, what is involved is not just the dialectics of the conscious and the unconscious and vice versa, but instead migrating to Pure Consciousness."[3] The noted scholar of Indian religion Mircea

[3] Som P. Ranchan, Revisioning the Gita, (Delhi: Konarak Publishers, 1991), p.16.

Eliade adds: "The *Jivanmukta* no longer possess a personal consciousness – that is, a consciousness nourished on his own history – but a witnessing consciousness which is pure lucidity and spontaneity."[4] The Gita views Freedom, Pure Consciousness and Spontaneity as not altered states but as expressions of the Self-knower. Western thinkers like Pierre Teilhard De Chardin emphasize the same generalization. He also accepts freedom, spontaneity etc. as the expressions of the Self. To quote Chardin: "The within, consciousness and then spontaneity – three expressions for the same thing. It is no more legitimate for us experimentally to fix an absolute beginning to these expressions of one and the same thing than to any other lines of the Universe."[5]

Freedom and Activity

The Gita presents activity not as a means to freedom, but expounds the theory of freedom in action. Freedom is achieved not as a result of work or abstention from work. The Gita explains *freedom in the midst of action* and *not freedom from action.* Activity itself is freedom. S. Radhakrishnan wirtes: "... spiritual freedom is not inconsistent with activity. Duty as such drops away but not all activity. The activity of the liberated is free and spontaneous and not obligatory."[6] According to the Gita activity

[4] Mircea Eliade, Immortality and Freedom, Tr. Willard R.Trask, 2nd. ed., (Princeton: Princeton University Press, 1969), p.363.

[5] Pierre Teilhard De Chardin, The Phenomenon of Man, (Glasgow: Williams Collins Sons and Co. Ltd., 1959), p.62.

[6] S. Radhakrishnan, The Bhagavad Gita, 6th Ind. rpt., (New Delhi: Blackie and Son (India) Ltd., 1977), pp.73-74.

is both self-giving and self-fulfilling. Activity and freedom are simultaneous phenomena. The Gita emphasizes duty and freedom as complementary. Elucidating this Radhakrishnan continues: "The aim of the Gita is not so much to teach a theory as to enforce practice, dharma. We cannot separate in theory what is not separable in life. ... *Dharma* is what promotes worldly prosperity and spiritual freedom. The Gita does not teach a mysticism that concerns itself with man's inner being alone. Instead of rejecting the duties and relationships of life as an illusion, it accepts them as opportunities for the realization of spiritual freedom. Life is offered to us that we may transfigure it completely."[7]

There is a distinct difference between the Gita concept of freedom and the Existential concept of freedom. A comparative examination of the two will vividly precipitate the difference. In Sartrean existentialism acting is decided by the choice of the actor. The agent can choose 'either-or'. He is free to act according to his selective consciousness. His "freedom lies in open choice."[8] According to The Gita freedom is not born of choice. Freedom is not selective consciousness but an accepting mode of consciousness. In the words of Sri Aurobindo: "The liberated man has the complete and total knowledge, *Krtsnavid*, and does all woks without any of the restrictions made by the mind, *Krtsnakrt*, according to the force and freedom and infinite power of the divine will within him."[9]

---

[7] S. Radhakrishnan, The Bhagavad Gita, 6th Ind. rpt., (New Delhi: Blackie and Son (India) Ltd., 1977), pp.79-80.

[8] Pratima Bowes, Consciousness and Freedom, (London: Methuen and Co. Ltd., 1971), p.154.

[9] Sri Aurobindo, Essays on the Gita, 8th ed., (Pondicherry: Sri Aurobindo Ashram, 1970), p.445.

The Lord speaks about integral acceptance and endurance of dualities. For Sartre freedom is that which divides the choices for a selection. According to Bhagavan, freedom lies not in dividing and comparing, creating a schism in between the choices, but in accepting both integrally allowing a wholesome vision. By using freedom in selecting, judging and discarding the other, one is 'contempt' to be bound by his selective action. Being free in accepting the facts, one transcends the baffling and opposing dualities.

In the Gita Bhagavan epitomizes the importance of integral knowledge – *samagram jnanam*. Integral perception is the right perception – *samyag darsanam* (Bhagavad Gita: VI.29). Integral knowledge is not the selective understanding of opposites but their integral understanding. To one who sees the differences distinctively but comprehensively, freedom is immediate and is not predicated by choice. To be aware of the differences and yet not to judge them by comparison is true freedom. Everything is unique in its own kind and hence to select one by discarding the other by a comparative analysis, is the expression of parochial vision. Every thing has its inherent value that is disclosed not through a process of comparison and selective judgment, but by seeing the thing as it is, in its own place. One is free when he sees things in their own respective place, without attributing the colors of judgment, allowing things to be as they are.

Freedom, according to the Lord, is having a perfect sense of proportion. Archie J. Bahm comments: "Anxiety, perturbation and discontent occur because we are unwilling to accept the universe. We want to be different … .The present is already as good as it can be, and its goodness is wasted when we fail to appreciate it."[10] Freedom itself is concealed when it is employed in viewing things according to mental modifications, ideas and images. It is for the same reason that Simone De Beauvoir interjects: "...the world's objects are made up of all the values one has endowed them with."[11] Reiterating the importance of proportionate perfection, the Gita warns against the dwelling in extremes. Selecting the extremes is indulgence. To avoid excess is to avoid bondage. Integrating the extremes by a middle path is meditation and freedom. It is not freedom from something or for something, but being free.

The mind that receives what life brings and yet is free from all modifications is a balanced mind. According to the Lord acceptance is transcendence. A Yogi is *nirdvantvah* – one who endures the dualities. By enduring the dualities he transcends them – *dvandvatitah*. He neither hopes for something yet unachieved nor attempts to preserve what is already acquired and hence is *vimatsarah* and *niryogaksema*. He is content with what is gained by chance, which comes unsought. He is described as *yadrccalabhasantustah*. Since he accepts gain and loss with an equanimous mind, he is never bound by action. "Satisfied with what comes to him by chance, rising above the pairs of opposites, free form envy, equanimous in success and failure, though acting he is not bound" (Bhagavad Gita: IV.22). Being free from identifications with the nature and notion of agency – *nirmamonirahamkarah* – he takes up all actions. "That man

[10] Archie J. Bahm, Tr. The Bhagavad Gita, (Bombay: Somaiya Publications Pvt. Ltd., 1970), p.19.

[11] Simone De Beauvoir, A Farewell to Sartre, Tr. Patrick O' Brain, (Britain: Penguin Books, 1984), p.413.

attains peace, who, abandoning all desires moves about without attachment, without selfishness, without vanity" (Bhagavad Gita: II.71). Even while engaged in activity he remains absolutely free, for activity and *brahmisthiti* – Karma and Self-abidance – are not different phenomena for him. The freedom of the Self-knower is not ordained by an external factor. He is free in his action since he always abides in his Self. To him activity is not against Self-abidance, but is from Self-abidance. A corollary to this generalization of the Gita concept of freedom can be found in the statement of A.C. Ewing in his book *The Fundamental Questions of Philosophy*. Ewing emphasizes: "Freedom lies in self-determination as opposed to determination by something else."[12]

Freedom and Happiness

If freedom is used in selecting either of the choices then there always remains a chance of bondage to be caused by the discarded other. Pratima Bowes on analyzing the relationship between consciousness and freedom writes: "Since he is free to choose either way he experiences anguish ... there is an immediate experience of the fact of freedom in the phenomenon of anguish."[13] Anguish and sorrow are always from the other. As per Sartrean existentialism it is "feeling of freedom which manifests itself through anguish ... characterized by a constantly renewed obligation to remake the Self and this is what designates

[12] A.C. Ewing, The Fundamental Questions of Phislosophy, (London: Routledge and Kegan Pual Ltd., 1951), p.189.

[13] Pratima Bowes, Consciousness and Freedom, (London: Methuen and Co, Ltd., 1971), p.154.

man's free being."[14] Swami Bodhananda says: "Sadness – *visada* – is the ultimate check post where you bump into Brahman. Your heart strings an array of beats and the fate plays on it. And that is anguish."[15] The separated view of the other always generates a tendency to move towards it or away from it. When Sartre considers this constant movement for remaking arising from anguish, as the freedom of the individual, the Gita enunciates a peaceful movement that springs from happiness. In the words of the Lord a happy person is a free person. His freedom is not impelled by the anguish caused by the 'other' but results from his integral vision. He never allows a separated existence of the 'other' to impede his freedom, but integrates it in his encompassing consciousness. On the Gita ideal of a free person M.M. Agrawal states: "The free human being is aware of the life-situation in a manner which does not impose upon it a false meaning and values necessitated by a psychological need to transform the difficult and unbearable reality into a personally acceptable and manageable one. Such a subject, it is clear, apprehends and lives in truth. ... Further this freedom-consciousness must in itself be a continuing source of true happiness, just as the presence of the compulsive psychological forces must always be a constant source of impatience, insecurity, irritation and therefore unhappiness."[16]

The Bhagavad Gita begins its discourse from the scenario of Arjuna placed between the armies in the battlefield. To the Arjuna

[14] Pratima Bowes, Consciousness and Freedom, (London: Methuen and Co, Ltd., 1971), p. 155.

[15] Swami Bodhananda in a discussion with the author in 1995.

[16] M.M. Agrawal, The Philosophy of Non-attachment, (Delhi: Motilal Banarasidass Pubs., 1982), pp.53-54.

who was anguished by indecisiveness either to fight or to quit the warfront, Bhagavan's first advice was not to grieve (Bhagavad Gita: II.11). The same advice is reiterated in the last chapter when the Lord says "*ma suca*." (Bhagavad Gita: XVIII.66). The central message of the Gita is to be always happy. The Gita cites Freedom and Happiness as synonyms of Pure Consciousness. Archie J. Bahm remarks in his translation work on the Gita: "The central philosophy of the Gita is simple: Do not worry. Worry is useless and evil. He who worries makes himself miserable."[17] A Yogi is one who is *antasukhi* and *antararama* – happy in the Self and rejoices in the Self. "Whoso has his joy within and his pastime within, and whoso has his light within only, that Yogin attains Brahman's bliss, himself becoming Brahman" (Bhagavad Gita: V.24). Anguish or grief apparently veils the potency of consciousness and lands one in indecisiveness. A Yogi never gives a place for grief. He is ever happy – *santusta satatam* (Bhagavad Gita: XII.14).

In the Gita a distinction is made between happiness and pleasure. What is meant by happiness is not the transient pleasure got from an object of experience. Happiness is *aksayasukham* (Bhagavad Gita: V.21) – the endless and perpetual joy. The Bhasyakara notes: "The pleasures that are caused by contacts of the senses with sense objects are only generators of pain, since those delights are caused by nescience" (Gita Samkara Bhasya: V.22). Hence the Self-knower does not procrastinate being happy. His joy has no reason, but is spontaneous and continuous. He does not make happiness an object to be attained, but

---

[17] Archie J. Bahm, Tr. The Bhagavad Gita, 6th Ind. rpt., (Bombay: Somaiya Publications, Pvt. Ltd., 1970), p.19.

constantly revels in happiness. "The emotional joy or happiness. For true or pure joy must be free from intentionality. It cannot be the product of a self-motivated series of cause and effect. True joy must be truly spontaneous."[18] Pleasure does have a beginning and an end. The contact of a sense organ with its object marks the beginning of a pleasure, and their separation, its end. This contact that brings about pleasure is mediated by emotion. Regarding the nature of emotion a remark made by Sartre is quotable in this context. Sartre opines: "A consciousness becoming emotional is rather like a consciousness dropping asleep."[19] In contradistinction to emotional joy happiness does not conceal or reduce the potency of consciousness. In fact Happiness and Pure Consciousness go together.

Happiness does not have a beginning or an end, for it is the very nature of the Self. "True happiness of human beings lies not in the possession of outward things but in the fulfillment of the higher mind and spirit, in the development of what is most inward in us."[20] A craving and reacting mind obscure happiness that is ones real nature. Association of mind with a desirable object undergoes a mental modification called *sukha* or pleasure. *Dukha* or pain is the modification undergone by the mind when it associates with an undesirable object. When these modifications are absent, the mind is transparent to the Self, its real nature – *svarupa* – being Happiness. The Gita describes: "He that is able

[18] M.M. Agrawal, The Philosophy of Non-attachment, (Delhi: Motilal Banarsidass Pubs., 1982), p.53.

[19] Jean Paul Sartre, Sketch for a Theory of Emotions, Tr. Philip Maiet, (London: Methuen and Co Ltd., 1962), p.78.

[20] S. Radhakrishnan, The Bhagavad The Gita, 6th Ind. rpt., (New Delhi: Blackie and Son (India) t. Ltd., 1977), p.363.

... to withstand ... the impulse of desire and anger, he is a Yogin, he is a happy man" (Bhagavad Gita: V.23) A happy man is ever content – *nityatrpta* (Bhagavad Gita: V.23) – and is free – *nirasraya* (Bhagavad Gita: IV.20) – being ever abiding in Pure consciousness – *satatayukta* (Bhagavad Gita: II.1). The Gita is emphatic in that happiness is not an object to be sought. The more happiness is sought, identifying it with desirable objects, the more elusive and far it will be. Research conducted by contemporary psychoanalysts and Depth psychologists also agree with this idea about happiness. The theory explained by the Gita is reflected in the words of Viktor Frankl, the founder of logotherapy when he says: "The pursuit of happiness amounts to a self-contradiction: The more we strive for happiness, the less we attain it. Peace of mind also must content itself with being a side effect, for it is self-destroying as an intention"[21]

The Gita describes Yoga as *dukhasamyoga viyogam*. This phrase describes happiness as the disjunction from the apparent union with grief. The union with happiness is the real and original union that is already there. An alert mind is a happy mind. Therefore Bhagavan says, "When thought is quiescent, restrained by the practice of Yoga; when seeing the Self by the self, he is satisfied in his own Self; when he knows that Infinite Joy which, transcending the senses, can be grasped by reason; when, steady (in the Self), he moves never from the Reality" (Bhagavad Gita: VI.20-21).

When according to Sartrean Existentialism, movement is triggered off by anguish, according to the Gita all movement is

---

[21] Viktor E.Frankl, Psychotherapy and Existentialism, (New York: Pocket Books, 1967), p.52.

calmed down by happiness. The Self-knower moves not, since he beholds consciousness everywhere. He sees the Lord everywhere – *samam pasyaniha sarvatra samavasthitamisvaram* (Bhagavad Gita: XII.28). "He sees who sees the Supreme Lord, remaining the same in all beings, the undying in the dying. Because he who sees the Lord, seated the same everywhere, destroys not the self by the self, therefore he reaches the Supreme Goal" (Bhagavad Gita: XIII.272-9). Knowing Pure Consciousness as *sarvalokamahesvaram* (Bhagavad Gita: V.29) – the Lord of the whole universe he rests in the midst of movement. He is motionless in movement. He is free to move anywhere since he is motionless and has nowhere to reach. Any movement does not overwhelm him, since he abides in Pure Consciousness that is sheer overwhelmingness. This nature of consciousness is described in the Gita as "... all desires enter as waters enter the ocean, which, filled from all sides, remains unaltered ..." (Bhagavad Gita: II.70).

Consciousness and Time

The Gita expounds the relationship between consciousness and time from a psychological and hermeneutic standpoint. When a person acts impelled by a desire for an object, his activity is impressed in his mind as a memory. It is the memory that is later defined as a thought and a further desire for the desirable object. The Gita views thought as time. Annie Besant traces the reduction of pleasure got form a desirable object into memory and thought, vividly in her book A Study in Consciousness. This description may help to understand the Gita concept of time better. To quote Annie Besant: "As the states of pleasure

and pain become more definitely established in consciousness, they give rise to the three aspects; with the fading away of pleasure there is a continuance of the attraction in consciousness, a memory, and this becomes a dim groping after it, a vague following of the vanishing feeling, a movement – too indefinite to be called an effort – to hold it, to retain it; similarly with the fading away of pain there is a continuance of the repulsion in consciousness, again a memory, and this becomes an equally vague movement to push it away. These states give birth to: memory of past pleasure and pain, indicating the germination of the Thought-aspect; longing to experience again pleasure, or avoid pain, the germination of the Desire-aspect; this stimulating a movement, the germination of the Activity-aspect."[22]

According to the Gita, thought is time, since it is the product of memory. Thought is an extension of the past into the present for its continuation in the future. The mind thinks in terms of the past when it is motivated by a desire to repeat the act. And the mind thinks in terms of the future when it expects a desirable result. A mind that is swayed by desire and expectation is constantly lured by a fictitious past and future. Such a mind is blind to the moment-to-moment newness of the present. The beholder of an expecting mind superimposes a non-existent elusive past into the real existent present by repeating acts. The Gita denotes that it is such a mind that awaits happiness to be got through pleasurable objects. Happiness is in the present time-scale. Hence the Gita advises to be *yadrcca labha santusta* and *santusto yenakenacit* – to be happy in what is received unsought.

[22] Annie Besant, A Study in Consciousness, (Adyar: The Theosophical Publishing House, 1980), pp.156-157.

The Gita admonishes desire and expectation and suggests non-attachment to results.

The fictitious nature of the past and future time scales which is expressed as desire and expectation, as explained by the Gita is admitted by thinkers like Merleau-Ponty as well as contemporary analysts of consciousness. A comparison of the Gita account of time and the modern interpretation of time is relevant in this context. In the view of Merleau-Ponty: "The past, therefore, is not past, nor the future, future. It exists only when a subjectivity is there to disrupt the plentitude of being in itself, to adumbrate a perspective, and introducing non-being into to it. A past and future spring forth when I reach out towards them."[23] George L. Kline expresses a corollary of this idea: "The future as indeterminate and the past as fully determinate are alike lacking in subjectivity. No past existent is a subject; and since there is no such thing as a 'future existent', there is, a fortiori, no such thing as 'future subject'. Subjectivity, and hence (ontological) privacy, experiential immediacy, decision, purpose and freedom are limited to subjects; which means that they are found only in the present. The past and future are both characterized by objectivity, although in slightly different senses: the objectivity of the past is an aspect of its real potentiality; the objectivity of the future is an aspect of its pure possibility or, more precisely, pure possibilities. There is no mode or type of being which is unique to the future. But since pure possibilities (in contrast to real potentialities) are not time-dependent, the future may be harmlessly characterized as the 'realm' of pure possibility, even

---

[23] M. Merleau-Ponty, Phenomenology of Perception, 4th imp., Tr. Colin Smith, (London: Routledge and Kegan Paul Ltd., 1962), p.421.

though, strictly speaking, possibilities as timeless, also have a kind of 'locus' in the present and the past. What the future 'holds' is (timeless) possibilities for present actualization."[24]

When Merleau-Ponty refers to subjectivity and being, they mean the empirical ego and the Self respectively. By subjectivity George L. Kline refers to Being or Self. Time exists when there is 'I' who mistakes her to be the agent and the enjoyer. This feature is elaborately explained in the Gita in the context of *Prakrti*, *Purusa* and *Jiva*. The past and future time scales are the fictitious products created by the Self-ignorant. The Self is always the present, which integrates the past and future. As per the hermeneutics of the Gita the past and the future are psychological time scales. The present is the real chronological time. Hence a Yogi is described by the Gita as one who works – *nirmamo nirahamkarah* – without the thought of 'I' and 'mine'. To him Activity is Self-actualization expressing the potency of the Self in manifold ways.

When the unending chain of memory causes activity, desire and thought it is prone to be victimized by time. Activity is then no longer creative but can only be a weak emotional expression. A desiring and expecting mind wants only to repeat the act. Repetition veils newness and creativeness. That is the characteristic of the present. According to the Gita creativity is not a process in time. On the Gita conception of creativity M.M. Agrawal notes: "In an actual act of creation, the awareness and

---

[24] George L. Klaine, Present Past and Future as Categorical Terms and the Fallacy of Actual Future, Ed. Jude P.Dougherty, The Review of Metaphysics a Philosophical Quarterly, Vol.XL. No.2, (Washington: Catholic University of America, 1986), pp.224-225.

the material production of the elements are so intimately linked together that one cannot significantly talk of a temporal gap between the two."[25] But when an individual acts motivated by a desire, his act can only be a projection of memory – the past – in the future. To him future is the repetition or continuation of the conditioned inner past, directed by memory and modified by imaginations. Such a person can-never be sensitive to the newness of the present. By his judgmental evaluation "the present is compared with the past and assessed in terms of the future. The present, what is given in experience, is caught in the conceptual net of the past."[26]

The Gita qualifies a Yogi as *anarambha* and *sarvarambhaparityagi* – one who abandons beginning. If an activity has a beginning then it has an end too. The in between interval is extended by expectation and anxiety. A Yogi works for no set purposes. Since he does not begin any action the time process does not catch him up. His action can be marked as creative for he is ever established in the Self. Being established in the Self he experiences timelessness in time. The Self-knower does not reduce his experiences into memory but integrates them in his accommodative consciousness. He acts not mechanically but spontaneously, being always in the present. Since the conceptual framework of past and future time scales in terms of desire and expectation does not bind his action he is free in action. His consciousness provides a point or orientation for different

[25] M M. Agraval, The Philosophy of Non-attachment, (Delhi: Motilal Banarsidass Pubs., 1982), p.58

[26] M M. Agraval, The Philosophy of Non-attachment, (Delhi: Motilal Banarsidass Pubs., 1982), p.58

contexts. This nature of consciousness as the focal point that integrates experiences is emphasized in the writings on recent studies in consciousness. Rudolf A. Makkreel says: "Despite the embeddedness of consciousness in historical-contextual systems, consciousness retains its relevance: it provides a point of orientation as the interpreter attempts to conceive how different contexts intersect and give meaning to their pasts."[27] Rohit Mehta in his explanatory work on the Gita clarifies: "The Being is al the time present in the process of Becoming—but its presence is so subtle that one misses it. The Being illumines the whole field of Becoming. ... Rooted in the experience of Being he goes forth into the diversified expression of Becoming. The Becoming is in the process of time, but the restrictive influence of time drops away when there comes into it the touch of the Timeless, which the Being fundamentally is."[28] In the Gita the Lord defines a thought-free mind as an alert mind that views the Becoming and the changeless Being comprehensively. An alert mind is a happy mind that is creative. As per the hermeneutics of the Gita Happiness, Alertness and Creativity are the expressions of Timelessness.

Integral Consciousness and Intentional Consciousness

Consciousness is described as intentional in nature, in Husserlian and Sartrean thought. The Gita describes consciousness as integral.

---

[27] Rudolf A. Makkreel, Hermeneutics and the Limits of Consciousness, Ed. Hector-Neri Castaneda, Nous, Vol. XXI. No. 1, (Indiana University, 1987), p.10.

[28] Rohit Mehta, From Mind to Super Mind, (Bombay: P.C. Manaktala and Sons Pvt., 1966), p.136.

According to Husserl, the transcendence of consciousness is due to intentionality brought about by consciousness. Pratima Bowes encapsulates the Husserlian notion of transcendence and intentionality in her words: "... transcendental intending of an object as an unitary something and not just as a mass of unrelated properties and the consequent intuiting of its essence – this transcendental function of consciousness is uncovered by reflection – is what is meant by the constitutive function of consciousness."[29] Sartre's conception is also affined, since in his view, "... consciousness is always consciousness of something.... It is nothing if it is not the revelation of that something."[30] Consciousness is substantial in so far it is intentional. Consciousness can be known only as intentional consciousness. Sartre upholds the non-substantiality or contentlessness of consciousness, if it is abstracted form the intentionality to world. "Consciousness ... is functional reality utterly devoid of all traces of substantiality ... it exist only to the degree to which it appears.... "[31]

From the Gita version of consciousness, intentionality can be explained in two ways – existentially and ontologically. Consciousness is intentional in the cognitive process. The Gita accepts the tripartite factors involved in a cognitive act as knowledge, known and knower – *jnanam*, *jneyam*, *parijnata* (Bhagavad Gita: XVIII.8). Consciousness is intentional as far as one separately views the object to be known, knower and the

[29] Pratima Bowes, Consciousness and Freedom, (London: Methuen and Co. Ltd., 1971), p.124.

[30] Pratima Bowes, Consciousness and Freedom, (London: Methuen and Co. Ltd., 1971), p.124.

[31] Pratima Bowes, Consciousness and Freedom, (London: Methuen and Co. Ltd., 1971), p.124.

resultant knowledge. This is the existential explanation for the intentionality of consciousness. The Gita explains intentionality also from the ontological plane, by assigning the intentionality of consciousness to one who is deluded by a separate existence, division and plurality. Bhagavan says, "Many-branched and endless are the thought of the irresolute" (Bhagavad Gita: II.41). The irresolute " by differentiation, sees in all the creatures various entities of distinct kinds..." (Bhagavàd Gita: XVIII.21). Intentionality is attributed to consciousness, when consciousness is mistaken to be the psychophysical complex – the ego. Intentionality is not essential – *svabhavika* – but only adventitious – *aupadika* – to consciousness. T.M.P. Mahadevan aptly remarks: "While it is true that there is no phenomenon without consciousness, there is no phenomenological evidence to say that there is no consciousness without the phenomenon."[32]

According to the Gita, the real nature of the Self is Pure Consciousness. It is not intentional but is integral;. Along with Bahm, R.C. Zaehner also translates Yoga as "integration".[33] The Bhagavad Gita itself is described as the science of integration – *yogasastra* – and the Lord is lauded as *yogesvara*. Annie Besant defines Yoga as the "rational application of the laws of the unfolding of the consciousness in an individual case."[34] K.M. Munshi notes: "... Yoga is the one comprehensive process by which man ascends in the scale of life by performing acts which

[32] T.M.P. Mahadevan, Ed. Spiritual Metaphysics, (New Delhi: Arnold – Heinemann, 1975), p.144.

[33] R.C. Zaehner, Tr. and Comm., The Bhagavad Gita, (Oxford: Clarendon Press, 1969), p.11.

[34] Annie Besant, An Introduction to Yoga, (Adyar: Theosophical Publishing House, 1908), p.19.

are the expression of a dynamic personality based on the complete coordination of all his powers."[35] Consciousness integrates the world as a web of existence – *madatma sarvabhutatma.* Intentionality is giving reality to a separated existence and division. Integral consciousness gives no reality to the apparent separation of the world, and divisions. In Integral Consciousness intentional plurality is absent. It is sensitive to the essential oneness in the seeming plurality. Feurstein remarks: "Fulfillment ... means the realization of the order in the universe and recovery of Selfhood."[36] "The Self abiding in all beings, and all beings (abiding) in the Self, sees he whose self has been made steadfast by Yoga, who everywhere sees the same." (Bhagavad Gita: VI.29). Integral Consciousness is not contentless consciousness, it being the content of everything. The content has no existence separate form consciousness. The content of consciousness is in non-separate relationship with consciousness.

Consciousness is not opposed to anything but integrate everything. The Self-knower who intent objects is not separate from Supreme Consciousness. He does not attribute reality to the intentionality of consciousness. To a *jnani* also, the appearance of sensations and experiences – *pratiti* – remains, but to him there is no comprehension – *pratyaya.* He sees the differences integrally and not intentionally. The Lord speaks about a state of subtle sensitivity – *adhyatmacetas* (Bhagavad Gita: III.30), which enables the vision of each and everything in its own proper

---

[35] K.M. Munshi, Bhagavad Gita and Modern Life, 6th ed., (Bombay: Bharatiya Vidya Bhagavan, 1962), p.36.

[36] George Feurstein, Tr. The Bhagavad Gita, (New Delhi: Arnold Heinemann (India) Pvt. Ltd., 1980), p.41.

place. Consciousness integrates even intentionality. Consciousness marks the dissolution of the intentionality of ego by integrating it.

9

Conclusion

yetra yogesvara krisna yetra partho dhanurdharah
tatra srivijayor bhutirdhruva nitimatirmama

Wherever there is Krisna, the Lord of Yoga, wherever there is Arjuna, the archer, there fortune, victory, prosperity and polity are established.

Bhagavad Gita 18:78

The Bhagavada Gita is a text that is vested with the teachings of philosophical, psychological, ethical and religious import. Along with the Upanishads and Brahmasutra, the Bhagavad Gita forms the Prasthanatraya, three foundations, of Indian philosophy. The eighteen chapters of the Gita form chapters XXIII to XL of the Bhismaparvam of the Mahabharata. The authorship of the Gita is given to Vyasa, and its date of composition, according to astronomical evidence cited in the Mahabharata, could be 3137 BCE. Many commentaries and elucidations were written on the Gita. Samkaracarya has given the earliest known commentary to the Gita, followed by Ramanuja, Madhusudhana, Nimbarka, Anandagiri etc. and modern commentators like Sri Aurobindo, Gandhi, Tilak etc.

Coming under the Smrti literature, the Gita integrates

different systems of thoughts and cults. Vyasa articulates the teaching of the Gita in such a way that it enables the vision of truth in its entirety, curbing any sectarian outlook. Different and divergent currents of thought such as the Vedic idea of sacrifice, the Upanishadic philosophy of the Absolute, the Bhagavata theism and the Samkhya dualism are refined, reconciled and made into a unique and holistic system of thought. The philosophy of the Gita is not meant for a particular sect of people or it is outdated into an historical time. The Bhagavad Gita is meant for people and minds of all times. Regarding the stupendous nature of the Gita, Sri Aurobindo makes a notable comment: "The language of the Gita, the structure of thought, the combination and balancing of ideas belong neither to the temper of a sectarian teacher nor to the spirit of a rigorous analytical dialectics cutting off one angle of the truth to exclude all the others; but rather there is a wide, undulating, encircling movement of ideas which is the manifestation of a vast synthetic mind and a rich synthetic experience. This is one of those great syntheses in which Indian Spirituality has been as rich as in its creation of the more intensive, exclusive movements of knowledge and religious realization that follow out with an absolute concentration on clue, one path to its extreme issues. It does not cleave asunder, but reconciles and unifies."[1] In the words of Sarvepalli Radhakrishnan: "The Gita is specially suited for the purpose, as it attempts to reconcile varied and apparently antithetical forms of the religious consciousness and emphasizes the root conceptions of religion which are neither ancient nor

[1] Sri Aurobindo, Essays on the Gita, 8th imp., (Pondicherry: Sri Aurobindo Ashram, 1970), p.6.

modern but eternal and belong to the very flesh of humanity, past, present and future."[2]

The Gita discusses both the subjective and objective aspects of life. What the Gita envisages through its systematic teaching is a harmony of the apparent extremes. The concepts like renunciation and action, work and meditation, *Purusa* and *Prakrti*, *Jnana* and *Bhakti* are introduced to integrate the polarities from a wholesome vision of the Self. A rigorous attempt is made by the Gita to revitalize and redefine these concepts and terms into their fuller and definite meaning, suiting to the needs of all times. The Gita conceives *Bhakti*, *Jnana* and *Dhyana* as the means to Yoga and the fruit of Yoga. The means and goal are envisioned form the subtle psychology of the individual. The Gita gives no room for a compartmentalized separation of devotion, work and meditation. Self-knowledge, detached work, meditation and devotion are mutually embracing and complementary to each other. This is the reason evident when the Gita enlists common characteristics of a *Jnani*, *Bhakta* and *Yogi*. We find a precise blend of theism and absolutism in the Gita.

The Gita defines a philosophy that gives equal importance to metaphysics, logic, ethics and individual psychology. The colophon at the end of each chapter in the Gita reiterates the nature of the Gita as the *Brahma-vidya* and *Yoga-sastra*. The Gita gives not only a metaphysical interpretation – *brahma-vidya* – but also a practical program – *Yoga-sastra* – to transform knowledge into experience.

The ideal of the Gita is a spiritually enlightened person.

[2] S. Radhkrishnan, The Bhagavad Gita, 6th Ind rpt., (Bombay: Blackie and Son (India) Ltd., 1977), p.7.

Sthitaprajna is a person of non-demanding devotion, who abides in the Self. She is an integrated person. The development of an integrated person is not possible outside the field of interactions and relationships. World is posited by the Gita as the necessary field for individual organization and actualization. Kurukshetra symbolizes the battlefield of the mind, in an allegorical sense. The negative tendencies of the mind are confronted by developing positive qualities. The Gita gives utmost importance to human mind and its dispositions. The destiny of an individual is framed by her thoughts and attitude of work. What the Gita envisions is a consciousness that is centered around and focused on the Self. The Gita defines Self-consciousness, not as an equivalent or alternative to ego, but as Self-knowledge itself. Consciousness in the sense of Self-knowledge is the central point referred to by the Gita as that which embraces every bit of existence, at the same time unfolding its potency in its entirety.

The analysis made, in the earlier chapters, on the concept of consciousness in the Bhagavad Gita, in the background of Darsanas, vouchsafes certain distinct features. The Gita presents a comprehensive and integral picture of the nature of consciousness from the ontological, epistemological and existential standpoints. A brief discussion on consciousness as presented in the Vedas, Upanishads and the classical Indian systems of philosophy helps to understand the nature of consciousness in the Bhagavad Gita from a wider background. The Gita reveals a comprehensive psychology of consciousness in the light of a profound philosophy. The Bhagavad Gita fills the gaps left by Darsanas in the analysis of consciousness and helps the apprehension of the much-discussed concept from a transpersonal point of view.

There is a marked difference in the methodology used in the West and in the East in analyzing consciousness. When occidental thinkers view consciousness as an epistemological concept, the oriental Darsanakaras analyze consciousness metaphysically relating to the Self, Self-knowledge, world, activity and freedom. Regarding the nature of consciousness Indian systems interpret consciousness variously as an epiphenomenon, a cognitive function, a quality of the Self, as the passive enjoyer and the essential nature of the Self. Though metaphysically we can find parallel lines of thought in the Upanishads and Advaita Vedanta, the subtle exposition of the ontological and hermeneutic nature of consciousness is unique to the Gita. With affinity to the Upanishadic metaphysics the Gita maintains that consciousness is the real nature of the Self. Consciousness is not an abstract quality but the true substance of the individual.

The germinal ideas of the elucidatory exposition of consciousness in the Gita can be traced to the Sruti – Upanishads. The Upanishads maintain consciousness as the ultimate reality. But the relation between consciousness, activity and freedom is given only in an aphoristic style. The Gita annuls this difficulty with its treatise on *Karma*. The study made in this book indicates that amongst the Darsanas the ideas elaborated in the Gita on consciousness is best expressed in Advaita Vedanta. Karel Werner says: "The view of the essential oneness behind phenomena, expressed fully and openly in the Upanishads, and made popular by the Bhagavad Gita, was later philosophically elaborated by

Samkara in his Advaita Vedanta system of thought."[3]

The Gita establishes the independence of consciousness as an apodeictic fact. Consciousness is not a quality emerging from a suitable collocation of physical elements. The Gita does not nullify the place of physical elements in relation to consciousness but clarifies the nature of material existence form a metaphysical hierarchy. Carvaka maintains consciousness to be an epiphenomenon that subsists with the body and disappears when the body disintegrates. According to the Gita, it is the *deha* – material body – that disintegrates. *Dehi* or the Self that propels the body is eternal. *Dehi* is Pure consciousness.

Buddhist schools define consciousness as a stream of thoughts, intelligence and emptiness. Both Madhyamika Buddhism and Sartrean Existentialism identify consciousness with voidness or nothingness so as to emphasize the intentionality of consciousness. They explain the real or the unreal existence of the world with reference to intentionality. The Gita recognizes intentionality as a cognitive process and does not give it ontological reality. The Gita accepts the tripartite factors involved in a cognitive act, which is intentional. Consciousness is intentional as far as there is a separation between object, subject and knowledge. But when ontologically examined this separation is not rigid but only adventitious and hence unreal. In reality, consciousness is not intentional but integral. The Gita introduces the term Yoga with this connotation. Consciousness integrates world as a continuum of existence. Hence the Gita advises to see oneself as the Self of every other being. The Gita posits

[3] Karel Werner, Yoga and Indian Philosophy, Ist ed. rpt., (Delhi: Motilal Banarsidass Pubs., 1980), p.4.

consciousness as the content of everything, in contrast to the contentless consciousness of Buddhist schools and Sartrean Existentialism.

By denominating consciousness as intentional, qualitative, or as one amongst the dual realities, we are faced with two major difficulties, as it is drawn in the present study. The first difficulty is in negotiating a stable relationship between the intentionality of consciousness and Pure Consciousness, or consciousness as quality and the substance, or consciousness as the passive principle and its active material counterpart. The second difficulty is in working out the nature of Self, from these premises. If consciousness is intentional then which is the primary truth or substance – consciousness or intentionality? The probe into this question ends up in a double-aspect answer, where we have to maintain the reality of one for explaining the reality of the other. The analysis of these situations that is made in the study of consciousness in the light of the Gita implies that such contention can land only in the relegation of consciousness to a teleological principle.

According to the Bhagavad Gita consciousness is that which is always existent. It is always present as the Self of the cognizer who intends objects. Consciousness is not telic but is ontic. Non-existence – *abhava* – cannot be attributed to the eternal – *Sat* – in terms of spatial or temporal order. Temporal limitation is negated when the Gita says in the second chapter that the Self is never non-existent. Spatial limitation is discarded when another verse of the second chapter asserts that consciousness as the Self in the bodies of all is eternally indestructible. Birth and death make their entry and exit in the abiding and continual presence of consciousness. The Self is not born nor does it ever perish. After having been it does not ceases to be. The Self is *avinasi* and *nitya*. No mode of material transformation affects the Self.

The Self as of the nature of consciousness is *sasvata* – eternal – and is not subject to conditional changes. The *Ksetrajna* – Self – is that which makes all changes knowable. Changes pertain to the field of matter – *ksetra*. *Ksetra* constitutes all that which falls in the field of consciousness. *Ksetrajna* is the *Upadrsta* – close witness, and *Anumanta* – sanctioner. The Gita distinctively defines the nature and function of consciousness and matter through the concepts of *Ksetra*, *Ksetrajna*, *Purusa* and *Purusottama*. By citing *Ksetrajna* as the Supreme *Purusa* – *Purusottama* – the Gita establishes the non-separate identity of individual consciousness and Supreme Consciousness. *Purusottama* is understood not merely as a theistic expression. It is an ontological term expressing the Absolute.

Darsanas interpret the relationship of matter with consciousness variously. Carvaka holds that matter is the raw material for the production of consciousness. Consciousness is an adventitious quality of the living body, as explained, by Nyaya Vaisesika. It is through the Self's association with the mind and body that consciousness results. Samkhya depicts consciousness and matter as of mutual co-existence. Neither is *Prakrti* dependent on *Purusa*, or *Purusa* dependent on *Prakrti*. Both are independent realities. From the Advaitic point of view *Prakrti* is *mithya* and *Purusa* is the *parmarthika satya* – the ontological real. Jainas maintain the relation between consciousness and matter as identity in difference. There is real identity between the Self and Karmic matter in the state of bondage. For Buddhists the Self as well as material objects are non-existent in the way we understand existence in common experience.

The Bhagavad Gita traces the union of consciousness and matter as of the nature of ignorance. Due to delusion, *prakrtisthapurusa* – the Self seated in the body – mistakes itself to be the doer and enjoyer. It is due to Self-ignorance that the existent nature of consciousness – *Purusa* – is superimposed on *Purusa*. Since the nature of the union of consciousness and matter is ignorance, the union does not affect consciousness. Samkaracarya vividly explains this feature in his commentary to the thirteenth chapter of the Gita.

Any contact or union of consciousness and matter to happen there should be a prior separation. Since the material world is non-separate from consciousness there is no contact between consciousness and matter. Matter is the creative appearance of consciousness. William Beidler remarks: "… the mark of the Gita … is that it avoids the schism between *Prakrti* and *Purusa*."[4] According to the Gita consciousness and matter do not have two ontologically different status. But they are phenomenologically explained as two. Hence if, from a nihilistic or absolutistic point of view, we fail to apprehend the world we miss the aesthetic aspect of consciousness. At the same time if the material world alone is admitted forsaking the whole, we miss to recognize the logical priority of consciousness. The Gita initiates a holistic vision in its chapters on *Vibhuti Yoga* and *Visvarupadarsana Yoga*. *Vibhuti Yoga* is the vision of consciousness in everything and *Visvarupadarsana Yoga* is the vision of

[4] William Beidler, The Vision of Self in Early Vedanta, (Delhi: Motilal Banarsidass Pubs., 1975), p.167.

everything in consciousness. A difficulty involved in the study of consciousness is that consciousness has to keep its relation with the mental states and yet retain its untouched purity. The Gita overcomes this difficulty by propounding the immanent nature of consciousness as *Prakrti* and its transcendence as *Purusottama*.

The concept of consciousness is best studied in the light of a theory of action. Activity is a standard that faces varied measurements in Indian Darsanas as well in the Western thought. Functionalist theories suggest a causal determinism regarding consciousness and action. For Carvaka, action is a hedonistic concept. For the Buddhists, activity is suffering and for the Jainas karmic matter forms the constituent of bondage. From the Samkhya Yoga perspective it is the activity of *Prakrti* that causes the bondage of *Purusa*.

The Gita initiates a deeper probe into the psychodynamics of action. The Gita theory of action can be rightly termed as ontological pragmatism. The Gita examines action from the psychology of the individual as well as from the ontology of the Self. George Mead correctly says: "The basic unit of psychology is to act – no longer Watsonian and behaviouristic, but the manifestation of self in historical time and social space. The act, however, becomes the true affirmation of the self only when it is the integrated expression of all the powers of the self."[5] The Gita accounts for *Karma* from its spiritualistic base. If *Karma* is solely a pragmatic notion then it will be nonetheless akin to the Carvaka hedonism. By elevating activity to the spiritualistic

[5] George Herbert Mead, The Philosophy of the Act, (Chicago: Chicago University Press, 1938), p.74.

realm, the Gita help to decipher the intricate psychology of the individual. Standing a step ahead to the Samkhya theory, the Gita theory of *gunas* gives a qualitative hierarchy of mental constitution. The *guna* or the psychological disposition of an individual can hind his awareness and at the same time can be a means to liberation by leading to the right performance of action.

Various theories equate activity differently with willed or voluntary action, intentional movement, result-oriented act etc. The general notion is that activity is that which causes bondage, and for the same season, abstention from activity is liberation. Jainas view *karmapudgala* as a quantitative hindrance to the liberation of the Self. For the Purvamimamsaka virtuous action is the door to heaven and vicious action pushes one to hell. They consider activity pragmatically by identifying it with ritualistic performance.

Jerome A. Shaffer enlists five theories of action of contemporary interest in his book "Philosophy of Mind". He stipulates that action can be intentional when it is prompted by a decisive mental state. But the cause of the intentional act is not an event or mental state but the agent himself. The performative theory of action holds that activity means to perform the act of assigning responsibility to the agent. Another theory is that activity is to be explained by citing a goal rather than a pre-existing state, event or agent. The contextual accounts of action claim that activity is to be conceived in a context of rules, norms or practices. The theory of action that is developed in Gita is a unique theory that comprehends the afore-mentioned connotations. The Gita enunciates *Karma* as a means to mental purity as well as the creative expression of a free mind. The Gita shows a rare insight into terms like agency, cause, mental state, action, inaction and non-action. A theory of action in general is centered on these terms. From the analysis of *Karma* given by the Gita, the subtlety of action is brought out in its entirety.

The primary question pertaining to the nature of action is that who intends action. The Gita propounds that the *Prakrti* does all forms of action. It is ones nature or *Prakrti* that operates as the direct and causative agent. Agency can never be attributed to the doer's Self which is a Pure Consciousness. It is due to Self-ignorance that one superimposes doership and enjoyership on the Self. The Gita theory of action is essentially connected with the theory of the Self. An unintegrated mind is constantly swayed by attachment or aversion to results. To such a mind discrimination between the Self and the not-Self is difficult. For a person with a tumultuous mind, Karma becomes a means to mental purity. Mental purity is gained by the composed reception of results. It is non-reaction to results. Acceptance of dualities marks their transcendence.

The Gita reiterates the importance of mental integration as the only means to win the meditative quality of mind. If work is done with expectation for the result then that will make work secondary thereby hampering its cumulative quality. Therefore action should not be intended from a pre-formative mental disposition but form an impartial awareness of the situation. The goal of action, then according to the Gita is *atmasuddhi* or mental integration.

The Gita lays down different contexts and norms for the performance of work, according to *adhikara-bhedha* or the mental disposition of different individuals. The activist is advised to work with non-expectation of results. To one who has won a non-reactive mind, the Gita advises to renounce the notion of agency. If renunciation of agency is difficult then he is called upon to dedicate all works before a higher and divine altar. The goal that is maintained by the Gita by all these norms is the exposure of ones mind to oneself. Such an exposition helps to negate the ideas and images superimposed on consciousness. G.E. Moore writes: "The moment we try to fix our attention upon consciousness and to see 'what', distinctly, it is, it seems to vanish: it seems as if we had before as a mere emptiness. When we try to introspect the sensation of blue, all we can see is the blue: the other element is as if it were disphanous."[6] In the process of introspection, the introspector itself is dissolved. This dissolution is not extinction but is the expansion of the agent. The Self-knower sees his Self in all and all in his Self. The Gita helps to orient a self-image in the light of a wholesome vision. Such a self-image will not be existentially alienated from the world but will integrate the essence of every being.

A theory of action in general considers renunciation as a term antithetical to activity. But the psychodynamics of the Gita brings forth the term *sanyasa* or renunciation as the essential definition of action. Action is not mere movement of the body and renunciation is not the physical giving up of activity. Renunciation or inaction is the essential nature of the Self. Action is the creative actualization of the individual. Renunciation is Self-knowledge in the sense it is the giving up of false images imposed on the Self. Action in the truest sense can be delivered

---

[6] G.E. Moore, Philosophical Studies, (London: Routledge and Kegan Paul LTd., 1922), p.25.

only by a renouncing mind. A renunciant does not lodge any kind of imaginations. His is a fluid personality which is creative every instant. Lawrence S. Kuble resonates this idea in his words: "... integrated, unified, all of a piece, one-pointed, totally organized in the service of the fascinating matter-in-hand. Creativeness is systemic; ie., a whole – or Gestalt – quality of the whole person ...."[7] The Gita depicts renunciation as the natural state of a *Karmayogi*. A contemporary analyst of Gita holds: "... splitting life three ways into knowledge, action, renunciation and making them into separate compartments is the hallmark of delusion."[8] Yet another radical postulate pronounced by the Gita is that activity is meditation. Work in its full quality can be initiated only by a non-reactive meditative mind. Psychologists like C.O. Evans also recognize the importance of meditation. Evans speaks about meditation using the term 'attention'. He says: "...attention not only produces an unprojected consciousness by the negative method of excluding certain elements form the forefront of consciousness but also produces unprojected consciousness in a positive manner through the dynamics of executive attention itself."[9] Meditation, to the Gita is not a passive process but a dynamic phenomenon. One can meditate only if he has gained thought integration by the right mode of work without attachment to the results. Activity and meditation are complementary to each other. Hence engaging in action is meditating on the Self. It is form the premise of this

---

[7] Lawrence S. Kuble, Explorations in Creativity, Eds. Ross L. Mooney and Taker A. Razik, (London: Harper and Row Pub, 1967), p.53.

[8] Som P. Ranchan, Revisioning Gita, (Delhi: Konark Pub., 1991), p.19.

[9] C.O. Evans, The Subject of Consciousness, (London: George Allen and Unwin Ltd., 1970), p.126.

postulate that the Gita declares *Dhyana* as *Yoga*. The Gita propounds a revolutionary theory of action by drawing continuity and simultaneity of Self-knowledge, Being and Activity.

Freedom is a concept that is studied concomitant to the study of consciousness. According to the Gita freedom is not a quality but he nature of the Self. Freedom is not becoming fee from action but being fee in action. Freedom is Self-knowledge. To the Gita, freedom lies not in the schizoid perception of choices but in their integral awareness. Being free in accepting the facts one transcends dualities. In contrast to intentional consciousness the Gita speaks of integral consciousness. Since consciousness is integral, it is not opposed to anything but to accommodate and encompass everything. The Self is not opposed to the not-Self. True freedom consists in the integral perception of the seeming contradictions. A free person is hence a *Yogi* and *Sthitaprajna*. Freedom is the nature of the Self-knower. At the same time freedom is reflected in his behavioral patterns. The Gita presents a behaviorist definition of a free individual by enlisting the attitudinal characteristics and responses of a *Yogi*, *Jnani*, *Gunatita*, *Bhakta* and *Sthitaprajna*. A comment made by Karel Werner is quotable at this juncture. He says: "Yoga ... is always a practical activity on the part of the whole individual. It appears to be a consciously adopted system of training or pattern of behavior aiming at enlarging or deepening man's direct experience of reality...."[10]

The exposition of consciousness in the Bhagavad Gita also

---

[10] Karel Wener, Yoga and Indian Philosophy, 1st ed. rpt., (Delhi: Motilal Banarsidass Pubs., 1980), p.XI.

exposes the nature of the functionalistic analysis of consciousness. Functionalistic analysis begins from the conception that consciousness is a psychic function. Theories accessory to it hold the Self to be the ego or non-ego. The Gita cautions these attempts. The riddles which are faced in the study of consciousness can be solved only if it is understood as the cognizer's Self and not as a cognitive function. The Self is not the ego or non-ego but is Pure Consciousness. Ego and non-ego are mental constructions. Even when it is dissected as a cognitive act, consciousness is present as the cognizer's Self, illumining the analysis. The Self as consciousness reveals both the ego and non-ego. What we understand from the metapsychology of the Gita is that, since consciousness is the most intimate Self, it can never be comprehended in objective terms. The paradox involved in the analysis of consciousness, mind and the cognition of the world, emerges form the unscrupulous superimposing of the objective and subjective realms. As a solution for the paradox, Gita gives neither an idealistic nor a realistic interpretation of consciousness. To the realist the Gita presents consciousness idealistically and to the idealist realistically. The Gita dissolves the bifurcation itself in conceptualizing consciousness and matter.

The Gita gives utmost importance to the analysis of the questioner than to the question. The answer to the question is apprehended n the analysis of the questioner. The conceptual study of consciousness in the light of the Gita has a definite scope in psychoanalytic explorations and experiments. The Gita has a stupendous role in the field of therapy too. Recent studies unanimously agree that there is a relationship between thoughts and the emotional disposition of the individual. The Gita enunciates the technique of *karmayoga* in such a manner that it will help the cultivation of positive emotions by reducing negative emotions. The negative tendencies of the mind such as frustration, anxiety etc, is annulled by the positive mode of acceptance. The Gita theory of meditation helps to strengthen the mental faculty by the therapy of watching thoughts. In short the Gita concept of consciousness will help to make a deep and fruitful probe into the real nature of the Being.

10

Epilogue

mamedamitham ca tathedamidrsam
tathahamevam na paro na vanyadha
vimutataivam na janasya kalpana sada
same brahmani cadvaye sive

Concepts of people such as 'mine', 'this', 'thus', 'this is so',
'I am so', 'another is not so', etc. are all due to delusion.
They are never in Pure Consciousness, which is auspicious,
the same in all and without a second.
Upadesa-Sahasri of Sankaracarya: X.11

Brain studies, cognitive sciences and cultural studies, jointly in the last ten years, have redefined the complexity of 'consciousness' by factorising two otherwise less important categories. These categories are: (i) analysis and understanding of the way we approach the problem itself, and, (ii) how that influences our definition of the problem. The major epistemological worry faced equally by the empirical analyst as well as the philosopher and psychologist is based on the central feature of 'consciousness' that is 'experience'. *Prima facie*, this worry could be described as how to have a theoretical explanation for the mutual influence of neural events and subjective experiences and which one (neural events or subjective experience) is the defining characteristic of consciousness. Nevertheless, it is recognised that the field of consciousness studies is no more a school of reductionism, whether it is the case of understanding segregated mechanisms for neural events or mystifying experiences under unexplained 'transcendences'.

Binding experiences is the single most issue in the centre of focus in the last decade of discussions on 'consciousness' crossing disciplines: neurobiological, quantum mechanical, computational, theoretical, psychological etc. Though the details of what constitutes 'experience' differ from method and perspective, a consensus has emerged that (i) to explain 'consciousness' is to explain 'experience'; (ii) to explain experience is to explain its unity and binding nature. Following this preliminary consensus, however implicit it was, many discussions take place from the first, second and third-person perspectives, though the mainstream discussion is still dominated to a greater extent by third-person approaches.

Today in consciousness studies, interestingly, it is seen that an attempt to understand 'experience', such as simple physical pain or much complex psychological pain, will have to cross the epistemological barriers of hierarchies and causal relationships, demanding a non-linear path. The classical description of consciousness as 'unitary' has even evolved, to accommodate the questions emerging in interdisciplinary dialogues, to present the term 'self' which was once considered metaphysical, but very much scientific today. The epistemological transition, however implicit it is, is from a third-person perspective to a first-person perspective. It is from linear thinking to non-linear thinking. The extent of the meanings imputed to 'consciousness' hence often crosses the empirical limits and sometimes becomes diffused to qualitative experiential descriptions.

A distinct trend in 'consciousness' discussions started with the theory of 'easy problems and hard problem' by David Chalmers (1995, Chalmers) which for the first time in the Western world made a semantic distinction between 'being conscious' and 'what is responsible for consciousness'. Both experimental and cognitive science recognised the strong presence of an 'explanatory gap' (1987, Jackendoff). Though the mainstream approaches still remain reductionistic, or at least dualistic in explanations, the complexity of 'consciousness' and its unique nature in contradistinction with any other phenomenon in the lab is being largely accepted. This acceptance has inspired theories favouring complex cognitive and social functions, neural and subneural structures, system-environment interaction etc. in order to fill the 'explanatory gap' and place 'consciousness' in its deserved seat.

Many views that are currently discussed and debated no more fall into a strict division of reductionistic and non-reductionistic approaches. The reason could be the recognition, in these approaches, of a distinct characteristic of 'consciousness', namely that it is not strictly linear. Perhaps, the need for bridging first person and third person worlds also discourages such classical schismatic approaches. One of the prominent views is that there is a distinction between subjective conscious experience and the biological mechanisms responsible, and their mutual non-reducibility based on the position that first-person data cannot be fully understood in terms of third-person data (2000, Chalmers). Biological explanations have also factored a hierarchy of functions in order to explain consciousness. One such view holds that consciousness is a highly complex motor response occupying 'the uppermost echelon of a hierarchy having the primitive reflex at its base' and that which 'arises from the systems' interactions with the environment'(2001,Cotterill).

Approaches to explain consciousness as an epiphenomenon, but not in the classical sense of emerging from a physical composite, also take into account that the primary problem for explanation is more than a theoretical divide between the empirical and the subjective aspects of consciousness. Therefore, some of these approaches hold that consciousness 'is formed in the dynamic interrelation of self and other, and therefore is inherently intersubjective' (2001,Thompson) or that it is a system of interactions between the animal and its environment and that it is not located in the brain (1991,Varela et.al.). Explanations which address the psychological and social dimensions of consciousness hold that consciousness is 'some pattern of activity in neurons' (1997, Churchland) or that it is best understood in terms of varying degrees of 'intentionality' (1991, Dennett), and in terms of 'memes' which are the units of cultural evolution (1976, Dawkins; 1999, Blackmore).

Yet another school of thought that strongly upholds the need for finding neural correlates for the subjective components of consciousness is interested in the scientific exploration of meditation techniques. This school acknowledges the contribution of Eastern philosophy and wisdom traditions for a very specific role, which is, towards understanding and practicing meditation techniques for transcendental and extra-ordinary states of consciousness and experiences (1999, Shear).

It is interesting to see that much of these discussions consider consciousness as a phenomenon to be understood and that it is much within the scope for investigation and dialogue like any other phenomenon. There is a degree of equal balance between two basic explanations/approaches for consciousness such as (i) neural-physical-social correlates (ii) extra-ordinary and meditational (transcendental) experiences mostly validated by neural or other third-person data.

'Consciousness' has become the umbrella term for debating many issues crossing disciplines yet connecting disciplines. This is interesting. Because, given the variety and differences in the themes and ideas for human discourse, to have a common factor in our dialogues seems to be difficult. The route and possible result of this dialogue is to connect and joint various streams of thought whether, empirical or intuitive, experimental or theoretic, in order to map and place consciousness. On a scale of meta-analysis, this is a linear and horizontal approach, essentially because our dialogues start from third-person working definitions we assume (however different they are) of 'consciousness'. Nevertheless, contributions made by dialogues which could be clubbed under the term 'consciousness' is eventful, since they are an attempt to harmonize and integrate otherwise divergent human thinking.

The Problematic of Experience

The questions we ask about consciousness have their bases on different kinds of experience, whether it is dream, states of mind, memory, pain (physical and mental) etc. But the analyses for these questions are based on segregated information about behavior or brain events and processes. Therefore the answers to these questions are given in terms of neural correlates and neural information processing and models thereof. This method takes away the essential aspect of 'being conscious' or 'consciousness' that is the 'person'. Questions asked as a result of first-person experience are given answers that are founded on third-person information. Essentially, there is a gap between the problematic of conscious experience and the attempts to address it, which I call as the 'harder problem' (Menon, 2001). The standards and criteria that we have followed for objective understanding are most often the criteria for third-person information. This method helps us build technologies and understand abnormalities transcending individual existences. The first-person qualitative methods give us opportunities to be sensitive to the individual nature, psychology, expressions and uniqueness.

If both methods are important then how is the 'harder problem' addressed? I do not have a ready answer for this question. But we could attempt a method that will not be mutually converting (information to experience and experience to information), reductionistic or solipsistic. Meaning, we should avoid the presumption of the larger picture of consciousness emerging out of solely by third-person methods or first-person methods. The 'harder problem' is not a question, I think, to be answered completely, or a complete theory about consciousness. Rather, it is the ontological essence of 'consciousness' that need to be addressed which ever method we adopt. This will help us *see* something more than or beyond third-person information and first-person experience.

I think there is an interesting and serious turn taking place in the current discussions on consciousness. This turn is based on and compelled by the intractable relationship of 'consciousness' with 'experience'. The nearest empirical idea for the unity and subjective nature of consciousness is 'experience'. Hence the scientific focus on 'experience'. The interesting part of the discussions is that though there is a recognition of experience as vital in the study of consciousness, the attempt itself is to strip 'experience' off the qualities which would make it of experiential nature (unitary and subjective) and study it on the basis of empirical standards such as causal connections, neural influences, neural locations etc. I am not suggesting that brain research is not needed or even less important. Certainly, it is very significant in its own right. But if our guidelines and methods are not based on our basic premise to study consciousness (experience, which is unitary and subjective) then certainly we cannot make a claim that brain studies apart from giving new knowledge about brain functions would also lead to a cŏmplete theory of consciousness. The puzzle in the current discussions on consciousness is that of the persistent conflict between epistemology and phenomenology.

Categories of Thinking

There is a general agreement that it is interestingly perplexing to be conscious and yet not to understand what brings about the phenomenon of consciousness. Why is it perplexing?

Our knowledge systems are mostly based on cognising the 'other', or at least about an objective world of information or experience that belongs to the 'other'. Mostly, we feel comfortable when prior objective knowledge is available about anything that we experience. To have an experience and still not to know 'how' and 'why' it came about is an intellectual discomfort for us. It cannot be that we do have an experience but still we do not know 'what' is there or 'how' it is there. The first-person experience gets a larger agreement of being natural or normal or not mystical only if it is validated by third person analysis and representation. The usual way of discourse for us cannot approve of 'having something' without knowing 'what it is' or 'how it came'. Is third-person representation and consensus necessary for all human expressions, is the question. Perhaps, we can have something, have many applications of it, without having the final third-person representation of it in terms of causal and local explanations.

The availability of 'consciousness' for our most intimate experiences and yet our inability to understand it *completely* in terms of third person information makes us think that 'consciousness' is a complex phenomenon, and that its complexity need to be addressed. We understand 'complexity' as an intrinsic characteristic of the 'other', the object of investigation, which we attempt to study. This notion of ours about 'complexity' is to be examined.

When we reduce the different expressions and features of a phenomenon to one or two or to some quantity, we have to remember that it certainly is the only possible way of understanding something so multifaceted and simultaneous, and therefore could be called as a simple method, but need not be the final and complete method, and not the complete third person representation of the first person phenomenon. Complexity could be the characteristic feature needed for the design for providing third-person representation. Perhaps, what we distinguish as 'simple' and 'complex' are not the intrinsic characteristics of the object of investigation, but the categories of thinking and understanding that we have formed according to the third-person information supplied to us by the tools we have designed. Hence, the question 'should design and tool be complex' becomes important.

Moreover, the standard scientific criteria of replication cannot be applied since the third-person representation cannot be a replica of the complete first-person phenomenon but only a *representation* of it from a particular framework that follows certain epistemological and empirical or theoretical parameters. If consciousness cannot be understood without looking at 'experience' then certainly experience cannot be reduced for convenient reductive (physical, psychoanalytic and cultural) methods of understanding. It will have to be open for a variety of meanings validated from first-person perspectives. This will question the scientific monopoly of explaining consciousness in a singular way from a reductive standpoint, and will encourage scientific methods to reexamine the normative criteria for 'truth' and 'reality'.

Dialogues on Larger Goals

According to Chalmersian theory of 'easy problems and hard problem' first-person data cannot be subjected to the standard method of reductive explanation. This theory also questions the basic fact of consciousness, that is, why is the performance of neural functions accompanied by subjective experience?

The 'why' question here is pertinent to understand the bases on which we found our primary, secondary and tertiary questions and methods for understanding 'consciousness'. Why 'why'? The 'why' question ('why neural functions are accompanied by subjective experience') assumes:

(i) Consciousness as a separate 'something' borne or unusual or non-natural,

(ii) (Neural) functions as basically having only mechanistic meanings, and,

(iii) Subjective experience as not the intrinsic nature of consciousness.

These criticisms, which are indirectly upheld by the camp of anti-reductionism, stem from the basic conflict between 'experience' and 'cognition'. The normative criteria for establishing 'truth' start from the objective reduction of whatever is posited. Here subjective experience falls out of normative standards for agreeing upon something as valid. So, the why-question as well as the assumptions arises from the conflict we encounter between epistemological necessity and experiential primacy. Both seem to be unavoidable and co-existent in human discourse.

It is difficult, if not impossible, to resolve a conflict if both the components of it are equally important. But the recognition of this unavoidable conflict itself, in our theories and models, will help us to widen the scope of investigation and prevent de-humanisation of the goals we seek for fulfilment. After all, both through third-person information and first-person experience what we ultimately seek are personal growth and health, co-existence and sharing, and a continuous exploration into the unknown and the unpredictable.

A prologue before we set forth the theorisation and definition of the problem will be helpful for a student of 'consciousness'. This prologue will elucidate the primary division of a set of agenda based on direct first-person experience and the consensus we share on perceived facts. The primary division will be of the meaning and scope of 'awareness of something' and 'awareness by itself'.

What exactly is 'self awareness'? It is awareness of something. It is either the awareness of: (i) the world outside, such as other states of mind, objects, etc. (ii) the world inside, such as 'my emotions', 'my perceptions', 'my body', 'my identity' etc. The 'world inside' cannot be understood without the intervention of self-reflection and self-participation. What is 'awareness itself'? Awareness itself can be seen as (i) uniting discrete thoughts, and the two worlds (inside and outside), (ii) as meta-awareness of the two (inside and outside world) awareness-es, (iii) as pure I-ness. Unless a distinct distinction is made of these different categories of existence for our thinking and analysis we will end up searching the needle in the same haystack for centuries without realising that the problem is not just the subtleness of the subject of our inquiry but our own inability to design a comprehensive search. The design of the comprehensive search is important because the way we search for it is going to alter the presence of it in the invincible heap. What is the relation between consciousness and happiness, consciousness and action, consciousness and freedom of will, consciousness and transformation of experience, consciousness and spiritual experience – these and many other questions that give focus for human expressions and possibilities from a transpersonal and humanistic standpoint will be significant in working out a road map for consciousness studies.

References:

Daniel Dennett, *Consciousness Explained*, London: Penguin Books, 1991

David Chalmers, 'The Puzzle of Conscious Experience', *Scientific American*, December 1995, pp.62-68

David Chalmers, *The Conscious Mind: In search of a fundamental theory*, Oxford University Press, 2000

Evan Thompson, 'Empathy and Consciousness', *Journal of Consciousness Studies*, vol.8, No.5-7, 2001, pg.1

Francisco Varela, Evan Thompson & E. Rosch, *The Embodied Mind: Cognitive Science and Human Experience*, Cambridge: MIT Press, 1991

Francisco Varela & Jonathan Shear, Ed. *The View From Within: First Person approaches to consciousness*, England: Imprint Academic, 1999

Paul S. Churchland & T. J. Sejnowski, *The Computational Brain*, Cambridge: MIT Press, 1997

Ray S. Jackendoff, *Consciousness and the Computational Mind*. Bradford: MIT Press, 1987.

Richard Dawkins, *The Selfish Gene*, Oxford University Press, 1976

Rodney M.J. Cotterill, 'Evolution, Cognition and Consciousness', *Journal of Consciousness Studies*, vol.8, No.2, 2001, pg.4

Sangeetha Menon, 'Towards a Sankarite approach to consciousness studies', *Journal of Indian Council of Philosophical Research*, Vol. XVIII, No.1, January-March 2001, pp.95-111

Susan Blackmore, *The Meme Machine*, Oxford University Press, 1999

11

Bibliography

Abhedananda. The Upanisadic Doctrine of the Self: An Analytical study of the nature of the Self as revealed in Upanisads. New Delhi: Oriental Publishers and Distributors, 1978.

Advarin, Dharmaraj. Vedanta Paribhasa. Ed and Tr. S.S. Suryanarayana Sastri. Adyar: The Adyar Library, 1942.

Agraval, M.M. The Philosophy of Non-attachment. Delhi: Motilal Banarsidass Pubs., 1982.

Aniruddha, Abhidhamatthasangaha. Tr. Bhikku J. Kashyap. The Abhidhamma Philosophy. Delhi: Bharatiya Vidya Prakashan, 1982.

Anirvan. Buddhi Yoga of the Gita and other Essays. New Delhi: Biblia Impex Pvt. Ltd.,1983.

Arapura, J.G. Hermeneutical Essays on Vedantic Topics. Delhi: Motilal Banarsidass Pubs., 1986.

Arnold, Edwin. The Song Celestial Shrimad Bhagavad Gita. New Delhi: Interprint, 1978.

Asvaghosa. Buddhacarita. Tr. E.H. Johnston. Acts of the Buddha. Delhi: Motilal Banarsidass Pubs., 1972.

Atreya, Jagat Prakash. Mind and its Functions in Indian Thought. New Delhi: Classical Pubs. Co., 1985.

Bahm, Archie J. Tr. The Bhagavad Gita or The Vision of Krishna. Bombay: Somaiya Pubs. Pvt. Ltd., 1970.

Bahm, Archie J. Yoga Union with the Ultimate 1st Ind. ed. New Delhi: Arnold Heinemann Publishers, 1978.

Baldev, Raj Sharma. The Concept of Atman in the Principal Upanisads. New Delhi: Dinesh Publications, 1972.

Beidler, William. The Vision of Self in Early Vedanta. Delhi: Motilal Banarsidass Pubs., 1975.

Belvalkar, S.K. and Ranade R.D. History of Indian Philosophy. Vol.1 and 2. Poona: Bilvakunja Publishing House, 1927.

Besant, Annie. A study in Karma. Adyar: The Theosophical Publishing House, 1975.

Besant, Annie. A Study in Consciousness: A Contribution to the Signs of Psychology. Adyar: The Theosophical Publishing House, 1980.

Besant, Annie. The Wisdom of the Upanisads. 6h ed. Adyar: The Theosophical Publishing House, 1974.

Bhattacharya, Sibajiban. 'The Nature of Consciousness'. Bulletin of the Ramakrishna Mission Institute of Culture. Vol.XLI. No.11. Calcutta: Ramakrishna Mission, 1990.pp.267-273.

Bodhananda, Swami. Rishi Vision. New Delhi: Sambodh Foundation, 1992.

Bodhananda, Swami. Meditations. New Delhi: Sambodh Foundation, 1991.

Bodhananda, Swami. Happiness Unlimited: Self-unfoldment in an interactive world. Delhi: BlueJay Books, 2003.

Bowes, Pratima. Consciousness and Freedom. London: Methuen and Co. Ltd., 1971.

Brentano, Franz. Sensory and Noetic Consciousness: Psychology From an Empirical Stand point. Tr. Margarette Schattle and Linda C. McAlister. London: Routledge and Kegan Paul Ltd., 1981.

Broad, C.D. Mind and its Place in Nature. London: Routledge and Kegan Paul, 1925.

Campbell, Joseph. Ed. Spirit and Nature: Papers from the Eranos Year Books. Vol. 2. London: Routledge and Kegan paul Ltd., 1955.

Capra, Fritjof. Uncommon Wisdom. London: Century Hatchinson's Ltd., 1988.

Chaitanya, Krishna. Freedom and Transcendence. New Delhi: Manohar Pubs., 1982.

Chatterjee, A.K. Readings on Yogacara Buddhism. Varanasi: Centre of Advanced Study in Philosophy. Banares Hindu University, 1971.

Chatterji, Pritibhushan. 'Consciousness in the Philosophy of Jean Paul Sartre'. Bulletin of th Ramakrishna Mission Institute of Culture. Vol.XXI. No. 1 and 5, Calcutta: Ramakrishna Mission, 1970.

Chennakesavan, Sarasvati. 'Mind and Consciousness A Comparison of Indian and Western views'. Philosophical Quarterly. Vol.26, 1954.

Chennakesavan, Sarasvati. Concept of Mind in Indian Philosophy. 2nd rev. ed. Delhi: Motilal Banarsidass Pubs., 1980.

Chethimattam, John B. Consciousness and Reality. Bangalore: Dharmaram College, 1967.

Churchland, Paul M. A Neurocomputational Perspective The Nature of Mind and the Structure of Science. London: The MIT Press, 1975.

Coomaraswamy, Ananda K. Buddha and the Gospel of Buddhism. 2nd ed. New Delhi: Munshiram Manoharlal Pvt. Ltd., 1985.

Date, V.H. Vedanta Explained Samkara's Commentary on the Brahmasutras. Vol.I Bombay: Booksellers Pub. Co., 1954.

Datta, Dhirendra Mohan. Six ways of Knowing. London: George Allen and Unwin Ltd., 1932.

Davids, Rhys. The Birth of Indian Psychology and its Development in Buddhism: A Rewritten and Enlarged Edition of Buddhist Psychology. London: The Quest, 1978.

Davids, Rhys. A Manual of Buddhism. 1st Ind. ed. New Delhi: Oriental Books Reprint Corporation, 1978.

Davidson, Julian M. and Richard J. Davidson. Eds. The Psychobiology of Consciousenss. New York: Plenum Press, 1980.

Davies, John. The Bhagavad Gita. New Delhi: Ess Ess Pub., 1983.

Dayananda, Swami. The Teaching of the Bhagavad Gita. New Delhi: Vision Books, 1988.

Desai, Mahadev. The Gita according to Gandhi. 5th imp. Ahmedabad: Navajivan Publishing House, 1970.

De Silva, Padmasiri. An Introduction to Buddhist Psychology.

London: The Macmillan Press Ltd., 1979.

Deussen, Paul. Outlines of Indian Philosophy. 1st Ind. rpt. New Delhi: Ess Ess Pubs., 1976.

Deussen, Paul. The Systems of Vedanta. Tr. Charles Johnson. Chicago: The Open Court Publishing Co., 1912.

Deussen, Eliot. Advaita Vedanta: A Philosophical Reconstruction. Honolulu: East-West Center Press, 1969.

Devaraja, N.K. An Introduction to Samkara's Theory of Knowledge. 2nd rev. ed. Delhi: Motilal Banarsidass Pubs., 1972.

Easvaran, Eknath. The Bhagavad Gita for Daily Living. Vols. 1,2 and 3. California: The Blue Mountain Centre of Meditation, 1984.

Edgerton, Franklin. The Bhagavad Gita. Harvard: Harvard University Press, 1952.

Edwards, Paul. A Modern Introduction to Philosophy Readings From Classical and Contemporary Sources. London: George Allen and Unwin Ltd., 1957.

Edwards, Paul. Ed. The Encyclopedia of Philosophy. Vol.17. rpt. ed. New York: Macmillan Publishing Co. Inc. and The Free Press, 1972.

Eliade, Koelman M. Gasper. Patanjali Yoga. Poona: Pontifical Atheneum, 1970.

Eliade, Mircea. Yoga Immortality and Freedom. 2nd ed. Tr. Willard R. Trask. New Jersey: Princeton University Press, 1969.

Evans, C.O. The Subject of Consciousness. London: George Allen and Unwin Ltd., 1970.

Ewing, A.C. The Fundamental Questions of Philosophy. London: Routledge and Kegan Paul Ltd., 1951.

Ey, Henri. Consciousness: A Phenomenological Study of Being Conscious and Becoming Conscious. Tr. John F. Flodstrom. Bloomington: Indiana University Press, 1978.

Frankl, Victor E. Psychotherapy and Existentialism: Selected Papers on Logotherapy. New York: Washington Square Press, 1967.

Feurstein, George. Tr. The Bhagavad Gita. New Delhi: Arnold-Heinemann (India) Pvt. Ltd., 1980.

Gajendragadkar, P.B. Ed. The Classical Upanisads. Vol.1. Bombay: Bharatiya Vidya Bhavan, 1981.

Gambhirananda, Swami. Tr. Brahma-Sutra Bhasya of Samkaracarya. 4th ed. Calcutta: Advaita Ashrama, 1984.

Gandhi, Kishore. Ed. The Evolution of Consciousness. New Delhi: National Publishing House, 1983.

Gispert-Sauch. G. Bliss in the Upanisads: An Analytical Study of the Origin and Growth of the Vedic Concept of Ananda. New Delhi: Oriental Publishers and Distributors, 1977.

Gosh, Jagneswar. Samkhya and Modern Thought. Calcutta: The Book Co. Ltd., 1930.

Glover, Jonathan. The Philosophy of Mind. London: Oxford University Press, 1991.

Gooch, Stan. Total Man: Notes Towards an Evolutionary Theory of Personality. New York: Penguin Press, 1972.

Gough, Archibald Edward. The Philosophy of the Upanisads. 1st Ind. rpt. Delhi: Ess Ess Pubs., 1975.

Govinda, Lama Anagarika. The Psychological Attitude of Early Buddhist Philosophy. London: Rider and Co., 1969.

Griffith, R.T.H. The Hymns of the Rgveda. Vols. 1 and 2. Varanasi: Chowkhambha Sanskrit Series, 1963.

Grimes, John. 'Some Problems in the Epistemology of Advaita'. Philosophy East and West: A Quarterly of Comparative Philosophy. Vol.XLI.No.3. Ed. Roger T. Ames. Honolulu: The University of Hawai Press, 1991.pp.291-301.

Guenon, Rene. Man and His Becoming. Tr. Richard C. Nicholson. London: Luzac and Co., 1945.

Gundappa, G.V. Advaita Faith and Practice. Bombay: Bhartatiya Vidya BhavaN, 1975.

Hall, Fitz-Edward. Ed. An Introduction to Sankhya-Pravacana Bhasya: A Commentary on the Aphorism of the Hindu Atheistic Philosophy. Delhi: Eastern Book Linkers, 1986.

Hill, Douglass. The Bhagavad-Gita. 3rd imp. London: Oxford University Press, 1969.

Hospers, John. An Introduction to Philosophical Analysis. New Jersey: Prentice Hall Inc., 1964.

Hume, Robert Ernest. The Thirteen Principal Upanisads. 2nd rev.ed. Delhi: Oxford University Press. 1931.

Humphrey, Nicholas. Consciousness Regained: Chapters In Philosophical Psychology. Oxford: Oxford University Press, 1983.

Hussain, Shamshad. Creativity Concept and Finding. Delhi: Motilal Banarsidass, 1988.

Husserl, Edmund. Ideas. General Introduction to Pure Phenomenology. Tr.W.R. Royce Gibson. Lodnon: George Allen and Unwin Ltd., 1985.

Indich, Williams M. Consciousness I Advaita Vedanta. Delhi: Motilal Banarsidass Pubs., 1980.

Isherwood, Christopher. Ed. Vedanta for the Western World. London: George Allen and Unwin Ltd., 1963.

Isherwood, Christopher. Iyer, .K.V. Advaita Vedanta. New York: Asian Publishing House, 1964.

Jha, Ganganath Mahamahaopaddhyaya. The Prabhakara School of Purva-Mimamsa. Delhi: Motilal Banarsidass Pubs., 1978.

Jnaneshwari. A Song-Sermon on the Bhagavad Gita. 6th Ind. rpt. Vols.1 and 2. tr. V.G. Pradhan. Ed. M.M. Lambert. Bombay: Blackie and Son (India) Pvt Ltd., 1972.

Joad, C.E.M. An Introduction to Contemporary Knowledge. Lodon: E.J. Arnold and Son Ltd., n.d.

Joseph, Martin P. The Bhagavad Gita. Goa: Franciscan Brothers, 1978.

Kapila. The Samkhya Philosophy of Kapila. Tr. Jag Mohan Leval. Edinburg: Orpheus Publishing House, 1921.

Kaveeshwar, G.N. The Ethics of the Gita. Delhi: Motilal Banrsidass Pubs., 1971.

Keith, Berriedale A. A History of the Samkhya Philosophy. 1st Ind. rpt. Delhi: Nag Pubs.,1975.

Keith, Berriedale A. The Krama Mimamsa. 2nd ed. New Delhi: Oriental Books Rpt. Corporation, 1978.

Kline, George L. 'Present, Pst and Future as a Categorical terms and the Fallacy of Actual Future'. Ed. Judge P. Dougherty. The Review of Metaphysics a Philosophical Quarterly. Vol.XL.No.2 Washington: Catholic University of America, 1986. pp.219-225.

Kunhan, Raja. C. Some fundamental Problems in Indian Philosophy. Delhi: Motilal Banarsidass Pubs., 1960.

Kyokai, Bukkyo Dendo. The Teaching of Buddha. Tokyo: Buddhist Promoting Foundation, 1985.

Lal, R.B. The Gita in the Light of Modern Science. Bombay: Somaiya Publicaitons, 1970.

Lloyd. The Man of Reason: Male and Female in Western Philosophy, London: Mehtuen and Co. Ltd., 1984.

Lussna, G. 'The Concept of Awareness in the Work of R.P. Kaushik'. East and West Quarterly. New Series. Vol.34. No.1-3. Italy: Institute Ittaliano peril Medio ed estremo Oriente, 1984. pp.267-299.

Lycan, William G. Consciousness. London: The MIT Press, n.d.

Madvacarya. Sarva-Darsana Sangraha. Tr. E.B. Cowell and A.E. Gough. Ed. K.L. Joshi. Ahmedabad: Primal Pubs., 1981.

Mahadevan, T.M.P Ed. Spiritual Metaphysics: Essays in Mysticism and Metaphysics. New Delhi: Arnold-Heinemann, 1975.

Mahadevan, T.M.P. Superimposition in Advaita. 4th ed. New Delhi: Arnold Heinemann Pubs., 1976.

Mahajan, S.N. The Science of Yoga and Consciousness. Agra: Y.K. Pubs., 1987.

Mahajan, Yogi. Geeta Enlightened. 2nd rev. ed. rpt. Delhi: Motilal Banarsidass Pubs., 1991.

Majumdar, Abhaykumar. The Sankhya Conception of Personality or A New Interpretation of the Sankhya Philosophy. Ed. Jatindra Kumar Majumdar. Delhi: Bharatiya Book Corpora-tion, 1981.

Makkreel, Rudolf A. 'Hermeneutics and the Limits of Consciousness. Nous. Vol.XXI.No.1. Ed. Hector-Neri Castaneda. Indiana: Indiana Unversity, 1987. pp.8-12.

Marcaurelle, Roger. Sankara's Hermeneutics on Renunciation in the Gita. Ed. Aravind Sharma. New Essays in the Bhagavad Gita. Bombay: Books and Books, 1987.

Mehta, Rohit. From Mind to Super Mind: A Commentary on the Bhagavad Gita. Bombay: P.C. Manaktala and Sons, 1966.

Merleau-Ponty, M. Phenomenology of Perception. 4th imp. Tr. Colin Smith. London: Routledge and Kegan Paul Ltd. 1967.

Minor, N. Robert. Bhagavad Gita: An Exegetical Commetnary. New Delhi: Heritage Pubs., 1982.

Mishra, S. Ramamurti. The Text book of Yoga Psychology. New York: The Indian Press Inc., 1963.

Mohanty, Phani. The Concept of Purusa nad Purushottama in The Commentary of Samkara on the Prasthanatrayi. Delhi: Grag Publications, 1986.

Mesney, Rose L and Taker A. Razik. Explorations in Creativity. London: Harper and Row Pubs., 1967.

Muller, Max F. Three Lectures on the Vedanta Philosophy. London: Longmans Green and Co., 1894.

Muller, Max F. The Six Systems of Indian Philosophy. 1st Ind. ed. New Delhi: Associated Publishing House, 1973.

Muni Shastri, Devendra. A Source Book of Jaina Philosophy. Tr. T.G. Kalghatgi. Ed.T.S. Devodoss, Udaipur: Sri Tarak Guru Jain Granthalaya, 1983.

Munshi, K.M. Bhagavad Gita and Modern Life. Bombay: Bharatiya Vidya Bhavan, 1970.

Murty, K. Satchidananda. Revelation and Reason in Advaita Vedanta. New York: Coloumbia University Press, 1961.

Newman, A. 'The Causal Relation and its Terms'. Mind: A Quarterly review of Philosophy. Vol.XCVII.No.388. Ed. Simon Blackburn. Oxford: Oxford University Press, 1988. pp.529-550.

Otto, Herbert R. and James A. Teudio. Eds. Perspectives on Mind. Dordrecht: D. Reidel Publishing Co., 1988.

Potter, Karl. Presuppositions of Indian Philosophy. Englewood: Prentice-Hall Inc., 1963.

Potter, Karl. Gen.Ed. Encyclopedia of Indian Philosophers. Vols.1,2,3 and 4 Delhi: Motilal Banarsidass Pubs., 1987.

Prasad, Jwala. History of Indian Epistemology 2nd ed. Delhi: Munshiram Manoharlal Pubs., 1958.

Radhakrishnan, S. Tr. Brahmasutra. London: George Allen and Unwin, 1960.

Radhakrishnan, S. Indian Philosophy. Vols. 1 amd 2. centenary ed. Delhi: Oxford University Press, 1989.

Radhakrishnan, S. The Principal Upanisads. Centenary ed. Delhi: Oxford University Press, 1989.

Radhakrishnan, S. The Bhagavad Gita. 6th Ind. rpt. Bombay: Blackie and Son (India) Ltd., 1977.

Radhakrishnan, S. Essentials of Psychology With a New Forewood by S. Gopal. Delhi: Oxford University Press, 1988.

Ranade, R.D. Vedanta: The Culmination of Indian Thought. Bombay: Bharatiya Vidya Bhavan, 1970.

Ranchan, Som P. Revisioning Gita. Delhi: Konark Pubs., 1991.

Radhakrishnan, S. New Sights on Gita. New Delhi: Ajanta Publications, 1987.

Rangacarya, M. The Sarva Siddhanta-Sangraha of Sankaracharya, New Delhi: Ajay Book Service, 1983.

Rao, Ramachandra S.K. Development of Psychological Thought in India. Mysore: Kavyalaya Pub., 1962.

Roer, E. The Twelve Principal Upanisads. Vol.7. 2nd ed. Adyar: The Theosophical Publishing House, 1931.

Russell, Bertrand. The Analysis of Mind. 10th imp. London: George Allen and Unwin Ltd., 1971.

Sachdeva, I.P. Yoga and Depth Psychology with Special Reference to the Integration of Personlaity. Delhi: Motilal Banarsidass Pubs., 1978.

Safaya, Raghunath. Indian Psychology. New Delhi: Munshiram Manoharlal Pubs. Pvt. Ltd., 1976.

Samkaracarya. Vivekacudamoni. Tr.P. Samkaranarayanan. Bombay: Bharatiya Vidya Bhavan, 1979.

Samkaracarya. Drg-Drsya Viveka. Tr. Swami Nikhilananda. 6th ed. Mysore: Sri Ramakrishna Ashrama, 1976.

Samkaracarya. Aparokshanabhuti, 7th imp. Tr. Swami Vimuktananda. Calcutta: Advaita Ashrama, 1989.

Saroja, G.W. Tilak and Sankara on the Gita. New Delhi: Sterling, Pubs. Pvt. Ltrd., 1985.

Sastri, Alladi Mahadeva. The Brahmasutra-Sankara-Bhasyam with Five Commentaries. Calcutta: Metropolitan Print and Pub. House, 1941.

Sastri, Alladi The Bhagavad Gita with the Commentary of Sri Sankaracharya. Madras: Samata Books, 1981.

Sartre, Jean Paul. Sketch for a Theory of Emotions. Tr. Philip Mairet. London: Methuen and Co. Ltd., 1962.

Satchidanandendra, Swami. The Method of the Vedanta: A Critical Account of the Advaita Tradition. Tr.A.J. Alston. London: Kegan Paul International Ltd., 1989.

Satyanand, D. Dynamic Psychology of the Gita of Hinduism. New Delhi: Oxford and IBH Publishing Co., 1972.

Seksena, S.K. Nature of Consciousness in Indian Philosophy. 2nd ed., Delhi: Motilal Banarsidass Pubs., 1971.

Shapiro, Dean H. Meditation: Self-Regulation Strategy and Altered States of Consciousness. New York: Aldine Publishing Co., 1981.

Sharma, B.N.K. The Brahmasutra and their Principal Commentaries: A Critical Expositon. Vol.1 Bombay: Bharatiya Vidya Bhavan, 1971.

Sharpe, Eric J. The Universal Gita: Western Images of the Bhagavadgita: a bicentenary survey. London: Gerald Duckworth and Co. Ltd., 1985.

Shrivastava, Umashankar, Geeta Vihar. Calcutta: M. Datta and Co., 1973.

Siddhanta-Chakravarthi, Nemichandra. Dravya Samgraha. Tr. and Ed. S.C. Ghoshal. Delhi: Motilal Banarsidass Pub., 1989.

Singh, Amar. The Heart of Buddhist Philosophy: Dinnaga and Dharmakirti. Delhi: Munshiram Manoharlal Pubs. Pvt. Ltd., 1984.

Singh, Balbir. Karmayoga: The Discipline of Action. New Dehi: Arnold Heinemann Pubs., 1981.

Singh, P. The Gita, a Workshop on the Expansion of Self. Bombay: Somaiya Pubs. Pvt. Ltd., 1977.

Singh, Santokh. Consciouness as Ultimate Principle. New Delhi: Munshiram Manoharlal Pubs. Pvt. Ltd., 1989.

Sinha, Jadunath. Indian Psychology, Vol.1 and 2. ed. Calcutta: Sinha Publishing House, 1958.

Sinha, Jadunath. The Philosophy of Vijananbikshu. Calcutta: Sinha Publishing House, 1976.

Sri Aurobindo, Essays on the Gita. 8th ed. Pondicherry: Sri Aurobindo Ashram, 1970.

Sri Aurobindo, The Upanisads: Texts Translation and Commentaries, Part 1. 3rd imp. Pondicherry: Sri Aurobindo Ashram, 1988.

Stout, G.F. Mind and Matter. Ed.G.N.A. Vesey. Body and Mind- Readings in Philosophy. London: George Allen and Unwin Ltd., 1964.

Strawson, P.F. An Essay on Kant's Critique of Pure Reason. London: Methuen and Co. Ltd., 1962.

Taita, Nathmal. Studies in Jaina Philosophy. Varanasi: P.V. Research Institute. Jainashram. Hindu University, 1951.

Taylor, Gordon Rattray. The Natural History of the Mind. New York: E.P. Dutton, 1984.

Telang, K.T. The Bhagavad Gita with the Sanat Sujatiya and the Anugita. Delhi: Motilal Banarsidass Pubs., 1965.

Tick, Donald H. The Concept of Maya in Samkara and Radhakrishnan. New Delhi: Chanakya Pubs., 1986.

Tilak, Balgangadhar. Srimad Bhagavd Gita Rahasya or Krama Yoga Sastra. Tr. B.S. Sukthankar, Poona: Tilak Brothers, 1935.

Tiwari, Kapil N. Dimensions of Renunciation in Advaita. Delhi: Motilal Banarsidass Pub., 1977.

Urguhart, W.S. The Vedanta and Modern Thought. Delhi: Gian Publishing House, 1986.

Vasubandhu, Abhidharmakosa. Tr. Theodore Stcherbatsky. The Soul theory of the Buddhists. 2nd rev. ed. Delhi: Bharatiya Vidya Prakashan, 1976.

Verma, C.D. Ed. The Gita in World Literature. New Delhi: Steerling Pubs., 1980.

Vidyabhusana, Satish Chandra M.M. Tr. The Nyaya Sutras of Gotama. Ed. Nandalal Sinha. Delhi: Motilal Banarsidass Pubs., 1930.

Vijnana Bhisku. The Samkhya Pravacana Bhasya. Vol.2 Ed. R. Garbe. Cambridge: Harvard Oriental Series, 1895.

Vivekananda, Swami. Rajayoga. 19th imp. Mayavati: Advaita Ashrama, 1990.

Vyas, R.N. The Bhagavad Gita and Jnan Yoga. New Delhi: Abhinav Pubs., 1985.

Ward, James. The Psychological Principles. Cambridge: Cambridge University, 1918.

Warrier, Krishna A.G. Srimad Bhagavad Gita Bhasya of Sri Samkaracharya. Madras: Sri Ramakrishna Math, 1983.

Whiteley, C.H. Mind in Action: An Essay in Philosophical Psychology. Oxford: Oxford University Press, 1973.

Wild, John. Ed. Studies in Phenomenology and Psychology, Oxford: North Western University, 1966.

Wilkes, Kathleen V. Real People: Personal Identity without Thought Experiments. Oxford: Clarendon Press, 1988.

Williams, Sir Monier-Monier, A Sanskrit-English Dictinary: Etymologically and Philogically arranged with special reference to Cognate-Indo-European Languages. rpt. new ed., Delhi: Motilal Banarsidass Pubs., 1990.

Wood, Ernest. The Bhagavad Gita Expalined. Califorina: New Century Foundation Press, 1954.

Woods, J.H. The Yoga System of Patanjali. Cambridge: Harvard Unviersity Press, 1927.

Yati, Nitya Chaitanya. The Bhagavad Gita: A Sublime Hymn of Yoga Composed by the Ancient Seer Vyasa. Tr. Nataraja Guru. New Delhi: Vikas Publishing House Pvt. Ltd., 1981.

Zaehner, R.C. The Bhagavd Gita with a commentary based on the original sources. Oxford: Clarendon Press, 1969.

Zimmer, Heinrich. Philosophies of India. Ed. Joseph Campbell. London: Routledge and Kegan Pual Ltd., 1951.